A Librarian's Guide to Engaging Families in Learning

A Librarian's Guide to Engaging Families in Learning

M. Elena Lopez, Bharat Mehra, and Margaret Caspe, Editors

Foreword by R. David Lankes

LIBRARIES
UNLIMITED®
An Imprint of ABC-CLIO, LLC
Santa Barbara, California • Denver, Colorado

Library of Congress Cataloging-in-Publication Data

Names: Lopez, M. Elena, editor. | Mehra, Bharat, editor. | Caspe, Margaret,
    editor.
Title: A librarian's guide to engaging families in learning / M. Elena
    Lopez, Bharat Mehra, and Margaret Caspe, editors ; foreword by R. David
    Lankes.
Description: Santa Barbara, California : Libraries Unlimited, [2021] |
    Includes bibliographical references and index.
Identifiers: LCCN 2021023903 (print) | LCCN 2021023904 (ebook) | ISBN
    9781440875830 (paperback) | ISBN 9781440875847 (ebook)
Subjects: LCSH: Libraries and families—United States. | Libraries and
    community—United States. | Education—Parent participation—United
    States. | Public libraries—United States—Case studies.
Classification: LCC Z711.92.F34 L53 2021 (print) | LCC Z711.92.F34
    (ebook) | DDC 021.2/4—dc23
LC record available at https://lccn.loc.gov/2021023903
LC ebook record available at https://lccn.loc.gov/2021023904

ISBN: 978-1-4408-7583-0 (paperback)
      978-1-4408-7584-7 (ebook)

25 24 23 22 21   1 2 3 4 5

This book is also available as an eBook.

Libraries Unlimited
An Imprint of ABC-CLIO, LLC

ABC-CLIO, LLC
147 Castilian Drive
Santa Barbara, California 93117
www.abc-clio.com

This book is printed on acid-free paper ∞

Manufactured in the United States of America

Contents

Foreword

R. David Lankes

Families come in all shapes, sizes, and configurations. They are an important structure for learning, and they are a key set of stakeholders for libraries. Families form a foundation for many adults and children in the ways they learn and in how they first see the world.

Librarians and the libraries they build and maintain should be key agents in learning. As families come in such variety, so, too, must the offerings of libraries. Yet as families shape the worldview of the learner, so, too, must library staff be constantly aware of the worldview they inhabit and project.

Will learning in a library be passive and focused solely on reading enrichment? Or will it be authentic and constructed around the learner? Will the engagement between librarian and family be transactional—content well developed and delivered to families to be consumed? Or will library staff build relationships as written about throughout these pages? Will librarians seek out learning that empowers citizens to question inherent inequities in our institutions, or will they simply reify the status quo?

It is essential that we ask these questions and interrogate the mission of librarianship and learning. For too long the value of libraries was assumed to be in the realm of learning by too many in and out of the field. The library simply was taken as a place of learning, and its role, with regard to tools such as collections, read-alouds, and programming, was beneficial to families as an article of faith: an uncritical assessment of the influence and obligations librarians have to their communities.

This take has deep roots: from Melvil Dewey considering the public library to be a coequal institution of learning with the public schools to Andrew Carnegie's philanthropy to build public libraries for the education of the masses. It is rhetoric that still populates the field with phrases such as the "university of the people." Yet what happens to this view when our understanding of both learning and the role of social justice has changed so dramatically in the past decades? For example, we still see the impact of Dewey's racism and Carnegie's support of class stratification on our libraries.[1] Instead of deleting their names, it is important to confront the realities they brought. We want the field not to erase and ignore but to confront and reform. What if, instead, John Dewey and his ideas of student-centered learning and education as a social function shaped learning as a concept in libraries?

We know now that we do not teach but that people learn. We know that learning is an internal conversation, constantly seeking to scaffold new ideas with old, building a view of the world that is constantly evolving and changing. The library can be a place like a functional family, where this learning is not only nurtured but where a zone of safety can be created for learners to engage dangerous and discordant ideas. However, libraries, like families, are not automatically such places. It takes deliberate and sustained effort to be a foundation for growth.

Over the past years, many public libraries have taken the idea of proactive educational engagement seriously. These pages are full of examples and ideas that have emerged from putting learning and the family at the center of what we do. From makerspaces to media production to writing clubs to tutoring services to full high schools in the library, librarians have sought to challenge the assumption of how libraries are learning places and instead sought to ensure that they truly are.

Then, of course, the world changed. The coronavirus pandemic closed our buildings, and in a matter of days, public libraries became virtual. For too many horrible months in 2020—when the death count from the novel coronavirus reached hundreds of thousands of lives worldwide; when our cities erupted to protest for racial justice and equality after the murder of George Floyd by police, bringing a voice for change to the street in spite of the danger of the pandemic; when librarians wrestled with the risks of reopening and with ongoing issues of vocational awe[2] that threatened to put the mission of librarianship ahead of the wellness of library staff—the library became a truly virtual organization. In an instant, all our words about learning and families and engagement were put to a very heavy test.

How many of the services we built to welcome families and transform the lives of learners were tied to the concrete and steel of buildings instead, no matter our rhetoric of inclusion and relationship? How quickly did our educational activities devolve into the lending of e-books? How many of our newly online engagements still served the rural child or the adult leaner who had struggled to make a living wage but was now out of work with no way to afford an internet connection?

To be sure, as the weeks of "stay at home" orders and a shutdown economy went by, learning crept back into what we did. Online story hours were matched with online tutoring and a new digital relationship with online courses. Librarians regained their footing and began to look to create a new normal.

I have said that the "community is the collection" and that librarians must face outward. The books on the shelves are tools to enhance, engage, and support the true genius of neighbors, artisans, and elders. Families are important structures in that vast and unique collection. They foster a sense of curiosity and wonder while instilling the power of agency in youth and adult alike. Families are the important connective tissue in neighborhoods, cities, and counties; they share not only the resources of a library but a grand sense of generational knowledge that is now needed more than ever as we seek a more just and equitable society.

Notes

1. Bharat Mehra and Laverne Gray, "An "Owning Up" of White-IST Trends in LIS to Further Real Transformations," *Library Quarterly: Information, Community, Policy* 90 no. 2 (2020): 189–239.

2. "Vocational awe describes the set of ideas, values, and assumptions librarians have about themselves and the profession that result in notions that libraries as institutions are inherently good, sacred notions, and therefore beyond critique": Fobazi Ettarh, "Vocational Awe and Librarianship: The Lies We Tell Ourselves," Library with the Lead Pipe, January 10, 2018, http://www.inthe librarywiththeleadpipe.org/2018/vocational-awe (accessed June 8, 2020).

Introduction

M. Elena Lopez, Bharat Mehra, and Margaret Caspe

Public libraries are beacons of hope and progressive change in the twenty-first century. During times of peace and progress as well as during times of crisis and need, they emerge as first responders to essential services of family learning, engagement, and community resilience. As vital information providers to enhance knowledge, skill, capability, and capacity in their communities, they transform everyday lives of besieged families and others to new opportunities and potential growth.

A Librarian's Guide to Engaging Families in Learning presents a diverse collection of chapters that illustrate thought and action in how public libraries are proactively adopting new ways of knowing families, building partnerships with families and their communities, and leading for impact. These carefully selected gems tell the story of contemporary public libraries as a significant community asset of knowing and becoming. Our book brings together emerging perspectives and successful case studies of family learning and community engagement. Reflective practices and critical thinking about the world of public library management, services, programming, and more help us understand the challenges libraries face and opportunities they offer in our multifaceted, complex, and uncertain reality.

Today, when we experience the public library, we witness a vibrant place of new beginnings and emergent happenings of people coming together in dialogue, discourse, learning, and engagement. This depiction is no longer one of passive and neutral libraries that tiptoe around issues of diversity, advocacy, activism, and social change. It now is in the very epicenter and vortex of the messiness of families in learning and everyday community lives. This has involved new kinds of alliances and partnerships to embrace diversity, adopt advocacy roles for making a difference, and embrace social justice to further fairness, justice, and equity for underserved families and communities on the margins of society. In these forward-looking ways of the present, the modern public library is the place that actively embraces every dimension of family and community learning. It looks toward a future of developing meaningful engagement to generate intentional, systematic, and community-wide changes. This collection is a select glimpse of public libraries' stories.

Public libraries, their families, and communities now come together in unique and novel ways to learn and grow with each other. In our criteria and process of selecting relevant materials to include in this collection, we weighed significant issues, preferring those where libraries recognized and built on the assets and strengths of their families belonging from a range of different communities. We also considered how individual contributors provided a distinctive perspective to represent this diversity of settings and learning, equity of service, inclusion of traditionally underserved users, and the collaborative nature of their partnership. Figure I.1 visualizes this varied scope, coverage, vocabularies, and content of the book in a word cloud created from the contributed titles.

We recognize that our selections do not include every and all instances of family engagement, for there are countless stories worth telling. Nor do they present a cookie-cutter strategy to deliver effective services while engaging families in learning. The nature of this collection is not comprehensive. It is illustrative of ways that demonstrate uniqueness and possibilities. The few examples selected here showcase the rich and complex ways that libraries develop meaningful experiences and value with their families and their communities. The collection contextualizes the embedded and situated nature of these interactions: the knowing and learning with families—and building partnerships with their communities—leading to generating impact and making a difference.

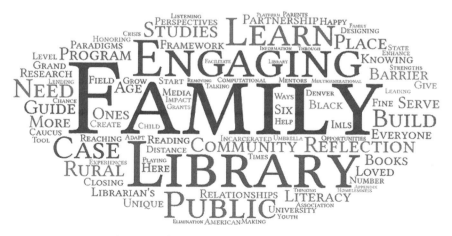

Figure I.1   Central Points of the Book

When we think about our own experiences with public libraries, most of us can remember one of our first visits there. Margaret remembers first visiting a branch of the New York Public Library as a young child with her grandmother. She remembers being enthralled by the grandeur of the building, the smell of the books, the calmness of the lights hanging over desks, but—most impressionably—the enormous wooden card catalog that used to exist back then. Touching the cards was a tactile delight: so much so, that to her grandmother's horror (and likely every librarian's horror as well), when no one was looking, Margaret began to remove cards from each of the drawers and place them in new ones! Her grandmother shrieked and then worked speedily and lovingly to place all of the cards in their rightful alphabetical place, and then the two walked off together to the children's room to borrow and read books.

Bharat can trace his roots as a social justice educator and advocate to his humble origins of everyday child abuse and domestic violence in India. Pursuit of books, reading, writing, and poetry and, later, academic scholarship were his escape and led him to libraries of all sorts, types, sizes, shapes, and forms. His search for knowledge brought him nearly every weekend to many a street vendor in the winding back alleys of Delhi's slums and depressed neighborhoods for secondhand books at dirt cheap prices. These adventures, at first, were an escape from a toxic family environment, and then over the years, they became a window to the lives of Martin Luther King Jr., Mohandas Karamchand Gandhi, Mother Teresa, and many more, as a source of inspiration and strength. Books transformed his life. Looking back and outward, he sees possibilities for libraries as sources of positive family engagement, learning, justice, shelter, and escape from dysfunctional circumstances.

Elena grew up in a country without a public library system. Her love of books came from a Filipino family that valued education and surrounded her with books. Before entering kindergarten, her mother found a teacher who taught her to read and write at home. She also asked Elena's godmother to give her books for a Christmas present every year. Her father was an avid and eclectic reader. He subscribed to three Philippine dailies and several American magazines—from *Time* to *Sports Illustrated*—and read every night after dinner. It is not surprising, then, that Elena values family engagement because it opens the door to lifelong learning, and she treasures American public libraries because they make books freely available to everyone, especially those who cannot afford to buy them.

These vivid recollections of public libraries and books and knowledge often lead us to frame our experiences there: times spent with grandparents, childhood experiences of refuge and learning, and memorable times that stayed with us in shaping who we are even today. What draws these stories together is family, engagement, learning, empowerment, and the process of transforming a reality to new opportunities and growth.

And this is the purpose of this book: to bring intentionality to how libraries engage families, to show the importance and power of this work, and to provide ideas and inspiration to shape how libraries transform to make it happen.

The notion of transformation was at the top of our minds as we wrote this book as well. As we were nearing completion of this edited collection, the world turned upside down. The coronavirus pandemic shut many of the nation's public library doors, but this didn't stop public libraries from serving families and communities. Public libraries kept Wi-Fi on, lent hotspots to those without strong internet connections, and offered curbside service. Libraries also suspended late fees, transitioned storytimes online, kicked off summer learning early, and offered even more online books and collections.

Compounding the pandemic, the murder of an African American, George Floyd, at the hands of a white policeman shook the nation and led to massive

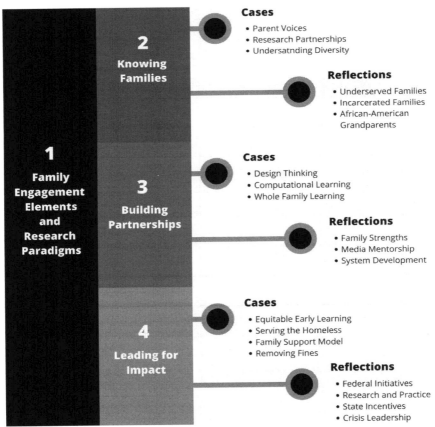

Figure I.2   Structure of the Book. (Source: Rachel Hanebutt)

protests condemning violence toward Black people and persistent racial injustice. Once again, the transformative role of the public library as an institution that can bring the community together came to the fore. In the words of Tony Marx, president of the New York Public Library, "We can all be proud that the mission of the Library—to educate, welcome and respect all perspectives, convene safe and productive conversations, and offer opportunity to all—directly combats divisiveness, ignorance, hate, and racism. It is and remains our founding idea: that everyone can learn and contribute, and must be respected. And in learning about others we learn about ourselves and hopefully find ways to live together, to embrace and better understand each other."[1]

So this is also the story of this book: how libraries are continually transforming to meet the needs of families and communities by knowing them, building partnerships with them, and taking the lead to impact their lives. This forms the structure of the book, which is divided into four major parts: perspectives on libraries, families, and communities (part 1); knowing families and communities (part 2); building partnerships (part 3); and leading for impact (part 4). Figure I.2 visualizes these relations for the reader as a mapping device for the book. The details of the chapters within each part are provided at the beginning of each part as a guide to ease readability and flow.

Acknowledgment

We would like to thank Rachel Hanebutt for the graphic display of the book's structure for this introduction.

Note

1. Tony Marx, "Tony Marx: Reflections on This Moment," New York Public Library, June 1, 2020, https://www.nypl.org/blog/2020/06/01/tony-marx-reflec tions (accessed June 6, 2020).

PART 1

Perspectives on Libraries, Families, and Communities

Introduction to Part 1

M. Elena Lopez, Bharat Mehra,
and Margaret Caspe

Libraries are about people. They are about people seeking a space where they can learn, find entertainment, and create knowledge. They are about people seeking connections around shared interests and experiencing a sense of community. For families, libraries are special places where children and adults can learn together and strengthen familial bonds. Children find lively learning activities and entertaining books and digital games. Parents can participate in energetic crafting with their children as well as find quiet moments to read and rest. Through these experiences, families nurture life-long learning.

In chapter 1, "Know, Partner, Lead: Family Engagement in Public Libraries," M. Elena Lopez and Margaret Caspe provide a framework of family engagement and a tool to guide librarians in their work on family engagement. Family engagement is a shared responsibility among families, schools, and communities for children's learning and development and family well-being. For families, it is an approach that activates their knowledge, attitudes, values, and behaviors to enable children to be motivated, enthusiastic, and successful learners. For public libraries, it is about empowering families with information and guidance and creating spaces for community connection. In this way, families are supported as teachers and learners and vital contributors to their communities. Although libraries are open to all community members, not all families have access to and participate in their services and programs. The authors offer a framework of action toward more equitable family engagement. This includes knowing families and communities, building partnerships, and leading for impact. By removing barriers and creating new opportunities for underserved families, public libraries can offer all families meaningful opportunities for learning among parents and children, developing strong parent-child bonds, building community, and creating pathways to lifelong learning.

In chapter 2, "Research Paradigms for Engaging Families in Public Libraries," Bharat Mehra and Scott Sikes acknowledge the gains libraries have made in family engagement but also point out that programs and practices are often ad hoc and unorganized. They are seldom integrated into strategic plans of libraries across metropolitan, urban, and rural contexts. An understanding about research paradigms is important to help move libraries forward into the development of programs and assessment procedures that are systematic, deliberate, and outcome driven. The chapter describes three types of research paradigms: (1) the positivist/postpositivist paradigm, based upon the understanding that objective social facts exist and can be understood through empirical observation and experimental testing; (2) the interpretivist/constructivist paradigm, which seeks to understand human experience from the premise that reality is created by individuals as they experience social life, and which relies heavily on qualitative data that give voice to the socially constructed experience of the subject; and (3) the critical paradigm, which is concerned especially with social and political structures and with systems of power and makes use of methods that foster conversation and reflection, thus allowing for the questioning and challenging of traditional entrenched structures and mechanisms of power. Each of these paradigms is illustrated in the design and implementation of library programs and assessments. As libraries review their current programs for children and families and plan future ones, they can use these research paradigms to inform the directions they can take to engage families meaningfully in the process.

CHAPTER ONE

Know, Partner, Lead: Family Engagement in Public Libraries

M. Elena Lopez and Margaret Caspe

American public libraries are places where people come to learn and connect with one another. From their beginnings in the 1800s, libraries have been gathering spots for reading and participation in community life (Wiegand, 2015). They also have a long history of developing collections and programs for children. At the dawn of the twentieth century, as an outgrowth of the efforts of child welfare advocates to oversee children's physical and moral development in public institutions, libraries developed programs tailored for their youngest members (Wiegand, 2015). Eventually, some libraries took children's programs to community settings through bookmobiles and visits to laundromats and public housing buildings, often to reach those who were the most underserved.

What stands out today is the engagement of *families* in children's literacy and learning. Librarians are shifting their focus from children's literacy experiences to partnerships with families in support of learning. This change in part grows out of consistent research findings on the benefits of family engagement. What matters for children's academic and social development, especially among low-income children and youth, are the learning opportunities provided by parents inside and outside the home as well as a safe and structured home environment (Longo, Lombardi, and Dearing, 2017). Family engagement is linked to children's school readiness and school performance, positive youth development, and high school graduation (Weiss, Lopez, and Caspe, 2018).

Family engagement is a shared responsibility for children's learning. For families, it is an approach to learning that activates their knowledge, attitudes, values, relationships, and behaviors to enable children to be motivated, enthusiastic, and successful learners. It is also about all family members becoming lifelong learners. For public libraries, family engagement is about building positive partnerships; it is not about "fixing" families. Libraries harness the strength and love that families bring to their children's lives and create opportunities for families and children to expand their horizons and spend time together learning and growing joyously. For example, the California State Library (n.d.) states that it is "shifting our thinking from asking children and their parents to join our system of service to finding ways in which we can join with families to support them."

Most importantly, family engagement in libraries is a social justice issue. Understanding and promoting family engagement in libraries is critical because, as free institutions, libraries offer services and resources to bring about educational equity. Due to lack of economic resources, families from low-income households are significantly less able to complement in-school learning with quality out-of-school-hours learning opportunities (Duncan and Murnane, 2014). Public libraries help close the "opportunity gap" by providing a safe and orderly space where students can find homework help and explore new interests and where families can relax and learn together. Compared to families from upper-income homes, parents from lower-income households say that the library helps them find information for their children, allows free access to the internet, and provides quiet study spaces, a broad selection of e-books, and the opportunity for interactive learning (Swan, 2014).

Over the past five years we have been on a journey to discover the many ways public libraries are engaging families. Much of our previous work on family engagement focused on schools and early childhood programs. Beyond formal educational programs such as these, we sought to explore communities as an important part of a child's learning ecology. Specifically, libraries provide learning opportunities in fun and creative ways and without the pressure associated with grades. And they are places where there is something for everyone, from infants to great-grandparents. Although there are similarities between family engagement in public libraries and schools— including an emphasis on supporting learning, trusting relationships, and promoting parents as advocates—there are also important differences. Libraries are often less structured and more informal than schools, provide opportunities for enrichment rather than formal education, support learning based on children's and families' individual interests, and focus on lifelong learning across various ages. Librarians are also not responsible for children's learning outcomes and data in the same way teachers are.

We began our exploration to understand family engagement in libraries by interviewing forty librarians throughout the country to get a sense of their relationships and experiences with families of both young and school-age children. We surveyed over four hundred public library directors and conducted in-depth interviews with leaders from eight state library administrative agencies. We published our findings in reports, blogs, and journal articles (Caspe and Lopez, 2018; Lopez et al., 2018; Lopez, Caspe, and Simpson, 2017; Weiss et al., 2016).

This chapter brings together what we have learned. We begin with four elements of family engagement in public libraries and explore the research behind why these elements matter for families and children. This is followed by an exploration of how libraries can deepen their commitment to equitable access and participation through knowing families and communities, building partnerships with families, and leading for impact. At the end of the chapter, we provide a tool to guide your family engagement work.

Family Engagement in Public Libraries: Supporting Families to Help Them Thrive

Public libraries partner with families to share educational materials, information, engagement opportunities, and guidance, so that

- families are lifelong learners who model a love of learning for their children through their engagement with library resources;
- families learn together through conversations and experiences that grow children's interests, curiosity, and creativity;
- parents and children develop strong bonds that encourage learning; and
- families build community to create supportive environments so that they and their children can thrive.

Families Promote Lifelong Learning

Families set the stage for their children's passion for learning and the pathway to their academic success (Harris and Robinson, 2016). They convey the importance of learning and introduce children to spaces where they can enrich their knowledge and hone their academic skills. These aspects of stage setting are found by accessing public libraries. Storytimes introduce young children and families to the world of books and fun-filled learning activities. For many parents of school-age children, academic success is aided through library programs such as homework help and summer reading. As of 2012 the online homework help offered by public libraries served the educational needs of over forty-two million K–12 students (American Library Association, n.d.).

When adult family members continuously learn, their children benefit. Parents' education is one of the constant predictors of children's school success. High educational attainment is associated with children's school readiness, academic achievement, and positive social behaviors. Through library programs such as adult education and English language learning, citizenship preparation, and computer literacy workshops, parents acquire important job and civic skills. By enrolling in adult education and GED classes, parents also model for children the value of an education and lifelong learning.

Lifelong learning takes on new urgency in a digital age where various types of media literacies are essential for communication, citizenship, and employment. The term "media mentorship" has emerged to describe the role of librarians to offer community members the information they need to make informed decisions about media use. Claudia Haines and Cen Campbell (2016) write that "media mentorship is not about having the latest and greatest technology. It is about library staff helping families find the best tool and creating the most positive experience possible." As Lisa Guernsey points out in chapter 13 of this volume, librarians can be successful media mentors by first listening to parents and understanding their family contexts.

Families Learn Together

Family engagement is about families learning together, or co-learning. In co-learning, adult family members learn alongside their children, guiding and scaffolding each other along the way. From a developmental perspective, it is about guiding children's early learning so that they increasingly take responsibility for their own learning. One example of how libraries support families learning together is around early language, literacy, and reading. Young children do not develop literacy skills on their own but need support from their families and other adults. Similarly, families benefit from ideas and ways to scaffold their children's language and literacy. So library staff are making spaces more family friendly and interactive and expanding their programming beyond book reading to creating fun and stimulating activities that give families new ideas to take with them while listening, asking questions, and talking and playing with their children at home and in the community (Neuman, Moland, and Celano, 2017; see also Celano and Neuman, and Todd-Wurm, chapters 15 and 17 of this volume, respectively).

The roles of families in motivating and engaging in reading are especially important given that by the time children turn nine, they read less frequently. Children's enjoyment of reading drops just when reading proficiency by third grade predicts long-term academic success (Scholastic, n.d.; Fiester, 2010). Family-oriented summer reading programs address this issue by encouraging both children and adults to read and participate in fun learning activities. Programs that libraries are already doing—from cooking demonstrations to kids' coding workshops and themed exhibits—encourage reading, inquiry, and conversations among family members.

Families Develop Strong Bonds That Support Learning

The nature of parent-child relationships has long been at the heart of family engagement efforts. Humans by nature are social creatures, and the ways that family members synchronize their language, facial expressions, and body movements with babies begin to set the stage for the bonds and relationships that grow across a child's lifetime. In the early childhood years, nurturing relationships provide an emotional refuge for children, fostering a healthy sense of belonging, self-esteem, and well-being. By the elementary school years, when parents characterize their relationships with their children around support, high expectations, respect and growing autonomy, children tend to do well academically and socially. Parent-child relationships remain important into early and late adolescence, as teens with supportive parents tend to make good choices, have a strong identity, and have career aspirations (Branje, 2018; Martin, Ryan, and Brooks-Gunn, 2007; National Institute of Child Health and Human Development Early Child Care Research Network, 2008). Although the style and form of parent-child bonds look different across different communities and cultures, their importance remains strong.

Libraries play a part in helping build these parent-child relationships. Compared with previous generations, families are changing and facing new, unfamiliar challenges. More mothers work outside the home, many parents are working longer hours or hold multiple jobs, and more children are being raised in single-parent households. The physical space of the library—with its quiet, peaceful, nonchaotic atmosphere—creates a natural setting for parents and children of all ages to get away from the hustle and bustle of their day and spend time together in relaxing, joyful ways.

And by promoting a love of stories and books, libraries are creating a context for parent-child relationships to thrive. Studies have shown positive associations between public library use and reading aloud, in which parents who own library cards and visit the library are more likely to read aloud to their children (Chen et al., 2016). This is beneficial not only for children's literacy and reading abilities but also because reading together promotes a strong, loving relationship and can increase parent interest in a child's life (Kassow, 2006).

Families Build Community

Peer connections are vital to family well-being. When family members form acquaintances and are part of a community, they are more likely to practice positive parenting and less likely to have trouble providing for their basic needs (Small, 2009). Libraries bring people together. They are spaces where people engage in conversations with each other and become active in the community (Klinenberg, 2018). Although social connections can happen spontaneously in libraries, they are also intentionally cultivated through programs and services. Maryland libraries, for example, bring families of young children together through cafés, an informal space for dialogue, reflection, and community building. While children participate in play activities, librarians hold conversations with parents that focus on lifelong learning and the excitement and challenges of raising young children. Parents support each other and share information that is useful for children's learning and parents' development. Through these cafés, librarians learn about what matters for families and ways that they can tailor services and collections to families' needs and interests (Weiss et al., 2016).

Libraries also share community knowledge. As R. David Lankes (2016; n.d.) points out, the community is the collection. Libraries become living spaces where people express and share their ideas and are active creators of knowledge. They are constantly evolving spaces where all families, especially those new to the United States—immigrants, refugees, and asylees—can join together, share their past, and build their futures in classes, workshops, or simple gatherings. Finally, libraries provide opportunities for families to make connections that improve communities. Family service learning is one approach for whole families—including children, parents, grandparents, and others—to volunteer to do projects in their community while spending time reading, learning, and conversing (National Center for Families Learning, 2015).

Advancing Equity through Family Engagement: The Competencies Library Staff Need

How might libraries best organize and support the four elements of family engagement? And how might libraries do this equitably so that they reach families who are often the most underserved? Educational equity requires a community effort. For public libraries, it is about equity of access to information and what Eric Klinenberg (2018) calls "social infrastructure" or the informal connections among people. Children from low-income homes are less likely to have access to high-quality, affordable preschool programs and often attend schools that are designated as needing improvement. And families who work low-paying jobs, without consistent hours, access to health care and other benefits, are often prohibited from spending time with their children and families in the ways that they would like. Public institutions such as libraries are able to do more to transform the lives of underserved children and families. And intentional outreach by libraries or through community partnerships can increase library use, especially among underserved families (Kreider and Lee, 2011; and see Lopez and Caspe, chapter 3, this volume). Celano and Neuman (chapter 15) will point out how libraries can go beyond leveling the playing field for all children and tip their assets toward those who are systemically disadvantaged.

Tipping the balance will require organizational changes to make library resources more accessible, relevant, and engaging among underserved children and families. It will also require leadership, vision, and funding. But most importantly, it means that librarians and other staff will need to navigate through the opportunities and challenges of engaging families in meaningful ways. To be successful, they must know families and communities, be able to build partnerships with them, and lead for impact (Caspe and Lopez, 2018).

Know Families and Communities

Librarians' knowledge and understanding of the communities and families they serve are inextricably linked to issues of equitable access and services. Knowing who uses library resources as well as those who don't and the barriers to access and participation can be a starting point for dialogue among library staff about how to best serve the community. Some promising approaches are described below. (See Mehra and Sikes, chapter 2, for research paradigms underlying these approaches.)

Uncover real-life experiences of those who have historically been marginalized or oppressed. Photovoice is a type of participatory research method that enables individuals to represent their lives through photography. Its value lies in empowering families to share their stories and from their perspective, in order to help librarians understand family strengths and the challenges families face (Wang and Burris, 1997). Participants are trained to take photographs of their daily surroundings to capture what is meaningful for them. They interpret their photos and talk about their choices with librarians, with other participants, and with the wider community. The Chicago Public Library has used this approach among refugees and political asylum seekers as a way to build connections in their new city and also educate the public about their lives (Public Library Association, 2018).

Use knowledge about families to create more diverse services and collections. Culturally and linguistically relevant books, written by authors representing the cultures of library participants, give children and families a sense of belonging to the library and community. A more diverse collection creates a platform for children's bilingual language development and for families to converse with their children about and validate their linguistic and cultural heritage (Dávila, Nogueron, and Vasquez-Dominguez, 2017). For example, in Milbridge, a small coastal town in rural Maine, librarians found that very few Spanish-speaking families spent time at the Milbridge Public Library mainly because there was a lack of books for adults and children in Spanish.

Through a partnership with a nonprofit organization, a Children's Day fundraiser was held. Money from the fundraiser was used to purchase Spanish-language books and magazines that families suggested for children and adults. Once the books arrived, the library threw a "processing party." Families from the community came to the library and helped to sort the books by category, placed Dewey decimal numbers on them, and entered them into the catalog system so that they could be ready for lending (Weiss et al., 2016).

Sponsor community dialogues. Community dialogues provide a structured opportunity for individuals from varying backgrounds to talk about what they enjoy about their library services and what they would like to see changed. This type of needs assessment provides library staff with important information to help enhance their services. For example, in order to open new channels of communication with community members around science, technology, engineering, and math (STEM) programming in its library, the Show Low Public Library in Arizona sponsored a series of community dialogues around the topic. Library staff quickly learned that families and community members found STEM intimidating and believed it was only for science-minded, college-educated people. This led to a conversation about how librarians might better communicate their vision of STEM as being for everyone; how they could educate their community on that vision led to improved programming (Holland and Dusenbury, 2018).

Build Partnerships

Libraries thrive when staff build trusting partnerships with families and communities that last over time. A key component of developing trust is cultural competence. Library educators think of cultural competence as librarians' ability to interact with families and communities of different cultures and to recognize, accept, and respect the legitimacy of the language, culture, and practices of nondominant groups. It is the ability to take families' perspectives, listen to them, depersonalize, and reflect (Caspe and Lopez, 2018).

Trusting partnerships develop when librarians are flexible and tailor their programs and services to accommodate different family configurations, including multiple generations of families learning together (e.g., young children, teens, and grandparents). Following are some promising approaches to building partnerships.

Build on families' funds of knowledge. Funds of knowledge consist of the skills and knowledge that are part of everyday household routines and work experiences (González, Moll, and Amanti, 2005). This approach acknowledges that all families have resources, strengths, and experiences that are assets for their children and the community. The funds-of-knowledge approach can be used to probe into family experiences with household chores, favorite TV programs, scientific knowledge, places they visit, and a host of other topics and then build programming based on these topics (Dávila, Nogueron, and Vasquez-Dominguez, 2017).

Denver Public Library's Community Learning Plaza embodies the idea of community members being more than "users" or "patrons" but active participants. The Plaza is a community-building platform tailored to meet the needs of immigrant, refugee, and asylee populations. Participants share mementos from home—a prayer rosary for a Hajj pilgrimage, a baby chair from godparents in Morelia, a deck of Chinese playing cards—and this helps build understanding and connection in diverse communities (Denver Public Library, n.d.).

Affirm family agency. Family agency refers to parents' belief that they have a role in children's learning and can make a difference in the development of their children's competencies (Hoover-Dempsey and Sandler, 1997). A welcoming climate and respectful communication create a sense of belonging to the library. At the Ignacio Community Library, a small rural library located within the boundaries of the Southern Ute Reservation in Colorado, library staff consistently think and talk about what they can do to make families feel welcome. Beginning with the simple question "How can I help you?" kindles a conversation about collections and library programs, two avenues whereby parents become active agents in their children's learning (Weiss et al., 2016). As Hillburn and Stahl (chapter 11) also report, parents are interested in structured learning activities with their school-aged children, and libraries have the assets to create programs that parents wish for.

Invite families into design thinking to build community. Design thinking is a community-building, problem-solving approach that allows families and librarians to connect and learn from one another while creating new services based on deep understanding and empathy (see Subramaniam, chapter 9). The process generally involves learning and creating in phases, including listening, observing, and talking with people to develop empathy and understand the challenges they face, brainstorming different ideas and ways to solve these problems, and testing out new ideas and solutions. Design thinking can help librarians actively engage the community in imagining new possibilities and piloting and refining practices over time.

For example, the Nashville Public Library used this process to create a new family literacy program for incarcerated teenage fathers. After a visit to a juvenile detention facility and conversations with the young men, librarians understood that their usual family literacy workshops would not work. They brainstormed what would be special and meaningful and came up with the idea of having the dads use rap to record a children's book, burning them onto CDs and placing them inside books that fathers could take home when they were released. The program has been successful in building community for these fathers and helping them think about literacy and ways to bond with their children (Atack and Cajigas, 2019).

Lead for Impact

Librarians are in a profession of public service that requires an obligation for social responsibility and inclusivity. The library profession expects librarians to be more than merely employees and to be champions of their library's mission. It calls for them to question assumptions about meeting the informational and service needs of families and communities and to confront racial, class, cultural, and other barriers that get in the way of access and participation (Caspe and Lopez, 2018). Serving all community members means not only fulfilling the needs of those who use library resources but also getting out of the librarians' comfort zone to focus on those who are least served. It means joining professional organizations and staying up to date on what is new and transformative to engage families in public libraries. It also entails removing barriers such as fines (see Jones, chapter 18) and learning from previous initiatives to identify effective practices and change less successful ones.

Following the May 2020 murder of African American George Floyd in Minneapolis and the ensuing nationwide protests, the responsibility of libraries to foster inclusion, mutual respect, and social justice has taken deeper significance. The Hennepin County Library in Minnesota issued this statement: "The staff of Hennepin County Library believe that Black Lives Matter. George Floyd was murdered because systemic racism supports police violence. The Library is a part of that system. We acknowledge that our buildings and our feet are on Dakota land and that our institutions and practices reinforce and perpetuate systems of inequity. . . . We are striving to listen, learn, educate and make critical changes that reflect our values as both community members and library staff" (Hennepin County Library, n.d.).

Following are some promising processes for reaching and engaging underserved families.

Raise the perspectives of socially excluded families and communities. Public libraries are institutions created by, for, and with communities. In community-led planning, the emphasis is on serving those members of the community who feel excluded. The approach, as described by Kenneth Williment (2009), shifts librarians' roles as experts in service planning to facilitators for the full participation of socially excluded groups in making library services relevant for them. The process goes beyond traditional needs assessment to include community outreach, conversations, codesign, and joint assessment.

Through processes such as these, librarians are able to create programs and services with and for families rather than "fixing" what librarians think are families' concerns or blindly adopting programs that other libraries have developed (Caspe and Lopez, 2018).

Reimagine partnerships. Creating partnerships goes beyond increasing participation numbers to provide children and families with meaningful and connected learning experiences across the home, library, and community. In Colorado, the vision for equitable access provided an impetus for state library leaders to use gaps in the state's early childhood policies and programs to enter into public-private partnerships for new initiatives. This led to the Growing Readers Together program that expanded family literacy services to unreached community members, family, friends and neighbors who care for young children (Lopez et al., 2019).

Create possibility. Leadership is about creating possibility to serve the varying needs and circumstances of families. Libraries are equipped to do this through their assets: the collection and use of data about library participants, space, and connections with the community. When data showed that many families who come to the libraries lacked shelter, health insurance, or medical care, the Pima County Library in Arizona added a registered nurse to its payroll. It partnered with the Pima County Health Department to expand nurse visitation to several library branches to serve adults, families with children, and teens (Weiss et al., 2016).

Reflections

Family engagement in public libraries is valued. Public libraries are attracting families through more diverse collections and a wide variety of innovative programs. They are guiding and modeling effective practices in early literacy and language development for parents and caregivers of young children. They offer structured after-school and summer activities that support family aspirations for their children's academic success. They are partnering with other organizations in order to enrich the learning experiences of children and families and link them to community services. Libraries are connecting families to one another through summer reading, workshops, and themed exhibits and programs. These events open opportunities for sharing knowledge and building community. All these reflect an expansive view of family engagement.

Still, public libraries can further their work by, first, adopting a family lens in designing their services. Libraries are divided into functional departments—children, youth, adults, community—that can make services for the whole family difficult to plan and implement. Looking at programs through a family lens requires a change in mindset: from viewing learning for children and teens to learning for the whole family, and from viewing parents as customers to recognizing them as partners. For these changes to happen, librarians will require supportive leadership and continuing education. As of 2018, the California State Library has trained more than three hundred library staff across thirty-four library systems on child development and relationship building with families. Suzanne Flint, consultant for the state, says, "It's pretty phenomenal, and we have librarians saying things like, 'I was very judgmental of parents. Matter of fact, I spent most of my time trying to avoid having to deal with them. I was there for the kids'" (Lopez et al., 2018).

Perhaps the most important challenge libraries face today is addressing equitable access and participation. Although the task is daunting, numerous examples from the literature, media, and the articles in this volume document how libraries are taking steps to make their services benefit underserved families and communities. In preparing this chapter, we read about how the Evanston Public Library in Illinois contracted a consultant to begin a process of racial healing. We spoke with a suburban library in Michigan whose bookmobile reaches geographically isolated and struggling families, providing them with books and backpacks and with food over the summer months so that eligible children do not go hungry when school is out. We learned about library innovations to serve homeless families, incarcerated fathers, and migrant families with young children. These examples are inspiring and encouraging.

Every library can do more to advance equity and expand community. The works in this collection provide a glimpse into programs, services, and innovations throughout the country that are meeting families where they are. In the appendix below we offer a short tool based on the themes emerging in this chapter, and the larger volume, to help support you in your journey to engage families in public libraries. Every library has something to offer and something to learn. We hope the examples we have provided offer inspiration to you as they have inspired us, and that this chapter is a stepping-stone for your continued growth.

References

American Library Association. "Homework Resources Offered, U.S. Public Libraries 2012." n.d. http://www.ala.org/tools/research/plftas/2011_2012 /hwresourcesmap (accessed October 1, 2019).

Atack, Elizabeth, and Klem-Marí Cajigas. "Design Thinking with Dads." Global Family Research Project, 2019. https://globalfrp.org/Articles/Design -Thinking-with-Dads.

Branje, Susan. "Development of Parent–Adolescent Relationships: Conflict Interactions as a Mechanism of Change." *Child Development Perspectives* 12, no. 3 (2018): 171–76. https://doi.org/10.1111/cdep.12278.

California State Library. "Early Learning with Families 2.0." n.d. https://elf2 .library.ca.gov/why/parents.html (accessed October 1, 2019).

Caspe, Margaret, and M. Elena Lopez. "Preparing the Next Generation of Librarians for Family and Community Engagement." *Journal of Education for Library and Information Science* 59, no. 4 (2018): 157–78. https://doi.org /10.3138/jelis.59.4.2018-0021.

Chen, Pamela, Corrinna Rea, Rebecca Shaw, and Clement J. Bottino. "Associations between Public Library Use and Reading Aloud among Families with Young Children." *Journal of Pediatrics* 173 (2016): 221–27. https://doi .org/10.1016/j.jpeds.2016.03.016.

Dávila, Denise, Silvia Nogueron, and Max Vasquez-Dominguez. "The Latinx Family: Learning y La Literatura at the Library." *Bilingual Review* 33 no. 5 (2017): 33–50. https://amaejournal.utsa.edu/index.php/br/article/view/290/278.

Denver Public Library. "Mementos from Home." n.d. https://www.denverlibrary .org/mementos-home (accessed October 1, 2019).

Duncan, Greg J., and Richard J. Murnane. *Restoring Opportunity: The Crisis of Inequality and the Challenge for American Education*. Cambridge, MA: Harvard Education Press, 2014.

Fiester, Leila. "Early Warning! Why Reading by the End of Third Grade Matters." Annie E. Casey Foundation, 2010. https://www.aecf.org/resources/early -warning-why-reading-by-the-end-of-third-grade-matters.

González, Norma, Luis C. Moll, and Cathy Amanti, eds. *Funds of Knowledge: Theorizing Practices in Households, Communities, and Classrooms*. Mahwah, NJ: Lawrence Erlbaum Associates, 2005.

Haines, Claudia, Cen Campbell, and the Association for Library Service to Children. *Becoming a Media Mentor: A Guide for Working with Children and Families*. Chicago: American Library Association, 2016.

Harris, Angel, and Keith Robinson. "A New Framework for Understanding Parental Involvement: Setting the Stage for Academic Success." *Russell Sage Foundation Journal of the Social Sciences* 2, no. 5 (2016): 186–201. https://www.jstor.org/stable/10.7758/rsf.2016.2.5.09.

Hennepin County Library. "A Message to Our Community from Your Library Staff." n.d. https://www.hclib.org/about/news/2020/June/we-stand-by -you (accessed June 21, 2020).

Holland, Anne, and Paul Dusenbery. "A Community Dialogue Guide for Public Libraries." 2018. http://www.starnetlibraries.org/wp-content/uploads /2018/10/Community-Dialogue-Guide100418.pdf.

Hoover-Dempsey, Kathleen V., and Howard M. Sandler. "Why Do Parents Become Involved in Their Children's Education?" *Review of Educational Research* 67, no. 1 (1997): 3–42. https://doi.org/10.3102/00346543067001003.

Kassow, Danielle Z. "Parent-Child Shared Book Reading Quality versus Quantity of Reading Interactions between Parents and Young Children." *Talaris Research Institute* 1, no. 1 (2006): 1–9. https://www.talaris.org/research /parent-child-shared-book-reading-quality-versus-quantity-of-reading -interactions-between-parents-and-young-children.

Klinenberg, Eric. *Palaces of the People: How Social Infrastructure Can Help Fight Inequality, Polarization, and the Decline of Civic Life*. New York: Crown, 2018.

Kreider, Holly, and Meredith Lee. "Family Engagement and Language Outcomes from a Shared Reading Intervention." Paper presented at the Annual Meeting of the American Educational Research Association, New Orleans, LA, March 18, 2011.

Lankes, R. David. "The Community Is Your Collection." n.d. https://davidlankes
.org/the-community-is-your-collection (accessed October 1, 2019).

Lankes, R. David. *The New Librarianship Field Guide.* Cambridge, MA: MIT Press,
2016.

Longo, Francesca, Caitlin McPherran Lombardi, and Eric Dearing. "Family
Investments in Low-Income Children's Achievement and Socioemotional
Functioning." *Developmental Psychology* 53, no. 12 (2017): 2273–89.
http://dx.doi.org/10.1037/dev0000366.

Lopez, M. Elena, Margaret Caspe, and Christina Simpson. "Engaging Families in
Public Libraries." *Public Library Quarterly* 36, no. 4 (2017): 318–33.
https://doi.org/10.1080/01616846.2017.1354364.

Lopez, M. Elena, Linda Jacobson, Margaret Caspe, and Rachel Hanebutt. *Leading
Family Engagement in Early Learning: The Role of State Library Administrative Agencies.* Boston, MA: Global Family Research Project, 2018. https://
globalfrp.org/Articles/Leading-Family-Engagement-in-Early-Learning
-The-Role-of-State-Library-Administrative-Agencies.

Lopez. M. Elena, Linda Jacobson, Margaret Caspe, and Rachel Hanebutt. *Public
Libraries Engage Families in STEM.* Boston: Global Family Research Project, 2019. https://globalfrp.org/Articles/Public-Libraries-Engage-Families
-in-STEM.

Martin, Anne, Rebecca M. Ryan, and Jeanne Brooks-Gunn. "The Joint Influence
of Mother and Father Parenting on Child Cognitive Outcomes at Age 5."
Early Childhood Research Quarterly 22, no. 4 (2007): 423–39. https://doi
.org/10.1016/j.ecresq.2007.07.001.

National Center for Families Learning. "Toyota Family Learning: East Palo Alto's
Neighborhood Cleanup." January 23, 2015. https://www.familieslearning
.org/blog/neighborhood-cleanup.

National Institute of Child Health and Human Development Early Child Care
Research Network. "Mothers' and Fathers' Support for Child Autonomy
and Early School Achievement." *Developmental Psychology* 44, no. 4
(2008): 895–907.https://doi.org/10.1037/0012-1649.44.4.895.

Neuman, Susan, Naomi Moland, and Donna C. Celano. *Bringing Literacy Home:
An Evaluation of the Every Child Ready to Read Program.* Chicago: Public
Library Association, 2017. http://everychildreadytoread.org/wp-content
/uploads/2017/11/2017-ECRR-Report-Final.pdf.

Public Library Association. "Photography, Storytelling, and Community Connections: How to Develop a Photovoice Project." August 29, 2018. http://
www.ala.org/pla/education/onlinelearning/webinars/ondemand
/photovoice.

Scholastic. "Kids and Family Reading Report." n.d. https://www.scholastic.com
/readingreport/home.html (accessed October 1, 2019).

Small, Mario Luis. *Unanticipated Gains: Origins of Network Inequality in Everyday
Life.* New York: Oxford University Press, 2009.

Swan, Deanne W. "The Effect of Informal Learning Environments during Kindergarten on Academic Achievement during Elementary School." Paper presented at the Annual Meeting of the American Education Research Association, Philadelphia, PA, April 4, 2014.

Wang, Caroline, and Mary Ann Burris. "Photovoice: Concept, Methodology, and Use for Participatory Needs Assessment." *Health Education and Behavior* 24, no. 3 (1997): 369–97. http://strive.lshtm.ac.uk/sites/strive.lshtm.ac .uk/files/wang%20concept%20and%09%20methodology.pdf.

Weiss, Heather B., Margaret Caspe, M. Elena Lopez, and Lorette McWilliams. *Ideabook: Libraries for Families*. Cambridge, MA: Harvard Family Research Project, 2016. https://globalfrp.org/content/download/73/436/file/IdeaBook.pdf.

Weiss, Heather B., M. Elena Lopez, and Margaret Caspe. *Joining Together to Create a Bold Vision for Next Generation Family Engagement: Engaging Families to Transform Education*. New York: Carnegie Corporation of New York, 2018. https://www.carnegie.org/publications/joining-together-create-bold -vision-next-generation-family-engagement-engaging-families-transform -education/

Wiegand, Wayne A. *Part of Our Lives: A People's History of the American Public Library*. New York: Oxford University Press, 2015.

Williment, Kenneth. "It Takes a Community to Create a Library." *Partnership: the Canadian Journal of Library Information Practice and Research*, 4, no. 1 (2009): 1–11. https://doi.org/10.21083/partnership.v4i1.545.

Appendix

This tool (table 1.1) guides you to reflect and take action on improving family engagement in your library. It is organized by the three main topics of this chapter and book: knowing families and communities, building partnerships, and leading for impact.

Column 1 represents ways librarians can partner with families and draws from the practices of libraries featured in this chapter and book.

Column 2 asks you to reflect on the level of proficiency of engaging families in children's learning and the lifelong learning of all family members. You can rate your library's practice as:

- 1 = We do not do this at all.
- 2 = We seldom do this.
- 3 = We do this sometimes.
- 4 = We do this frequently.
- 5 = We do this all the time.

Column 3 asks you to consider the ways you can improve your knowledge, partnerships, and policies and services for children and families.

Table 1.1 Assessing family engagement in your library

	Level of Proficiency, 1–5	Ways to Improve
Knowing Families and Communities		
Know and understand families to promote equitable library access and participation.		
We reach out to families, especially the underserved, to uncover real-life experiences of those who have been historically marginalized or oppressed and to learn about their routines, everyday lives, and their dreams and desires for themselves and their children.		
Use research, evaluation, and data to help improve library services for children and families.		
We seek to learn in different ways what is needed and meaningful for different types of families.		
Identify community assets and family strengths to build a vibrant library that serves all community members.		
We use what we've learned to engage families with diverse library collections, services, and resources that enhance and build on their strengths.		
Building Partnerships		
Build relationships based on family strengths.		
We learn about family interests and what excites parents and caregivers when they are with their children.		

(continued)

Table 1.1 (continued)

	Level of Proficiency, 1–5	Ways to Improve
Build relationships with families by supporting agency, decision-making, and active learning.		
We create a welcoming and respectful environment that affirms family agency—the belief that parents can make a difference in their children's learning—and empowers parents and caregivers to use library resources in ways that promote literacy and learning.		
Build relationships with families by fostering community.		
We provide space(s) where families can connect and learn from one another.		
Leading for Impact		
Lead to further social justice in underserved communities.		
We raise the perspectives of socially excluded families and communities.		
Lead through connections and participation in national library networks and initiatives.		
We keep abreast of family learning models, best practices, and documented evidence of success as we design library services for children and families.		
Lead to remove barriers to family engagement and create possibility for programs and services uniquely tailored to state and community contexts.		
We examine our policies to remove barriers to access and participation.		
We strive to take our work to the next level of services that benefit children and families, especially the underserved.		

CHAPTER TWO

Research Paradigms for Engaging Families in Public Libraries

Bharat Mehra and Scott Sikes

Public library services and support geared intentionally toward family well-being and increasing literacy across all ages are becoming more widespread. A wide range of programs and activities are being offered in order to create space and time for children and parents or caregivers to interact in positive ways. This reflects a more recent and broader understanding of family engagement and of the ways children and adolescents learn beyond formal schooling. Learning, discovery, and a cultivation of curiosity can take place in any environment, which is critical for academic and social development as well as lifelong learning.

As free, trusted, and safe places in their communities, public libraries are key to the provision of learning resources and information in fair and equitable ways. Libraries are also uniquely suited to offer a space where children and adults can learn together and strengthen familial relationships. However, historically these efforts have been ad hoc and unorganized in terms of integrating into the strategic planning process and in the development of strategic actions plans of the public libraries across metropolitan, suburban, and rural contexts.

An understanding of research paradigms is important to help move forward into the twenty-first century the development of programs and adoption of assessment measures that are systematic, deliberate, and outcome driven beyond past efforts. Yet an awareness of research paradigms also goes beyond providing a "system-centric," internalized value to the library agency in the telling of its story. It extends practitioner-friendly ways for the library staff to understand and document user-centered behaviors and individuals' use of library services in order to make them more effective and meaningful to local and distant users. Knowledge about research paradigms can address some questions such as, Have you ever wondered about the experience families are having at your library? How are families changing as a result of participating in your services? Or even, How are your library services impacting the greater community?

This chapter explores three research paradigms and the resulting application of methods that developed in public library service evaluation in historical and contemporary practice to gather feedback and engage with family users, patrons, clients, or customers. Characteristics of research paradigms in shaping the development and use of data collection and data analysis methods are highlighted. These include strategies to gather quantitative, qualitative, or mixed datasets as well as formal and informal approaches to engaging families in public library settings. Select studies briefly highlight illustrative practices in engaging families and other library stakeholders.

Dictionary.com defines "paradigm" thus: (1) a framework containing the basic assumptions, ways of thinking, and methodology that are commonly accepted by members of a scientific community; and (2) a cognitive framework shared by members of any discipline or group (www.dictionary.com). Guba and Lincoln (1994) expand research paradigms as a set of fundamental belief systems representing a worldview with their own specific ontological (i.e., nature and form of reality to be explored), epistemological (i.e., nature of relationship between knower and what can be known, namely, knowledge), and methodological assumptions (i.e., how the inquirer can find knowledge).

Three significant paradigmatic categories underlying most research tactics are touched upon in this chapter with their preferential relationship to specific methods and strategies as relevant to engaging families in rural communities. These are the positivist/postpositivist, interpretivist/constructivist, and critical paradigms. With the dissemination, adoption, and impact of "research" across all sectors of life, including those in public libraries, these paradigms become an important aspect of knowledge management to develop effective information systems and services to meet the needs of all users. In this chapter, the understanding of a paradigm is applied to ways of knowing as well as methods developed to gather patron feedback about specific programs. For example, a public library might frame a practice so that the data collected about the program from patrons are gathered in a positivist way; it might also determine that the initiative and project design itself is positivist.

Positivist/Postpositivist Paradigm

The positivist paradigm is based upon the understanding that an objective and independent reality exists. What is real can be observed and measured following an empirical process of discovery and analysis (Mertens, 2019). Table 2.1 highlights select strengths and weaknesses of the positivist/postpositivist paradigm as relevant to evaluating family learning in public libraries and provides a case example. Research within this paradigm relies on observation, measurement, and statistical analysis (O'Leary, 2017). Investigations of the social world can be conducted in the same way as research in the realm of the natural sciences, using a value-free, experimental approach that seeks to minimize the beliefs and biases of the researcher. Thus, positivistic research is generally aligned with quantitative methods of data collection and analysis (Mertens, 2019).

The shift to a postpositivist paradigm acknowledges that there can be no completely objective view of reality; however, understanding is still built upon empirical observation and experimental testing of existing theory. Although objective social facts exist, they are open to interpretation and subject to uncertainty. The demonstration of objectivity becomes the responsibility of the researcher through a detailed description of the research process (Pickard, 2013).

The positivist/postpositivist perspective carries useful implications and plays a role in the realm of family learning in several ways. Assessment and evaluation of family learning programs can be based on clear, measurable learning outcomes and goals. Statistical analysis of quantitative data may offer conclusive evidence of the efficacy or ineffectiveness of family learning. The development of skills related to literacy or to STEM subjects can be quantified and evaluated over time using a positivistic approach to research. Data may be used in the objective measurement of outcomes such as expanded knowledge and skills or behavior. These are just a few examples.

Applications of the Paradigm

Across libraries in Maryland, Family Information Centers were designated libraries specifically charged with information and resource provision to support early childhood learning experiences. The Family Information Center, in cases with a unidirectional information flow from the public library to

Table 2.1 Strengths and weaknesses of positivist/postpositivist paradigm and methods as relevant to family learning and service evaluation in public libraries

Paradigm	Positivist/Postpositivist
Methods	Predominantly quantitative: • Experiments • Quasi-experiments • Tests • Scales
Strengths (Advantages)	Empirically tested data. Permits analysis of causal relationships. Framework for making predictions and testing of hypotheses. Follows strongest standards of scientific investigation. Generalizable results. Allows wide range of statistical analysis. System-centric.
Weaknesses (Limitations)	Methodological inflexibility. Attempts to apply natural science perspective to investigations of complex human behaviors and social issues. Difficult to remove human fallibilities and biases from experimentation. Neglects consideration of the human users of information systems. Understanding that social laws can be universal and binding despite ethnic, racial, and other diversities.
Relevance to Family Learning	Assessment based on clear, measurable learning outcomes and goals. Development of skills such as literacy can be quantified and evaluated over time. Outcomes can be reflected in improved school attendance or behavior.

Table 2.1   *(continued)*

Paradigm	Positivist/Postpositivist
Case Example	Libraries adopt quantitative counts and observations during a suburban public library event. A staff member observes for fifteen minutes at the top of the hour throughout the course of an event. Data are collected for the number of people attended, where they live and what transportation they took to get there, amount of time people stayed during the event, number of people who walked away or rushed past, number of people who asked questions, etc. (Farrell and Mastel, 2016).

families, represented an application of the positivist/postpositivist paradigm. This one-way transmission assumed that information about literacy—based on scientific evidence—was factual and objective and that families would find the information helpful. Little effort was made to interact with families from the outset in order to elicit their interpretation of the information before it was widely shared.

Family Information Centers were implemented as part of the $50 million federal "Race to the Top–Early Learning Challenge Fund Grant" awarded to the Maryland State Department of Education (2021a). The grant (January 2012 through December 2015) from the U.S. Department of Education was designed to "create a seamless Birth-to-Grade 12 reform agenda" and guarantee state support for all young children and their families to overcome school readiness gaps and propel early childhood education forward. Every public library system in Maryland located in or near Title 1 attendance areas was expected to identify one or two branches that would place an informational table or kiosk in the library to provide information around issues and questions related to early literacy and early learning, and to highlight applicable community resources for library patrons (Maryland State Department of Education, 2021b). Often, family resource kits were provided with information to assist in learning of young children, especially kids with high needs, such as those with autism or English language learners (Maryland State Department of Education, n.d.).

The positivist/postpositivist approach was used to assess program effectiveness. Data collection included survey items such as how many people used the centers, how many people asked questions and spoke to organizers about them, how many times interactions took place with librarians, how many times the resource kits were used, how many times the children interacted with the resources, and so forth. The use of resource kits was easily assessed in quantifiable ways. Relevant transactional data logs provided web content evaluation in identifying limited usability and accessibility issues and patron usage counts. Staff observations and anecdotal staff feedback revealed details on user behavior and patron interactions. Maryland's *2016 Final Performance Report* reported that sixteen libraries had created Family Resource/Parent Information Centers and, through partnerships with the schools, "improved the quality of parents' interactions with library staff; increased the frequency of children and families' engagement with libraries, including obtaining library cards for children; and encouraged families to take greater advantage of other social services in their communities" (U.S. Department of Education, 2017, p. 13).

Interpretivist/Constructivist Paradigm

The interpretivist/constructivist paradigm seeks to understand human lived experience from the premise that reality is created by individuals as they experience social life. It puts forth the idea that a single, objective reality does not exist (Mertens, 2019; Cohen, Manion, and Morrison, 2017). The scientific methods of the positivist/postpositivist type are ill-suited to research human behavior and social phenomena, as they cannot reflect the multitudinous complexities of human interaction. The focus of research in the interpretivist/constructivist paradigm then becomes centered on the viewpoint of the participant with the recognition that our understanding of the world is shaped by individual background and experience (Creswell, 2017). For example, collecting data on patron feedback about how children and parents feel, think, or act during storytimes represents the interpretivist/constructivist paradigm's quest for individual perceptions and understandings.

Such a perspective relies heavily on qualitative data, which gives voice to the socially constructed experience of the subject and allows for meaningful and vivid description of phenomena. Using mixed methods, quantitative data may also be generated in order to provide further support or to deepen understanding.

Within the framework of family learning, an interpretivist/constructivist approach can be seen through the understanding of family as an educational entity. Learning in the familial environment involves a researcher's interaction, collaboration, and sharing among family members. In family learning, knowledge is created by means of observation and conversation. In this way, there is a development of shared meanings among those within the family unit, and the researcher, practitioner, or librarian becomes an active participant in the experience. A family narrative is created together. Table 2.2 highlights select strengths and weaknesses of the interpretivist/constructivist paradigm as relevant to family learning evaluation in public libraries.

Table 2.2   Strengths and weaknesses of interpretivist/constructivist paradigm and methods as relevant to family learning and service evaluation in public libraries

Paradigm	Interpretivist
Methods	Predominately qualitative though quantitative methods may also be used or a mix of methods: • Interviews • Focus Groups • Ethnography • Case Studies • Observations • Documentary analysis • Visual data analysis
Strengths (Advantages)	Seeks a deeper understanding of social contexts and human behaviors and interactions. Research happens in natural settings. Focus on the needs and behaviors of users. Explores thoughts, values, perceptions, and feelings of subjects. Accepts diversity and complexity of the human condition and of society.
Weaknesses (Limitations)	Contextual instead of generalizable. Reliance on a subjective ontological view. Analysis open to interpretations of the researcher and impacted by belief systems, values, and cultural experiences. Lack of attention to issues of power and agency.
Relevance to Family Learning	Family recognized as an educational institution. Processes involve interaction, collaboration, and sharing. Knowledge created through observation and conversation. Development of shared meanings among family members; a family narrative.

(continued)

Table 2.2 *(continued)*

Paradigm	Interpretivist
Case Example	Libraries organize focus groups with users of a specific rural public library service such as a storytelling event. Small groups of users are prompted to discuss feelings, perceptions, and thoughts about the service and to provide feedback and suggestions for its improvements.

Applications of the Paradigm

Most public library programs engaging with families in ways that are interactive, and dynamic and that involve active participation of multiple users are representative of the interpretivist/constructivist paradigm. The Family Place Libraries (FPL) initiative—started in 1996 by former library advocacy organization, Libraries for the Future—to identify and award model parent programs in a public library is one such example (see Todd-Wurm, chapter 17). The FPL's (n.d.) mission is to "increase the capacity of libraries throughout the nation to recognize and realize their full potential as community hubs for healthy child and family development, parent and community involvement and lifelong learning beginning at birth." The Columbus-Lowndes Public Library in Columbus, Mississippi, is one of three designated Family Place Libraries in the state. Programs are held weekly. Since 2008, children and parents/caregivers enjoy free play and socialization in developmentally appropriate centers for forty-five minutes followed by circle time that includes a story and music (Miller, 2014). Parent and caregiver involvement are central to the programming.

Reflecting an understanding of the family unit as a principal channel for learning and encouraging sharing and collaboration, the Parent-Child Workshop goes beyond traditional storytime programming to include interactive and developmentally relevant space design, safe toys, and age-appropriate books for children aged birth to five years. Mingling of specialists (e.g., speech language pathologists, nutritionists, and fire safety coordinators) as guests during specific sessions provides families with opportunities to bring up their questions and address their concerns; they are always encouraged to share program evaluations and suggestions for improvement.

Assessment includes recording the quality of experiences and social interactions the families are having, and documenting types of comments and application of their use in the design of activities. Positive library benefits have included the collection of family stories about various library programs, such as the "1-2-3, Play with Me," increased attendance at other children's programs, and greater circulation of materials and library visits. For example, one parent reported, "As a stay at home mom, [1-2-3, Play with Me] sessions and our family centered library offer lots of opportunities for us to get out and be around other kids in an appropriate learning environment. My son loves attending 1-2-3, Play with Me and Wee Babies music program every chance we get. We live about 30 minutes away and don't make it as often as we wish we could (Miller, 2014)."

Critical Paradigm

The critical paradigm is concerned especially with social and political structures and with systems of power (Giroux, 1986; Guba and Lincoln, 1994). A critical approach makes use of methods that foster conversation and reflection, thus allowing for the questioning and challenging of traditional entrenched structures and mechanisms of power. The critical position is focused on social justice and social change. Research may make use of qualitative, quantitative, or a mix of tools for data collection and analysis, as it seeks a deeper understanding of the widest and most diverse array of voices, values, and experiences in order to change imbalanced social power dynamics throughout the community (Frankfort-Nachmias, Nachmias, and DeWaard, 2015; Mehra, Rioux, and Albright, 2009).

With regard to engaging families in public libraries, the critical paradigm opens the sphere of its activities beyond engagement with their stronghold middle-class constituencies in urban, rural, and other settings (Mehra and Rioux, 2016). Critical theory recognizes perspectives of all stakeholders in any given situation. A critical paradigm calls for an inclusion of the points of view of the underrepresented in order to "do justice to a diversity of socially defined perspectives while providing a grounding for the evaluation of controversial problems" (Endres, 1996, p. 176). Including "invisible" voices (e.g., families from low-income backgrounds, families of color, LGBTQ+ families) in the process of information service design and development integrates a critical outlook by giving voice to an underrepresented group (Mehra and Bishop, 2007). Table 2.3 highlights select strengths and weaknesses of the critical paradigm as relevant to family learning evaluation in public libraries.

Applications of the Paradigm

A critical paradigm in public libraries is represented in the outreach efforts and programming activities that address changing community demographics (see Risley, chapter 6). The activities cater to ethnic and racial minorities in shaping library services—e.g., content, delivery, cultural sensitivity, structure, time offerings, and staff leadership—in response to the

Table 2.3 Strengths and weaknesses of critical paradigm and methods as relevant to family learning and service evaluation in public libraries

Paradigm	Critical
Methods	Generally qualitative methods with quantitative and mixed methods.
	Descriptions of contextual and historical factors especially as related to issues of power and oppression.
	Wide range of tools.
Strengths (Advantages)	Seeks reform, social justice, economic justice, and solutions to contemporary social problems.
	Explores and identifies connections among economic, political, social, and cultural issues of society.
	Attempts to explore, identify, and solve imbalances of power, inequalities, and economic injustices.
Weaknesses (Limitations)	Difficult to observe social change.
	Theory may be removed from practical, real-world solutions.
	Implication that society can be positively affected by outcomes of research.
Relevance to Family Learning	Focus on building deep community ties not based on hierarchical structures.
	Promotion of lifelong learning and engaged citizenship.
	Returning power to users for seeking learning and knowledge.
	A diverse conception of families.
	Can improve socioeconomic status.
Case Example	Libraries work with students to conduct a space study of an underutilized study area in an urban public library. Assessment is participatory and collaborative. The students independently select a mixed-methods approach that involves interviews, observing the space while in use, and asking other students to draw an ideal study space (Magnus, Belanger, and Faber, 2018).

particular needs and expectations of the targeted group. The "critical" is reflected in the strategic planning of the program as well as implementation of an information service design process. This might be from an understanding of demographics, critical review of community changes, reaching out toward different populations for their involvement, outreach to community leaders and community agencies, and effective needs assessment, to name a few.

Several public libraries represent the critical paradigm in their programming for families from low-income backgrounds. Such initiatives are "critical" in that the public libraries reach beyond their traditional middle-class customer base. For example, the Waukegan Public Library in Illinois launched an environmental scan in 2012 as its community was changing. It created the "Promotores" or Community Ambassador Program to leverage the personal networks of dedicated volunteers to gain information about the Latinx community. The ambassadors were charged to find out the barriers keeping the Latinx community from success, down to details such as whether people had a driver's license, access to a doctor, and levels of literacy. According to Amanda Civitello (2017), "the results of the environmental scan revealed deep inequities, along with opportunities for positive intervention." Based on the results of its scan as well as library administrative data, the library launched a new strategic plan in 2014 that committed to developing the programs and services the community said it wanted and needed. The plan has a significant focus on functional literacy, including early childhood education and grade-level reading, conversational ESL, and health awareness. Its website is in both Spanish and English.

The community ambassadors meet families and work with them to assess their needs. They help connect with families by alerting them to all available services that can be found at the library, such as bilingual storytimes and conversational ESL programs (Civitello, 2017). As the ambassadors are embedded within the communities, this program exhibits a focus on building deep community relationships not based in structures of hierarchy and power, which is central to a critical approach. It is also based on a diverse understanding of families and of citizenship and seeks to return power to users for learning and seeking information (Lake County Journal, 2013).

Conclusion

Public libraries are changing the way they engage with entire families, especially in the light of increasing diversity, both culturally and linguistically among families. Their methods and approaches toward engaging families have also shifted in becoming more systematic and organized, strategic and intentional, and impact driven and focused (Mehra, Elmborg, and Swee-ney, 2019). Integrating elements of a critical paradigm is important to con-tinue moving forward in these efforts.

Conversations over the past several decades have highlighted the shortcom-ings of the information theory–library practice divide in intellectual discourse. The narrow understanding of "research" in mainstream academic scholarship illustrates this triviality (Mehra, 2021). This chapter helps to address the lim-ited understanding of "theory" and its perceived distinction from practice. The use of information is embedded in every aspect of the library practice. Many initiatives through which libraries engage families can integrate multiple para-digmatic research elements to shape the philosophy and design and delivery of culturally appropriate information and services that are effective, meaningful, used, useful, and usable (Mehra and Elder, 2018). Characteristics of different paradigms integrated in the application of specific methods within the project or program design can provide complementary aspects to strengthen its over-all operationalization and implementation. This is especially relevant in assess-ing the value of emerging technology offerings in public libraries engaging diverse families, an area of work that will continue getting more attention as compared to the past. Knowledge about the research paradigms is important in this regard as well as for emerging library initiatives. When the research paradigms are integrated in the decision-making surrounding the creation of information offerings and services in public libraries, they hold the potential to engage families meaningfully in the process.

References

Civitello, Amanda. "Going Beneath the Surface: Outreach to Latino and Other Communities." *Illinois Library Association: Because Libraries Matter* 35, no. 1 (2017). https://www.ila.org/publications/ila-reporter/article/56/going -beneath-the-surface-outreach-to-latino-and-other-communities.

Cohen, Louis, Lawrence Manion, and Keith Morrison. *Research Methods in Edu-cation*. 8th ed. New York: Routledge, 2017.

Creswell, John W. *Research Design: Qualitative, Quantitative, and Mixed Methods Approaches*. 5th ed. Thousand Oaks, CA: Sage, 2017.

Endres, Ben. "Habermas and Critical Thinking." In *Philosophy of Education*, ed. Frank Margonis (Urbana, IL: Philosophy of Education Society, 1996), 168–177. https://educationjournal.web.illinois.edu/archive/index.php/pes/ article/view/2259.pdf.

Family Place Libraries. "About Us." n.d. https://www.familyplacelibraries.org /about-us (accessed December 20, 2019).

Farrell, Shannon L., and Kristen Mastel. "Considering Outreach Assessment: Strategies, Sample, Scenarios, and a Call to Action." *In The Library with* the *Lead Pipe*, May 4, 2016. http://www.inthelibrarywiththeleadpipe.org/2016/considering-outreach-assessment-strategies-sample-scenarios-and-a-call-to-action.

Frankfort-Nachmias, Chava, David Nachmias, and Jack DeWaard. *Research Methods in the Social Sciences.* 8th ed. New York: Macmillan, 2015.

Giroux, Henry A. "Critical Theory and the Politics of Culture and Voice: Rethinking the Discourse of Educational Research." *Journal of Thought* 21, no. 3 (1986): 84–105.

Guba, Egon G., and Yvonna S. Lincoln. "Competing Paradigms in Qualitative Research." In *Handbook of Qualitative Research*, edited by N. K. Denzin and Y. S. Lincoln. Thousand Oaks, CA: Sage, 1994. 105–17.

Lake County Journal. "Waukegan Public Library Wins National Award, Will Meet First Lady." *Lake County Journal*, May 3, 2013. https://www.lakecountyjournal.com/2013/05/03/waukegan-public-library-wins-national-award-will-meet-first-lady/ad4idva/?page=1.

Magnus, Ebony, Jackie Belanger, and Maggie Faber. "Toward a Critical Assessment Practice." *In the Library with the Lead Pipe*, October 1, 2018. http://www.inthelibrarywiththeleadpipe.org/2018/towards-critical-assessment-practice.

Maryland State Department of Education. "Maryland's Race to the Top: Early Learning Challenge Grant Supports Children and Families of Hispanic Origin and Children Learning English." n.d. https://earlychildhood.marylandpublicschools.org/system/files/filedepot/3/suppforhispchild_101512_0.pdf (accessed December 20, 2019).

Maryland State Department of Education. "Race to the Top Early Learning Challenge Grant." 2021a. https://earlychildhood.marylandpublicschools.org/bout/race-top-early-learning-challenge-grant.

Maryland State Department of Education. "Grant Projects: Project 8—Family Engagement and Support." 2021b. https://earlychildhood.marylandpublicschools.org/about/race-top-grant/grant-projects.

Mehra, Bharat. "Overcoming Interrelated Challenges to 'Diversity by Design' in the LIS Tenure and Promotion Process in the American Academy." In *Humanizing LIS Education and Practice: Diversity by Design*, edited by Keren Dali and Nadia Caidi. Abingdon, UK: Routledge, 2021.

Mehra, Bharat, and Ann Peterson Bishop. "Cross-Cultural Perspectives of International Doctoral Students: Two-Way Learning in Library and Information Science Education." *International Journal of Progressive Education* 3, no. 1 (2007): 44–64. http://inased.org/v3n1/mehrabishop.htm.

Mehra, Bharat, and Abbey Elder. "Benefits to Collection Development Librarians from Collaborating with 'Community-Embedded' Librarians-In-Training." *Collection Management* 43, no. 2 (2018): 120–37.

Mehra, Bharat, Jim Elmborg, and Miriam Sweeney. "A Curricular Model in a 'Social Justice and Inclusion Advocacy' Doctoral Concentration: Global Implications for LIS." *Proceedings of the Association for Library and*

Information Science Education Annual Conference: ALISE 2019. Westford, MA: ALISE, 2019.

Mehra, Bharat, and Kevin Rioux, eds. *Progressive Community Action: Critical Theory and Social Justice in Library and Information Science*. Sacramento, CA: Library Juice Press, 2016.

Mehra, Bharat, Kevin Rioux, and Kendra S. Albright. "Social Justice in Library and Information Science." In *Encyclopedia of Library and Information Sciences*, edited by Marcia J. Bates and Mary Niles Maack. New York: Taylor & Francis Group, 2009, 4820–36.

Mertens, Donna M. *Research Methods in Education and Psychology: Integrating Diversity with Quantitative and Qualitative Approaches*. 5th ed. Thousand Oaks, CA: Sage, 2019.

Miller, Lindsey. "Family Place Libraries: Recognizing Best Practices in Child Development." *SLIS Connecting* 3, no. 1 (2014): Article 5. https://doi.org/10.18785/slis.0301.05.

O'Leary, Zina. *The Essential Guide to Doing Your Research Project*. 3rd ed. Thousand Oaks, CA: Sage, 2017.

Pickard, Alison Jane. *Research Methods in Information*. 2nd ed. London, UK: Facet, 2013.

U.S. Department of Education. *Early Learning Challenge: 2016 Final Performance Report, Maryland*. Washington, DC: U.S. Department of Education, 2017. https://www2.ed.gov/programs/racetothetop-earlylearningchallenge/2016apr/md2016finalapr.pdf.

PART 2

Knowing Families and Communities

Introduction to Part 2

*M. Elena Lopez, Bharat Mehra,
and Margaret Caspe*

Knowing and understanding families is about library staff listening to families, learning about their routines and everyday lives, and recognizing their dreams and desires for themselves and their children. It's about recognizing and honoring how families vary in how they are configured, the decisions they make for their families, the resources they have available, what they believe, and how they structure learning opportunities. Most importantly, knowing and understanding families require thinking about and making extra efforts to connect to those families who are often underserved.

The chapters in this part all highlight different ways that librarians come to know and understand families and the communities they belong to. Three major themes emerge:

- Knowing families is integral to equitable library access and participation.
- Research and evaluation can help improve library services for children and families.
- Knowing families means building on community assets and family strengths.

Knowing families is integral to equitable library access and participation. In chapter 3, "'The Library Has to Be More Than Books': 'Voices' of Latinx Mothers," M. Elena Lopez and Margaret Caspe capture the voice of four Latinx mothers as they reflect on their experiences with libraries with their young children. The mothers explore the importance of libraries in making collections and services linguistically accessible and ensuring that libraries are spaces not only for learning but for community building. They also favor more diversity in librarianship.

In chapter 4, "The Partnership for Family-Library Engagement: A Unique Library-University Collaboration," Michelle Taylor, Megan Pratt, and Mariko Whelan explore how *a research and evaluation partnership—between a public library and a university—can help librarians* become aware of who participates in programs and why, what they like about programs, and how programs can improve in reaching out to families who might be underserved. "The Partnership for Family–Library Engagement" illustrates the combination of three research approaches described by Mehra and Sikes in this volume. The positivist approach offers demographic and participation data, the constructivist approach involves the library and research partners collaborating on curriculum revision and a theory of change, and the critical approach surfaces the issues of equity and participation, and leads to engaging underserved families in a process of continuous improvement in program design and evaluation.

Knowing families means that libraries build on community assets and family strengths to enhance their own programs. Kaurri Williams-Cockfield's chapter 5, "Finding Home: One Book, One Community," looks at what happens when libraries, schools, and families join together to approach with humility an awareness of refugee populations and their experiences by inviting an entire community to read the same book.

The reflections in this part also underscore the diversity that families bring and the policies that promote equitable access. In chapter 6, Carine Risley asks, "Who Do We Need to Serve?" She highlights what serving everyone—no matter their race, age, gender, religion, sexuality, immigration status, or abilities—looks like in a community with diverse geographic, economic, and cultural characteristics. In chapter 7, "Closing the Distance: Reaching Incarcerated Loved Ones," Nick Higgins delves into how libraries, by building on family strengths, can provide support to families with loved ones who are incarcerated. Finally, in chapter 8, "Reading Is Grand! A Family Literacy Program of the Black Caucus of the American Library Association," Karen Lemmons and Tamela Chambers remind us that families take many forms and that today's African American grandparents are assuming more responsibility for raising and educating children than ever before. So librarians must think about who we assume parents might be and, also, how community elders can be tapped to bring their history and wisdom to inspire learning among young people.

Together the chapters show the importance of librarians developing cultural humility in their understanding and knowledge of the diversity of whom they serve.

CHAPTER THREE

"The Library Has to Be More Than Books": "Voices" of Latinx Mothers

M. Elena Lopez and Margaret Caspe

Sprinkled with words in English and Spanish, the beautifully written children's book *Planting Stories: The Life of Librarian & Storyteller Pura Belpré* (Denise, 2017) tells the story of the first Puerto Rican librarian in the New York Public Library. Hired as a bilingual library assistant to work with the Spanish-speaking community in the early 1920s, Pura quickly saw that the *cuentos*, stories, from her homeland were absent from the library's collections. So Pura began to tell, write, and share her stories for children and families to come and hear. Nearly a century later, Pura's legacy lives on as many public libraries promote the development of collections to include Spanish-language materials, actively recruit bilingual and bicultural library professionals and staff, and develop programs to meet the needs of the Latinx community. This mission is upheld today in many ways, especially through REFORMA (the National Association to Promote Library & Information Services to Latinos and the Spanish Speaking), an affiliate of the American Library Association dedicated to improving library services for the nation's Spanish speakers (REFORMA, n.d.). Creating public libraries that honor and value language and culture, especially for the Latinx community, is important not only so that families feel empowered utilizing resources and materials but also so that families have equitable opportunities to access and use them (Dávila, Nogueron, and Vasquez-Dominguez, 2017).

In order to build culturally responsive and sustaining library spaces, librarians must come to know and understand the families and communities they engage. Knowing and understanding families and communities impact the visions librarians will have for them, their conceptualization of the librarian-community-family relationship, the actual interactions they have with them, and the ways they build relevant collections, services, and programs. Beyond knowing the broad demographics of a community, gaining insight into the experiences of families and their desires and expectations can lead to better community services.

Most importantly, knowing families begins with listening to them. It is about taking the time to hear their stories about the meaning of public libraries in their lives. In this chapter we attempt to present the "voices" of four Latinx mothers that we came to know through two nonprofit organizations in the western United States that work to support children and families, particularly those that are bilingual. Both of these organizations connect families to a variety of learning institutions within their communities, including early childhood programs and libraries. Between September and October 2019 we spoke with the mothers informally both in person and over the phone about their experiences using the public library in their communities. We use first names only, as some expressed that they did not want to be identified. These are their four stories.

Audocia

Audocia is a mother of three and an active member of her school district's English-language advisory council, whose goal is to support the academic success of all students.

The library is a place for education. For many of us who grew up in Mexico during my time, there were no books except those found in the school. We had no library. Things have changed now, but [when I was] a student, a teacher came to our pueblo, and we had a small notebook to write down what we learned. That was how we got an education.

Coming to this country there are many educational opportunities offered through the library. I learned about the library in 2004 through my daughter's preschool teacher. The teacher gave an orientation for parents and encouraged us to go to the library for our kids to learn and to develop their knowledge. Neither the children nor the parents in our group knew anything about the library. I never entered the library before that.

I have three daughters aged twenty-one, thirteen, and nine. My oldest daughter is in college now. When she was in middle school and having a hard time, she used the library's telephone tutor to help with homework. My two younger children often go to the library during the summer but not as much during the school year. In the summer they borrow books every week, return them the following week, and then check out more books. During schooldays, they have homework and can borrow books from the school, and so they only visit the library about twice a month.

My children borrow books in English and Spanish. My youngest is fluent in English and enjoys reading. At school her teacher asks her to translate for her classmates who are recently arrived immigrants and do not know the language. When she asks whether she can borrow library CDs, I tell her, "Two CDs and eight books." Of the eight books, two have to be in Spanish so as not to forget the language.

I tell my children to borrow the books they will enjoy and not check out books that they will not read. I try to teach them to be responsible about books. I tell them to put the library books in a bag inside the closet where they can pick up and return the books. In this way, they will not lose the books or forget them when it comes time to return them. One time when the children forgot to return books, the fine was about thirty dollars. I talked with the librarian, who was very understanding, and I did not have to pay the fine. But there are parents who do not go back to the library when they know that they have to pay fines. [Editor's Note: Following a nationwide trend, this library removed fines for overdue books.]

I know how to use the library, but for those who are new to this country, we need more Spanish-speaking librarians and more Spanish books, CDs, and videos. The library has flyers for parents with recommended books by grade level from preschool to third grade. It would be helpful to have them in Spanish too.

The library is not only valuable for children but also for parents, for them to continue reading and learning. My husband works two jobs and has no time for reading, but I love to read and borrow books in Spanish. Right now, I am reading *Amor y Respeto*, which is about developing relationships with your children, your husband, your coworkers. I also attend programs in the library about how to be a better parent, like how to deal with teenage daughters.

The library is a place to read and study and advance oneself. I would tell people who are new to this country to go to the library and get a library card.

Marilin

Marilin is a mother of two boys and working toward obtaining her General Education Development certification. She aspires to go to college one day.

This is a country where education is highly valued. People never stop learning and educating themselves. In the Mexican town where I came from, the library was mostly for students, but here you find people of all ages, and I am impressed with the senior citizens who tutor students and do community service. I came to know about the library when my children were in preschool and the teacher brought parents and children to the library. My children are now aged nine and thirteen, and we still borrow books and attend programs. I join the ESL conversation club at the library on Tuesday afternoon. I also take ESL classes at the Adult Education Center and took noncredit courses at the local community college. My goal is to get my GED.

It is not easy to be a parent, and the library is one place to help our kids with education. I cannot help my son with his homework. I have no family here to ask for assistance. My son uses the library program with live online help from expert tutors. It is also difficult for parents to communicate with teachers because they speak English, and the library is one place to learn English.

The library has many resources. My son takes violin lessons, and he found that you can borrow books to learn how to play music. My children enjoy summer programs, where they learn about robotics, and there is even a teen program that the older one attends.

We go to the library because it is a safe place. It has a calm atmosphere, and I find welcoming persons. I do not have family, but in the library, I do not feel alone. I meet other people like the parents of my kids' friends. My one wish is for more multicultural programs to bring people from different cultures to get to know each other and learn to live together as a community.

Erika

Erika is a mother of five children whose ages range from three to ten years. She is currently a stay-at-home parent whose passions are baking and volunteering at her children's school.

We are a military family and move around a lot. I came here two years ago from a base in Louisiana. We had a library at the base, and my kids and I could walk over in five minutes. We had access to books and storytimes, and the kids could get out of the house and socialize with other children of their own age. The library made a real effort to keep the kids busy, too, on holidays and during the summer, not only with books but with arts and crafts. There was always something to do.

Now my family has not been to the library. It's a twenty-minute drive to the library, and we have only one car, and there is no public transportation from the base to downtown. I am not able to go library events for children because of the times they are scheduled. We would go to the library if it was more accessible. There used to be a library at this base, but with budget cuts it closed. The families here have set up a little library where you can drop off and pick up a book. They had to do this to make books available.

Going to the library was part of my childhood. We did not have a car, but we had access to public transportation. After picking us up from school, my mother would take us to the library. We were at the library nearly every day! My love of reading comes from my mom. My mom would check out books on arts and crafts that we could do at home. We did not have to buy books. We could go to the library and check them out for two weeks. When I got older, my parents split up. The library then became my way to escape from home. I would just read books.

I love books and always like to read. Books are still part of my family's life. We have a little bookshop in the base. My kids use the school library, and there is a preschool where the younger ones go to. I get information about our local library from Facebook. The library's pretty good on social media, and it posts what events are going on. I do appreciate what the library does, like bringing theater groups to the library and even a mariachi band for *Día de los Muertos*. But you have to go to the library; the library does not come to you.

Marilu

Marilu is a mother of four children. She is a member of her city's leadership program for Spanish-speaking residents that brings information about the city's resources to community members whose first language is not English.

When I arrived in this country, I asked my landlady where I could go to read books. She told me about the library, but when she mentioned that it had a security guard, I was afraid I might be asked many questions and did not go. The first time I took a tour of the library happened when my child went to preschool. The teacher brought parents and our children to the library, and it was such a welcoming place so I started going to the library with my kids.

The library is a special place. When my children were younger, they enjoyed the librarian who entertained the children with puppets and story-telling, and he gave them the motivation to read. One of my daughters later volunteered at the library reading books in English and Spanish to the young children. I am very thankful to the preschool teacher and the library because my daughters learned to love reading and that has made them successful in school and especially in AP composition. They read novels, cookbooks, humorous books, and they also check out a program to learn different languages. The *New York Times* subscription helps my older one with her schoolwork.

The librarians are friendly and respectful, and that makes a big difference. The library recently did away with fines. It's a good policy because fines can increase and then the kids cannot pay and do not go the library anymore. I tell my kids that they have to be responsible and that the new policy shows that the library is confident that they will return the books.

When I think about how my library can be improved, I would like the teen area to have someone to guide and empower the kids, someone to support them so that they can learn and extend their knowledge. Few librarians speak Spanish, but it would be helpful if those who did had a badge that says, "I speak Spanish."

The library is the heart of knowledge. My father used to say that a book is one's best friend. I pass this on to my children. My father visited us, and he fell in love with the library, and even if he did not know English, he spent a lot of time at the library with my kids.

Conclusion

Through their stories we come to know the strengths that the four mothers bring to their children's education and the role that libraries play. They inculcate a love of learning and disciplinary habits to make parents and children responsible family and community members. These findings are in line with previous research showing that although it is not a monolith, the Latinx community tends to share cultural and social values including upholding the Spanish language, prioritizing family and extended families, conveying values through storytelling, and socializing children to consider others with respect and positive regard (McWayne and Melzi, 2014). The mothers value the library for opening the door to literacy for their young children and expanding their children's as well as their own knowledge. As one mother put it, "La biblioteca es el corazón de conocimiento" ("The library is the heart of knowledge").

Following in Pura Belpré's footsteps and based on these mothers' stories, we offer three strategies libraries can focus on to better serve families, especially Latinx families.

Equitable Access

If libraries are to be for all community members, they have to ensure equitable access to their collections and services. Community partnerships provide one way to bridge access gaps. One mother misses the lack of transportation to the library. Three of the mothers came to this country as immigrants. They had little knowledge about the library or had fears about approaching a government institution. Through a partnership the library had with an early childhood program, they came to value the library. Beyond physical access, the mothers talk about better access to collections in Spanish, the removal of fines, and importantly, relationships with library staff and the need to feel welcomed and supported.

Community Building

Libraries are spaces for being with community. The mothers visit the library for rest and relaxation and for bonding with their children and other people. Through storytimes and adult programs such as learning English and preparing for the GED, they expand their social networks. This is particularly important for parents who feel isolated from their community. For them, the library offers a sense of belonging.

Advancing Diversity in Librarianship

The mothers commented on the need for more Spanish resources as well as staff whom they could communicate with. Part of equitable service to all community members is to be able to meet their information needs. In part, this means hiring library staff who are representative of their communities and who have the competency—based on personal and professional experience—to efficiently meet the information needs of diverse families. While recruitment and career development require broad policy and system changes, libraries can also take immediate steps to listen to Latinx families and other underserved groups in an effort to improve their programs and services.

References

Dávila, Denise, Silvia Nogueron, and Max Vasquez-Dominguez. "The Latinx Family: Learning y La Literatura at the Library." *Bilingual Review* 33, no. 5 (2017): 33–50. https://bilingualreview.utsa.edu/index.php/br/article/view/290/278.

Denise, Anika Aldamu. *Planting Stories: The Life of Librarian & Storyteller Pura Belpré.* New York: HarperCollins Publishers, 2019.

McWayne, Christine M., and Gigliana Melzi. "Family Engagement in Children's Preschool Experiences among Low-Income Latino Caregivers: The Validation of a Culture-Contextualized Measure." *Journal of Family Psychology,* 28, no. 2 (2014): 260–66. https://doi.org/10.1037/a0036167.

REFORMA. n.d. https://www.reforma.org (accessed January 27, 2020).

CHAPTER FOUR

The Partnership for Family-Library Engagement: A Unique Library-University Partnership

Michelle Taylor, Megan E. Pratt, and Mariko Whelan

The Scottsdale Public Library (SPL) is a well-established library system serving the city of Scottsdale, Arizona, and its surrounding areas with five locations (Scottsdale Public Library, n.d.). More than 1.1 million people visit SPL libraries each year. Located in the Phoenix metropolitan area, SPL reaches an economically diverse population that ranges from low- and moderate-income residents to relatively affluent households, making it necessary to provide a full spectrum of services for patrons. The mission of SPL is to put people at the heart of dynamic library services by preserving the past, enriching the present, and illuminating the future. This mission has driven the library system to evolve and meet the needs of the community by providing innovative book-lending services while adding experiential learning opportunities, including classes and educational programming.

System-wide, SPL offers more than 1,700 programs annually for families with children aged birth to five at no cost to parents/caregivers; attendance at these programs exceeds 57,000 each year. Although SPL provides programs for patrons of all ages, one of its particular strengths is a strong focus on serving families with young children to foster healthy development and family well-being. As a part of the Family Place network of libraries focused on transforming libraries into family-friendly community centers (see chapter 17), many of these programs expand upon a traditional storytime format to create enhanced storytimes. In the latter, library staff lead a class attended by parents/caregivers and children together with the goal of promoting effective parenting via parenting tips and suggestions. To improve the quality of these early learning programs, SPL has collaborated with university-based researchers with expertise in quality early learning, evaluation, and parenting. This collaboration, named the Partnership for Family-Library Engagement, has brought a number of benefits to children, families, and library staff themselves. In this chapter we explore one particular series of enhanced storytimes called "Knowing and Growing." We explore the value of library-university partnerships to improve these programs, and highlight findings from evaluations of this work.

Knowing and Growing Enhanced Storytimes: A Model of Intergenerational Learning

Knowing and Growing Enhanced Storytime programs are a series of six-week programs that promote positive parent-child interactions and healthy development through literacy and play (Knowing and Growing Enhanced Storytime Programs, n.d.). All of the programs in the series are aligned with the Arizona Early Learning Standards and are designed to share information to parents while supporting playful parent-child interactions. The programs were designed by early childhood experts and library staff with funding support from the Arizona State Library and First Things First, a voter-initiated, statewide organization that funds early education. One program, Fun with Math & Science, focuses on supporting preschool-age children's cognitive development and includes lessons on using the senses, counting and comparing, geometry, sorting and classification, patterning, sequencing, measurement, and hypothesizing. Another program, Books Can . . . , focuses on supporting the social and emotional development of children aged birth to five years and includes lessons on attachment, trust and emotional security, feelings, self-awareness, self-regulation, relationships, and effective praise.[1]

Although each Knowing and Growing Enhanced Storytime program focuses on a different topic, all use a similar framework for each forty-five-minute session. Specifically, in each session, the programs provide (1) opportunities for playful learning interactions between children and parents/caregivers, (2) explicit suggestions for adults on how to support children's development, and (3) exposure to books, songs, and rhymes that families can use to support literacy and learning in the home. Seeing a need for this programming beyond the walls of the library, SPL also offers Knowing and Growing Enhanced Storytime programs at local community and family resource centers throughout the city. Further, SPL recognized that to ensure sustainability of quality programming, there was a need for a systematic evaluation of the implementation and effectiveness of these programs. As such, a partnership was formed between local university researchers and the SPL system.

Program Evaluation: The Partnership for Family-Library Engagement

Since 2014, SPL has collaborated with the authors—university-based researchers with expertise in quality early learning, evaluation, and parenting—to document, understand, and improve the quality of early childhood education programming for children and families through public library programming. This collaboration, named the Partnership for Family-Library Engagement, was designed to develop an infrastructure for conducting research that could be used to design, improve, and sustain effective library programming. By partnering with researchers to systematically engage in program evaluation, public libraries can create and refine their offerings to be culturally relevant and developmentally appropriate, and they can ensure the implementation is directly aligned with program goals. The research process enables libraries to more clearly identify measurable outcomes, make adjustments to better fit the needs of community members, and to identify areas for staff training and support.

Working together, the Partnership developed a set of shared goals, a system for meeting and communicating, and a work plan with clear and measurable outcomes. To date, the partnership has achieved three main milestones:

1. It has improved the quality of SPL's Knowing and Growing Enhanced Storytime programming by creating an explicit theory of change, aligning program content to current research and best practices, and collecting preliminary data on program participation and effectiveness.

2. It has developed and evaluated a professional development training for library staff to improve knowledge and skills important for interacting with families with young children, including culturally responsive practices and child development information.

3. It is currently completing a three-year rigorous (randomized control trial) impact evaluation of one of the programs, called Books Can. . . .

Process for Evaluating the Knowing and Growing Enhanced Storytime Programs

We began the evaluation with conversations about the program and its evaluation goals. We collaborated to revise the curriculum and create a mutually agreed-upon theory of change (i.e., identifying what change you want to see in caregivers by attending the program, and how the program does this). Our goal was to observe changes in key outcomes (i.e., parent

knowledge, beliefs, and practices) measured among the program participants. A secondary goal was to understand who was attending the programs
demographically. This was the library's first time to ask program participants
about who they were, including details like the adult's relationship to the
child(ren), race/ethnicity, primary language, and age of children.

The evaluation was conducted utilizing a nonexperimental pretest/post-
test design. This means that evaluators surveyed families before the first session and after their participation in six weeks of either Books Can . . . or Fun
with Math and Science. This pretest/posttest evaluation was a preliminary
step in the process of establishing a base of evidence for the Knowing and
Growing Enhanced Storytime programs. Further, in terms of building the
partnership, it was also a first step in introducing the research process to the
SPL library staff and patrons. Because the library context is a shared public
community space, much attention and care went into deciding what questions were asked of participants and designing the recruitment process in a
way that maintained a welcoming atmosphere.

Data were collected across three time periods—fall 2014, winter 2015,
and spring 2015—in five different library sites and one community center.
Programming was offered in both English and Spanish. All families who
participated in programming were invited to participate in the evaluation
study.

Study Sample. Overall, 228 parents (table 4.1) and children (table 4.2) participated in the study. A total of 116 families participated in the Books
Can . . . program evaluation, and 112 families participated in Fun with Math
& Science program evaluation. Most of the participants were upper-income,
white, and well-educated mothers. Nearly half of the children were in center-
based or home-based childcare, and nearly another half were taken care of at
home.

Preliminary Evaluation Findings

Results from the study provide an exciting first look at the experiences of
caregivers, sharing what they learned about parenting and the public library
in general. They offer important insights related to program access and
potential areas for improvement.

1. *Parents learn new and important information about social-emotional development* (see figure 4.1). The preliminary evaluation of Books Can . . . provides
initial evidence that parents and caregivers who participate in the program
learn new and important information about children's social-emotional development (Taylor et al., 2020). Specifically, by comparing the pre- to postpro-
gram surveys, it was found that after participating in the program, caregivers

Table 4.1   Demographics of adult participants across all programs

	Percentage (%)
Relationship to Child	
Mother	82
Father	8
Grandparent	4
Caregiver (relative or nonrelative)	7
Language Spoken in the Home*	
English	87
Spanish	24
Other language	24
Parent Education	
8th grade or less	<1
High school diploma/GED	4
Some college	9
Technical training/certificate	6
Two-year degree (AA, AS)	6
Bachelor's degree (BA, BS)	38
Master's degree (MA, MS)	28
Doctorate (PhD, MD, JD)	7
Parent Ethnicity	
Black	2
Native American	<1
White	60
Hispanic	16
Eastern Asian	5
Asian Indian	10
Middle Eastern	<1
Biracial (selected multiple)	6
	M(SD)
Economic Hardship	
(lower number = less hardship)	
Inability to make ends meet (range 1–5)	1.85(0.88)
Financial Strain (range 1–5)	1.1(0.37)
Parent Age (range 19–72 years)	36.37(8.12)

*Some families selected more than one language.

Table 4.2   Demographics of child participants across all programs

Child Characteristics	%
Child Sex	
Male	45
Female	53
Child Special Needs or Disabilities	4
Attends Childcare	45
Type of Childcare	
Center-based	42
Home-based	5
Own home	46
Other	8
	M(SD)
Child Age (range 13 weeks–6 years)	2.79(1.32)

Figure 4.1   A Group Session at the Scottsdale Public Library. (Source: Scottsdale Public Library [AZ])

- more strongly endorsed the importance of supporting their child's social-emotional development early, modeling appropriate behavior, and praising effort over personal characteristics.
- indicated that they had increased opportunities to interact with other caregivers, were more comfortable talking about their child with others, and felt more confident in their ability to parent their child.
- reported increased reading behavior at home.

The survey also asked open-ended questions that allowed caregivers to describe the benefits of the program in their own words. For example, when asked to "describe one new skill they learned after participating in Books Can . . . ," most participants cited learning about the importance of identifying and talking about emotions with their child, and how to do this. Others also mentioned the importance of praising their child's effort in completing a task rather than praising the child or task completion. These skills are illustrated in the following quotes:

- "Remembering how important talking about emotions is, even with young children."
- "The book *The Way I Feel* has been a great tool for helping my child verbalize his emotions. The other day he said, 'I'm frustrated' rather than acting out."
- "Be specific to what I'll be praising my child for."

2. *Parents learn new skills in promoting children's math and science development.* Initial evidence was also established in support of the effectiveness of the Fun with Math and Science program (Gaias et al., 2018). Specifically, parents are more likely to report that

- they play an important role in their children's math and science learning.
- they feel more prepared to use everyday learning opportunities to teach math and science to their children.
- when playing, they follow their children's lead rather than directing the play themselves.
- they observe that their children engage in more prosocial behavior.

When asked to describe one new skill they learned after participating in Fun with Math & Science, the most common response was that caregivers benefited by learning how to ask open-ended questions that encouraged children to think critically. Participants also shared that they were able to identify everyday opportunities to incorporate math and science concepts at

Figure 4.2   Children Engaging in Play with Blocks. (Source: Scottsdale Public Library [AZ])

home, particularly with respect to finding patterns (see figure 4.2). These skills are illustrated in the following quotes:

- "I have become better at asking my son open-ended questions."
- "Allowing my child to take [the] lead in what is interesting to him."
- "Talking about patterns throughout our day, and shapes. Noticing things in our everyday environment that can help her learn."

    3. *Parents learn about the library as a place for families.* This evaluation aimed to capture the role the library plays in families' lives beyond the specific programs described above. For example, in response to the question, "What do you like best about the public library as a place to bring young children?" parents frequently cited the library environment, with one participant describing the library as a "fun and safe place for kids to learn and play." Many parents described SPL as having child-friendly spaces with books, toys, and other learning materials, and that it is a place where they can go so their children can interact with peers while they meet with other parents. Parents also mentioned SPL resources and storytime programming. For example,

- "It feels like an [extension] of home. Teaches my son to respect the community property."

- "I like the interaction with other kids and being able to talk to other parents."
- "I like that they associate reading with fun and have enjoyable learning experiences during storytime and programs."

In response to the question, "What could the library do to be a better place to bring young children?" the majority of participant responses were related to requesting more options for participating in library programs—more age-specific programs and more days and times to offer programming, including weekends and evenings. A large number of participants did not have suggestions for improvement and made statements such as, "I love [it] how it is" and "Keep doing what they're doing."

4. *Parents differ in accessing and perceiving the benefits of the program.* The evaluation revealed variation in motivations and benefits of the programming. For example, when we examined the caregiver reports of program benefits, those who spoke a language other than English at home tended to be more focused on how the program enhanced their children's learning and promoted their development, whereas families speaking English only were more likely to focus on the social benefits of connecting with other parents/caregivers with young children.

Additionally, we observed that the location and timing of the program influenced who accessed the programs. For example, programming in community spaces outside the library and programs at nontraditional times (e.g., weekends) tended to be more accessible to working families and families facing increased economic hardship. One program is located at a community center that is easily accessed via public transportation and provides a range of services from employment support to a food pantry. This location is well situated to serve traditionally underserved families who may not otherwise access such programming in a library that is harder to get to or is located in a higher-income neighborhood where they may not feel welcome.

These results have highlighted the importance of understanding how SPL and Knowing and Growing Enhanced Storytime programs can reach and engage traditionally underserved populations. One of the next steps of the Partnership is to recruit families living in low-income neighborhoods and families whose primary language is Spanish for a second, more rigorous evaluation study.

Next Steps

One of the unique strengths of public libraries is their ability to adapt to the needs of their local communities. As a result, many library locations across the United States provide enriching and innovative programming that improves the lives of children and families. However, serving diverse communities also comes with real-world challenges. In our experience these challenges have included (1) how to reach a diverse audience, including children and families that may need the programs the most, and (2) how to provide culturally relevant interactions and environments. There remains a lot of work to address these challenges, but our evaluation provides a couple of suggestions for how to make progress on these issues.

First, collecting data on program participation is extremely valuable for understanding who is being served well and who is not. Collecting this type of potentially sensitive information within community settings such as libraries requires substantial trust building among partners and library patrons. However, by collecting basic demographic information on program participants, libraries can then identify who they are reaching and start thinking through why it may be easy to reach some audiences and more challenging to reach others. Some questions libraries might consider in terms of reach include:

- Is this an issue of access?
- Do some families not know about the programs? Are the programs offered at times or locations families cannot attend?
- Is the content of the programming meaningful and relevant to the lives of children and families in given communities?
- Is the program offered in the home language of children and families?
- Do our staff have the training and skills to build relationships with diverse children and families?

Second, public library-university partnerships are mutually beneficial and work to solve community identified needs (Taylor, Pratt, and Fabes, 2019). Specifically, public libraries are experts on their community and how to provide information and resources to improve the lives of individuals across the life course, while developmental researchers backed by the resources of the university can bring a skill set for designing and conducting research and program evaluation to answer questions important for program development and improvement efforts, such as staff training.

Research partners can help libraries craft strong theories of change and help come up with ways to measure this change. These efforts can then help fund and sustain the work of libraries while increasing access and effectiveness. The Partnership for Family-Library Engagement is an example of such work, as we work together to continue to engage in community-based research with the goal of supporting family engagement in library settings that promotes optimal parenting and enhances children's school readiness (Taylor, Pratt, and Fabes, 2019).

One question the Partnership is currently addressing is one of equity. Libraries have the potential to be an especially impactful support for low-income families that often face multiple barriers to accessing information and resources. In addition, low-income families do not often engage in traditional parenting classes, possibly because these programs can be hard to access and are often perceived negatively (Kazdin, 1997; Spoth and Redmond, 2000). In the evaluation described here, however, the majority of families who participated were from households considered upper income. With funding from the Brady Education Foundation, the Partnership conducted a three-year randomized control trial of the Books Can . . . program with an economically and linguistically diverse sample of parents and their preschool-age children. To ensure that families who might be the most underserved are able to participate, families were intentionally recruited from a variety of low-income community locations in partnership with a trusted advocate who was well connected and known across a variety of settings, including neighborhood centers, family resource centers, Head Start programs, Title I schools, and residential neighborhoods. This study was the first to evaluate the effectiveness of the Books Can . . . program using a random-assignment comparison group that allows for more robust claims of causality and program effectiveness.

Results from the study including 212 parents and preschool-age children indicate that Books Can... is effective for improving parental support for children's early learning (e.g., played counting games, singing songs, telling a story) and for children's emotional development (e.g., using emotion words, expressions, and encouragement when playing). However, it appears to be more effective for parents who report English as their primary language (Taylor, Pratt, and Eggum-Wilkens, 2020). These findings emphasize the promise for parent education programs that involve the child in interactive activities for enhancing parenting skills. They also point to the need to better tailor programming to meet the preferences and needs of socioeconomically, linguistically, and culturally diverse parents of preschool-age children. This is something our partnership is continually working toward, and the findings will provide empirical support for such efforts. In terms of program benefits, results of this study suggest that by providing parents with opportunities within the sessions to practice the skills they were learning, this storytime program was able to significantly improve parenting practices related to children's school readiness.

Third, continuous improvement is essential to implement quality early childhood programs that focus on engagement of the whole family across culturally diverse communities. SPL provides extensive training for staff to enhance knowledge and skills in the realm of child development, intentionality, scaffolding, and cultural responsiveness in instruction, which has led to confident, well-equipped staff who enthusiastically engage in providing programming to diverse audiences in multiple languages. In addition, the library system continues to develop new enhanced storytime programs to add to the menu of programs available to patrons. The latest addition to the Knowing and Growing Enhanced Storytime programs is Step Up to Learning,[2] which focuses on supporting children's approaches to learning and covers concepts such as initiative and curiosity, attentiveness and persistence, confidence, creativity, reasoning and problem-solving, and working as part of a community. The programs, which require registration, are highly sought by patrons, and most sessions are full and have a waiting list. Attrition rates are low, with the majority of families committing to attending all six weeks of the program. We are confident that the Partnership and what we learn from our evaluation are contributing to these results.

Notes

1. Fun with Math & Science and Books Can . . . are copyrighted by the City of Scottsdale Public Library.
2. Step Up to Learning is copyrighted by the City of Scottsdale Public Library.

References

Gaias, Larissa, Megan Pratt, Diane Gal, Michelle Taylor, and Lauren van Huisstede. "Improving Parenting to Promote School Readiness: An Evaluation of the Fun with Math and Science Public Library Program." Poster presented at the 2018 Society for Prevention Research Annual Meeting, Washington, DC, May 2018.

Kazdin, Alan. E. "Parent Management Training: Evidence, Outcomes, and Issues." *Journal of the American Academy of Child & Adolescent Psychiatry* 36, no. 10 (1997): 1349–56. https://doi.org/10.1097/00004583-199710000-00016.

Knowing and Growing Enhanced Storytime Programs. n.d. https://www.scottsdalelibrary.org/knowingandgrowing (accessed April 16, 2021).

Scottsdale Public Library. n.d. https://www.scottsdalelibrary.org (accessed April 16, 2021).

Spoth, Richard, and Cleve Redmond. "Research on Family Engagement in Preventive Interventions: Toward Improved Use of Scientific Findings in Primary Prevention Practice." *Journal of Primary Prevention* 21, no. 2 (2000): 267–84. https://doi.org/10.1023/A:1007039421026.

Taylor, Michelle, Megan E. Pratt, and Richard A. Fabes. "Public Libraries as a Context for the Study of Development." *Journal of Higher Education Outreach and Engagement,* 23, no. 2 (2019): 51–62.

Taylor, Michelle, Megan E. Pratt, Larissa M. Gaias, Lauren van Huisstede, and Diana E. Gal-Szabo. "Improving Parenting to Promote School Readiness: An Evaluation of the Books Can . . . Public Library Program." *Journal of Education and Training Studies* 8, no. 2 (2020): 47–57.

Taylor, Michelle, Megan E. Pratt, and Natalie D. Eggum-Wilkens. *Enhancing Child Development through a University-Library Partnership: Evaluation of Books Can...* Chapel Hill, N. C.: Brady Education Foundation, 2020. https://doi.org/10.11114/jets.v8i2.4544.

CHAPTER FIVE

Finding Home: One Book, One Community

Kaurri C. Williams-Cockfield

"You need to read this book," the sixth grader replied when the assistant director of his school asked his class to recommend a new book. "I bought it at the book fair and can't put it down." Little did the student imagine that the book would become the center of a community-wide reading project. *Refugee* by Alan Gratz is an award-winning young adult book that recounts the immigration experiences of three children at different points in history: the Holocaust, the Cuban rafter crisis, and the Syrian Civil War. In a predominantly white community, the teaching staff observed a growing interest in *Refugee* and started a blog in which students expressed their connection and empathy with the book's characters. They saw that the middle schoolers understood that there is more that connects than divides people of color. Impressed by the power of the book, the Blount County School District (Tennessee) and the Blount County Public Library took the opportunity to create a platform for the community to discuss timely issues of immigration and diversity. Thus the 1READ project was born (Bradshaw, 2018). The project promoted the common reading of Gratz's book among students, their parents, and the larger community, and a dialogue about the meaning of home.

This case study demonstrates how a community lacking cultural diversity can have meaningful discussions on the topics of immigration, culture, and identity. Blount County sits at the foothills of the Great Smoky Mountains and has an estimated population of 131,000 people, of which 94 percent are white (U.S. Census Bureau, 2018). The African American, Hispanic, and

Asian residents—of smaller numbers—relocated to Blount County for work in the manufacturing industries. They have created small pockets within the county where they live and work, with interactions with whites commonly occurring in public schools and government services. The county library staff members have noted the lower participation in family programming by African American, Hispanic, and Asian families and have prioritized them for the library's three service pillars: celebrating history, creating connections, and inspiring imagination. Although the library did not conduct a formal evaluation, library staff have noted that activities related to the 1READ project provided a context for more cross-cultural dialogue among families, encouraged Hispanic families to request copies of *Refugee* in Spanish, and increased participation of minority families in library youth programs.

THE BLOUNT COUNTY PUBLIC LIBRARY

The library is located in a 65,000-square-foot facility, employs 52 staff members (of which 11.2 FTEs hold MLIS degrees), and is open 70 hours a week across 7 days.

In 2018–2019, the library circulated 750,000 items, held 3,341 library programs, of which 651 were youth services programs, and had 378,000 visitors.

The Blount County Friends of the Library has a membership of 1,300 people. It provides all funding for library programs as well as serves as a strong volunteer base for program implementation.

The Project Brings Community Institutions Together

The 1READ project developed as a community collaboration. A committee composed of the Blount County Public Library, the Blount County School District, the Blount County Friends of the Library, and other community stakeholders such as Maryville College, the Maryville American Association of University Women, and the League of Women Voters, met monthly from the spring through the early fall of 2018. The committee created a sequence of activities in six segments designed to meet its goals, which were to create an immersive literature-based, community-wide reading project for middle school students and bring the community together around a book. The six segments were

1. Cross-curricular work during one nine-week period in four middle schools, which culminated in a final student project.

2. A daylong cultural festival for the community held at the library.
3. An author visit in which Alan Gratz spoke to each of the four middle schools.
4. A student writing workshop with the author, held at the library.
5. A library-sponsored community author talk and book signing.
6. An evening of performance and exhibits at Maryville College that provided students from all four schools the opportunity to present their final projects to the community.

The project created a new level of partnership between the library and the school district. Historically, library staff participate in and provide a variety of activities for the school district, including library tours and story programs, outreach programs, other community-wide reading programs, school registration activities, and parent-teacher events. However, the 1READ project was different: it was the first time that library staff engaged with district administration and teachers in the planning and curriculum design phase of a project, which made it possible to develop common goals and outcomes across both entities at the outset of the project.

Both district and library staff identified the importance of "access to books, family involvement, and expanded learning opportunities" as "defining features of the project" (Kuo 2016, p. 199).

Access to Books

The county's four middle schools with students in sixth to eighth grades participated in the project. In the original 1READ plan, the goal was to purchase a copy of *Refugee* for each middle school student; however, the price was prohibitive, and the decision was made to purchase classroom sets. The district, in partnership with the Blount County Friends of the Library, implemented a public sponsorship program whereby businesses and individuals could sponsor a class for $250. The community came together to donate funding, and a local bookstore in partnership with the publisher ordered the books at cost for the project, making it possible to stretch this funding so every middle school classroom could have a set of books.

The district administration and classroom teachers began the curriculum-planning phase in the spring of 2018. The project structure for students was designed to encourage connections with the book's characters, help students develop empathy, and read other books. The middle schools' focus during the first nine weeks was getting students to think about their similarities and differences as well as what unites people and what divides them. The district administration and middle school teachers planned the curriculum across all content areas on the themes found in *Refugee*. All students were required to read the book and focus on learning activities about culture, time, place, and

Figure 5.1   Student Display for 1READ Project. (Source: Jennifer Spirko, Blount County Public Library Youth Services Coordinator)

identity; survival in challenging environments; and how literature reflects "finding home." For example, students created a reading graffiti wall, a boat display of the migrants' travels, and maps that showed the journeys made by the three characters in the book (see figure 5.1) along with middle school students' own journeys. School libraries put up these displays to generate conversation and reflection on "finding home." One important outcome was that students learned to think about the hard decisions migrants have to make. In many situations, migrants do not want to leave home but have to (Bradshaw, 2018).

Schoolwide events included book fairs to encourage reading and musical performances by administrators and teachers to enrich the learning experiences of students. Each of the four schools had program cheerleaders who developed and implemented a variety of events and activities designed to build enthusiasm for the book, inspire conversations about "finding home," and expand the student conversations outside the classroom.

Family Involvement

Public libraries support the development of lifelong learning pathways when they "intentionally" design and implement children's programs that encourage participation from parents, educators, and community members (Weiss et al., 2016). Additionally, family engagement in a child's learning is key to helping them navigate difficult social and cultural issues such as immigration and diversity.

The structure of the 1READ project enabled parents to guide their middle school students through meaningful conversations on these issues as well as participation in the library-sponsored events described in the next section.

The library purchased twenty-five copies of *Refugee* (digital and print) so that homeschool students, parents, and other family members would have access to the book. The library set up a display encouraging parents and community members to read the book and provided parents with copies of the "Refugee Discussion Guide" (Scholastic, n.d.) to start a dialogue.

Neither the library nor the school district conducted formal evaluations with parents during this project, but parents shared anecdotally with teachers and library staff their children's positive experiences. One parent had this to say about the project, "Changing hearts and minds . . . so much of that happening through reading . . . thank you all for your amazing contributions and for being the kinds of teachers, parents, and community members who together can make a positive change in this community" (Terri Bradshaw, email to author, November 25, 2019).

Expanded Learning Opportunities

The project expanded learning opportunities for students and their families as well as the community by inviting author Alan Gratz to explore immigration and culture issues more deeply and by creating public events before, during, and after his visit.

In September 2018 the library kicked off Gratz's two-day visit with a cultural festival. The festival, which was attended by over four hundred people, featured a panel discussion with three refugee immigrants currently living and working in the Knoxville area. This discussion began with a presentation on the history of immigration in East Tennessee by Maryville College professor Dr. Doug Sofer. The three panelists answered questions about their immigration experiences and where they are now on their journey. One young boy was interested in the connection between fiction and real life. He asked a Cuba-born panelist who came to the United States as a young boy in 1961 if his immigration experiences were similar to how the book described them, and his answer was yes. During this discussion, all three panelists shared that they felt as if they had found home.

The library designed its space to encourage cross-generation and interactive learning. The main gallery area of the library was transformed into a Cuban café featuring food from Cuba, Syria, and Germany. The middle school culinary students prepared a dish from each of the countries and, as they served the food, shared with their parents and community members where the recipes came from and how they were prepared. Participant responses to the festival experience reiterated that the festival was a great way to connect with the three cultures. Many comments focused on the food provided by the student chefs, how articulate the students were on the food and its origins, and on the quality and taste of the food offerings (Jennifer Spirko, interview by author, December 19, 2019).

The festival's expanded learning activities engaged families with children of different ages. Families interested in gaming were able to participate in the large-size board game Ticket to Ride, a cross-country train adventure where players collect cards of various types of train cars that enable them to claim railway routes connecting cities in various countries around the world. The day also included a screening of the animated movie *An American Tail*, which is about a mouse who immigrated to America and, being separated from his family, must find a home in a new country. The movie was included to provide some context on the issue of immigration for younger children.

Additional exhibits and presentations during the day enabled students, families, and community members to develop their awareness about immigrants. The information came from Bridge Refugee Services, the Peace Corps, the Maryville College Center for International Education, and the League of Women Voters. Drosella Mugorewera, executive director of the Bridge Refugee Services as well as a Rwandan refugee, expressed appreciation for the opportunity to connect with the students, their families, and the community to share her immigration story. Based on informal comments made by participating family members, library staff do feel that this project created more dialogue between white families and those with different cultural backgrounds.

During his visit, Mr. Gratz spent time at all four middle schools talking about his book and holding informal discussions with students in the school libraries. The library hosted Mr. Gratz on the second day of his visit, where he conducted a writing workshop for a select group of middle school students from the four participating schools. He also gave an empowering community presentation on his writing process, *Refugee*, and his other books. This event was attended by approximately 250 students, parents, and community members.

The audience for the community author talk was full of middle school boys asking relevant questions and demonstrating their passion for the book and for reading. Students questioned the fate of the migrants and why some of the book's characters died or failed to be reunited with their loved ones. They came away with an understanding that not all refugees have a happy ending (Bradshaw, 2018). Parent comments included a father who noted that his son was now full of questions about immigrants and the conflicts discussed in *Refugee*. He expressed that it was great that his son was talking about difficult issues with other kids his own age. Student comments ranged from "I can't stop reading it" to "It was really sad, but in a good way" (Miller, 2018).

In October, after Gratz's visit, a sampling of student projects was showcased at a public event held in the Lambert Recital Hall on the Maryville College campus. This event featured musical performances, original poetry readings, cookbooks, board games, Choose Your Own Adventure–style history games, paintings, and sculptures—all representing the students' interpretation of the immigration experience and what "finding home" meant to them. After the public event, the art and games exhibits were moved to the library for an extended time for community viewing.

Success Factors

The 1READ initiative exemplifies the type of literary activity with the capacity to make a significant impact on student reading, their engagement with books, and their lifelong learning. It created a learning environment that encourages compassion and empathy as well as a love of reading among participating students and their families. One homeschool parent, in response to the library's community author event, posted on the library Facebook page "I've seen my son voraciously reading as a result of these books. I saw kids showing up 45 minutes early to this event, books in hand and eyes wide. I saw a line of kids stretch across the library eagerly awaiting their signed copy. I can't wait for next year, what a wonderful gift for the young readers in our county!" (Park, 2018). The success of 1READ was that the effort was led by students who were excited about the book even before the initiative was conceived. The support they got from the school, their families, and community institutions reinforced a deeper exploration of immigration, diversity, and inclusion. Library staff have noticed an increase in participation in youth programs by African American, Hispanic, and Asian families since the 1READ project.

The 1READ project planning and implementation represented a significant investment of time and resources from all partners, but it was key to the success of the project. Three processes were particularly important:

Cost sharing. The total cost of the 1READ initiative came to $14,000 and was divided across the program partners. The direct campaign held to raise funds for purchasing copies of the book generated around $8,000. The Blount County Friends of the Library provided the additional $6,000 to cover the costs associated with the author visits, the cultural festival, and the community author talk and book signing.

Clearly defined partnership roles. Project activities were delegated across 1READ'S committee membership, with the school district personnel taking responsibility for booking the author, for developing all the school-based activities, and for communicating with parents and students about 1READ. The library and school district worked together to plan the library activities, including the writing workshop and the two community-wide events to be held in the library: the cultural festival and community author talk and book signing.

The 1READ project provided the library with the opportunity to engage with Asian, African American, and Hispanic community members by working through the school-student-parent relationship. Notably, the library received requests for Spanish-language versions of *Refugee*, which the library did provide.

Multiple social media and print communications. Library staff created and maintained the 1READ Facebook page and handled all the external communications for the project including cross-marketing of events, community and donor outreach, media engagement with the local newspaper and NPR, and a strong social media push across library Facebook and Twitter accounts. Promotional signs (printed six-foot signs and digital media display slides) were posted around the library and through the digital signage system.

Next Steps

The 1READ project has profoundly changed the library staff and reinforced the importance of outreach to diverse populations and the creation of organizational partnerships that support these populations. The library staff are now focused on identifying and eliminating existing barriers to library resources and programs by building the next cycle of strategic directions around the theme of "Building Bridges." Goals include the review and edit of library policies and procedures for greater inclusion, staff training on trauma-informed service and sensitivity to cultural differences, and a plan to move library services into locations where the community already congregates, making it easier to access library resources.

The 1READ project was developed with the idea that it would become an ongoing, biannual event. However, the time needed to implement a school-library project of this depth makes it unlikely that future incarnations will follow the same structure. Planning was underway for a second 1READ project to be held in the spring of 2020, but the project was canceled because of the coronavirus pandemic. The public library staff and the Blount County Friends of the Library will seek ways to expand their roles so the program quality and level of family engagement will be maintained and, hopefully, expanded as the library begins implementation of the "Building Bridges" strategic directions.

References

Bradshaw, Terri. Interview by Hannah Martin. WUOT 91.9 FM, September 14, 2018. https://www.wuot.org/post/blount-county-schools-1read-program.

Kuo, Nai-Cheng. "Promoting Family Literacy." *School Community Journal* 26, no. 1 (2016): 199–221. http://www.schoolcommunitynetwork.org/SCJ.aspx.

Miller, Amy Beth. "Sixth-Graders Work with William Blount High School Culinary Students to Cook for 1READ Finding Home Festival at Blount

County Public Library." *Daily Times*, September 9, 2018. https://www
.thedailytimes.com/news/sixth-graders-work-with-william-blount-high
-school-culinary-students/article_f516f4d1-55cd-5a43-9de7-ed0a3f
2babcb.html.

Park, Dustin. "Thank You to Vandy Kemp. . . ." Facebook, September 12, 2018.

Scholastic. "Refugee Discussion Guide." n.d. https://www.scholastic.com/teachers
/ lesson-plans/17-18/refugee-discussion-guide (accessed July 18, 2018).

Spirko, Jennifer. "1READ Participant Feedback". Unpublished interview by Kaurri
C. Williams-Cockfield. Blount County Public Library, December 19, 2019.

U.S. Census Bureau. "Population Estimates, July 1, 2019 (V2019) — Blount County,
Tennessee [Race and Hispanic Origin]." *Quick Facts*, 2019. https://www
.census.gov/quickfacts/blountcountytennessee.

Weiss, Heather B., Margaret Caspe, M. Elena Lopez, and Lorette McWilliams. *Ideabook: Libraries for Families*. Cambridge, MA: Harvard Family Research Project, 2016. https://globalfrp.org/content/download/73/436/file/IdeaBook.pdf.

CHAPTER SIX

Who Do We Need to Serve?

Carine Risley

Libraries are increasingly identifying equity as a critical concern, which is both necessary and exciting and makes me feel optimistic for the future. In San Mateo County, California, equity means we must serve our entire community, not just the economically advantaged residents of our community who already use the library. Our 2018–2019 annual report states, "We're steadfast in our commitment to assuring that everyone—no matter their race, age, gender, religion, sexuality, immigration status, or abilities—has access to our libraries and feels welcome" (San Mateo County Libraries, 2019). We hold ourselves accountable to that charge—and collect data and focus on results to give us an indication of how successful we are. For example, in vulnerable communities, we keep track of the number of library meals served to youth and adults. We also record the number of participants in the monthly book club conversations with incarcerated youth. We commit to learning with generosity and open hearts from partners and families who help cocreate and share our services. And we share our findings with the community through annual reports.

San Mateo County is an area of stark contrasts. It is home to many affluent professionals but also has an increasing number of low-wage working families who are being squeezed out of the housing market by the growth of tech companies. Between 2017 and 2019, the homeless population increased by

12 percent (Angst, 2019). According to the *U.S. News and World Report* index on educational equity, San Mateo County's neighborhood and racial disparities are higher than national averages are (U.S. News and World Report, n.d.). Split by the Santa Cruz Mountains, the eastern portion of the county is urbanized while the western half is more rural, with vast stretches of protected land. The geography of this place disperses people and isolates rural communities from needed services.

Transforming Outreach

What has helped us introduce change—and then keep on changing—is a laser focus on *who* we need to be serving. One major area of work for us has been to diligently spot opportunities to deliver services beyond our buildings. When we first identified this as a strategic priority, outreach was an occasional activity. It has now grown into a core part of our public services roles. Our staff embed themselves at farmer's markets, WIC clinics, medical waiting rooms, the County Fair, housing complexes, playgrounds, parks, festivals, and more to connect with families wherever they are. Our outreach is about bringing a full expression of what the library is to where the people are—engaging families in activities and learning opportunities. We take out book bikes fully equipped with books, media, free Wi-Fi, and even portable 3D printers.

We also engage families and build community by offering fun learning experiences that cross generations. Our Lookmobile turns any place it visits into a learning landscape with hands-on exhibits. Created in collaboration with San Francisco's Exploratorium, this custom-built trailer highlights the county's unique composition, features, and perspectives. The Lookmobile promotes inquiry-based learning and offers visitors six core interactive experiences: evocative map exhibits, mapmaking activities, perspective drawing windows, a pinhole camera wall, a camera obscura, and a fog tricycle. We encourage visitors to continue their exploration beyond the Lookmobile by reading related materials in our collection. In this way we reinforce literacy and learning.

Channeling Resources to Ensure Equitable Access

The other strategic priority that has been essential in the sea change we have experienced in serving families has been to employ resources in new ways to ensure equitable access.

In 2019 we went fine-free (see Jones, chapter 18). Our goal is to ensure that all members of our community have equitable access to library books and other valuable resources and materials. Studies have shown that late fines can be a significant barrier to access and can drive borrowers away, particularly individuals with low or fixed incomes. We introduced fine-free library cards for children and teens in 2016, which increased the use of youth material and gave us the success to include the whole family. We saw a 15 percent increase in library circulation and a 25 percent increase in new student library cards (San Mateo County Libraries, 2019).

To fill nutrition gaps in our vulnerable communities, we offer a free, year-round meal program open to all ages. Our meal service not only allows us to fight hunger but also helps us nourish and engage the community so families can enjoy time together at the library. The healthy, balanced meals are served five days a week, with additional snacks offered in the summer season. This daily program has resulted in positive feedback and overwhelming support from the community. Our program eliminates the stigma of getting help with food and strengthens the bond we have with our community members. In 2019, we provided over 26,815 meals.

To reinforce the educational aspirations of families, we offer early education. Eager students get ready to tackle a new school year thanks to an uplifting experience with our Big Lift Inspiring Summer camps and the support of county funds. Serving seven school districts, our camps aim to transform early learning and help reverse summer learning loss. In summer 2019, 1,193 children attended, with a retention rate of 91 percent. Throughout the four years of the program, children have gained an average of 1.5 months of reading skills based on pre- and posttesting. The four-week, full-day summer camps are free to low-income families with children entering kindergarten through second grade. The program includes a morning literacy component, an afternoon STEAM (Science Technology Engineering Art and Math) enrichment segment, and two healthy meals. The enrichment curriculum offers engaging activities such as yoga, crafts, and science experiments.

Family engagement presentations and activities are a pivotal component of our summer camps. They include themed workshops on children and technology and supporting literacy development. In addition, all children receive a set of three books to take home to read with their parents. Parents who are English language learners receive a free copy of the Oxford English-Spanish picture dictionary to support their English literacy growth.

For several years now, in partnership with the LENA Research Foundation, we have offered our Talk Read Sing program in English and Spanish and expanded the program's offerings with partners such as the San Mateo County Housing Authority. Using patented LENA technology, "talk pedometers" track the number of words children are hearing throughout the day. The analyzed data the pedometers yield help families easily see how children learn language. Hosting these workshop series with community partners and working with previous graduates of the class have been essential to the ongoing success we have seen with this program.

Sharing Our Lessons

Once you identify fully serving underserved families as a priority, you'll find that the electrifying potential and innate flexibilities of public libraries are gifts. Lots of things either won't work or won't work as you thought they should. Our lesson has been to keep trying, to invite additional perspectives, to understand where and why our well-intentioned services aren't connecting with a given population, and to make adjustments. The nuanced, more effective, and authentic experiences that have resulted from our work in our communities has changed lives, changed our organization, and changed our county. And the work is just beginning!

References

Angst, Maggie. 2019. "As RV Dwelling Soars, San Mateo County's Homeless Population Rises 21 Percent." *Mercury News*, July 2, 2019. https://www.mercurynews.com/2019/07/01/as-rv-dwelling-soars-san-mateo-countys-homeless-population-rises-21-percent.

San Mateo County Libraries. "Annual Report 2018–2019." 2019. https://d4804za1f1gw.cloudfront.net/wp-content/uploads/sites/22/2019/09/23202226/2018-19-Annual-Report-Booklet.pdf.

U.S. News and World Report. "Overview of San Mateo County, CA." n.d. https://www.usnews.com/news/healthiest-communities/california/san-mateo-county (accessed December 19, 2019).

CHAPTER SEVEN

Closing the Distance: Reaching Incarcerated Loved Ones

Nick Higgins

We launched TeleStory at the Brooklyn Public Library in 2014.[1] The idea was to invite kids and families to connect with an incarcerated loved one during a free, one-hour video visit from a safe and welcoming community library. Video visits take place in meeting rooms that are filled with books, toys, puzzles, and craft supplies to create a destigmatizing and resource-rich environment for people ensnared in the criminal justice system. During sessions, families are provided with children's books and encouraged to read together, sing songs, and play. Children's librarians and other staff begin each video visit that includes young children with a book reading, song, or fingerplay. Each visit presents opportunities for referral to services and programs offered by the library or external partners. Every new visitor is given a welcome packet full of helpful library resources, along with a questionnaire for families that identifies any additional areas of need, such as housing, immigration, employment, or literacy.

Omaira was one of our first TeleStory users in 2014. "I tried to get people to use it," she said. "Especially the ones who had kids. It was really convenient." Her family was using the library already to get books, and her kids would use the computers. From the time she started using TeleStory, she preferred to combine it with in-person visits. "When my husband was in Rikers, I used to visit him in person three times a week. And then when I started using TeleStory, I changed it to visiting twice a week and calling from the library once a week.

He would do homework with my son. In person, we weren't allowed to bring any of that stuff in. So I could do more on the call. But in person you can show affection. It's different, but together it balances out. Then the facility banned me for a year, so TeleStory helped. I started going twice a week."

Expanding the Vision

In 2016, with funding from our City Council and the Knight Foundation, TeleStory was expanded to twenty-five libraries across five boroughs in all three of New York City's public library systems. By providing multiple, community-based access points across the city, Brooklyn Public Library, New York Public Library, and Queens Library are now providing families impacted by incarceration with a free and easily accessible way to visit and read together, strengthening relationships and creating a bridge back to the community for people who are incarcerated (see textbox).

We've hosted over four thousand TeleStory sessions since 2014. Sessions have taken place in Arabic, English, Polish, Russian, and Spanish. Over two-thirds of families have attended more than one video visit at the library.

Shahidah learned about TeleStory after overhearing someone mention it in the visitor intake center. She hadn't been a library user previously. Now she and her two-year-old visit weekly with her husband through video. Compared to the correctional facility, "the library is more polite, more pleasant, more peaceful," she says. "I feel like I'm here for myself. More independent, no one restricting you. Less harassment. At Rikers, they harassed me for my religion. They made me take my hijab off. We both agreed no more visiting when he moved to Rikers. The baby hasn't been there. Calling on the phone and using TeleStory is good enough for me. This makes me feel like I am doing something instead of nothing, and it allows me to relax. My son can move around, no restrictions."

We rarely ever position video visitation in libraries as being about leveraging new technologies. Rather, we talk about this service as advancing just policies for individuals and families impacted by the system. NYC's libraries have quickly emerged as leaders in providing ethical and family-friendly models of visitation services. We're getting better at supporting justice-involved families and increasing visit opportunities to help reduce recidivism. We aim to reduce the stigma of incarceration and to help generate greater empathy among library staff and community members while providing a trusted community-based referral source that empowers librarians to discover and share relevant services and programs within their communities.

A longtime TeleStory patron, Michelle, began using the program in 2014 after first learning about it during an information session at Rikers. "Everyone

---

RESOURCES FOR VIDEO VISITS WITH INCARCERATED PERSONS

This study was used in our efforts to craft an argument for noncommercial and community-based interventions in the proliferating market of for-profit video visitation schemes:

> Rabuy, Bernadette and Peter Wagner. *Screening Out Family Time: The For-Profit Video Visitation Industry in Prisons and Jails.* Prison Policy Initiative, 2015. https://www.prisonpolicy.org/visitation/report.html.

We created a toolkit for other library systems that are interested in starting their own video visit program:

> Brooklyn Public Library. "Telestory Toolkit." https://www.bklynlibrary.org/outreach/telestory-toolkit.

We contracted with the Vera Institute of Justice to conduct a comprehensive evaluation of our library-based video visit model. The report was published in February 2021.

> Digard, Léon, Jessi LaChance, and Jennifer Hill. *Closing the Distance: The Impact of Video Visits in Washington State Prisons.* Brooklyn, NY: Vera Institute of Justice, 2017. https://www.vera.org/downloads/publications/The-Impact-of-Video-Visits-on-Washington-State-Prisons.pdf.
>
> Pitts, David and Lionel Smith. *Brooklyn Public Library's TeleStory Video Visitation Program: A Process Evaluation.* Brooklyn, NY. Vera Institute of Justice, 2021. https://www.vera.org/publications/brooklyn-public-librarys-telestory-video-visitation-program.

---

attending this overview session at Rikers was angry——angry about being there, angry about their situation. When they started talking about TeleStory, I first thought it was a class, and I started listening. When I got my son to look into it, we decided to try it. Previously, it had been traumatizing to bring my son to Rikers. We wouldn't get home until eleven o'clock at night, and he would have school the next day. TeleStory is awesome."

Using TeleStory to Reach Families in Different Ways

In late 2017, BPL staff began planning a monthly support group for TeleStory families at our Bedford Library. Several branch librarians shared their experiences assisting formerly incarcerated patrons, many of whom are referred from the nearby Bedford Armory shelter. The consensus among the

Bedford staff was that meeting the needs of the neighborhood's reentry population should be a higher priority for the library. They suggested that in addition to family support groups, certain branches should have designated reentry navigators—preferably people who have gone through the justice system themselves—to implement a library-wide reentry strategy.

When asked about the relationship between TeleStory and overall library usage, Michelle mentions that her local branch is "wonderful. There is a resource coach available and visible to help you. I think the gatherings specifically for TeleStory families are extremely useful. People talk specifically to our issues, you don't have to sit there thinking, 'This is not for me,' just waiting for them to get to a part that you need. It is all helpful, all relevant."

TeleStory is an essential service for families in Brooklyn. Prior to the coronavirus pandemic, in one year alone, we hosted 2,388 video visits for 1,799 (unduplicated) family members. Sixty-three percent of them (1,140) came back to the library for more visits with their incarcerated loved ones. On average, each visit was attended by three people, usually a caregiver, child, and incarcerated parent. Forty-four percent of branch visitors were children (ages 0–17), 56 percent were adults (ages 18 and above). We have had family members who are unable to visit Rikers Island due to physical disabilities, conflicting work schedules, fear of exposing young children to a jail environment, and fear of immigration enforcement. We are able to provide a helpful and humane intervention. Although nothing should replace in-person interaction with a loved one, visiting through video can help strengthen relationships between separated family members and between families and the library.

Conclusion

A decades-long appetite for retributive justice and "tough on crime" policing in the United States has led to the current incarceration of 2.3 million people. The total disappearance from American civic life of a population the size of Houston has had devastating effects on those 2.3 million individuals and the countless others who are left behind. Neighborhood-based institutions such as public libraries witness this devastation at the ground level every day, and it's our responsibility as leaders in our communities to build thoughtful and compassionate responses on behalf of the people we serve. In Brooklyn, as in other towns and cities across the country, too many families have been separated by the justice system. Our library's response is to help collapse the distance between people separated by incarceration and to simply afford them the right to read and play together like everyone else. Your library may try a similar intervention. Or you may choose to deliver books to the local jail or state prison. You might create a writing program at a teen detention facility, throw a pajama party at a family shelter, or host a lecture on the collateral consequences of mass incarceration. Whatever your response—big or small—know that you and your library are helping to restore an increasingly rare part of civic life that powerful systems have been eroding for generations.

Note

1. You can learn more about TeleStory at https://www.bklynlibrary.org /outreach/telestory

Reading Is Grand! A Family Literacy Program of the Black Caucus of the American Library Association

Karen Lemmons and Tamela Chambers

Today's grandparents are assuming more responsibility for raising and educating children. Among racial and ethnic groups, Black children are the most likely to be cared for primarily by a grandparent. According to a Pew Research Study (Livingston, 2013), 7.7 million U.S. children—or 1 in 10—lived with a grandparent in 2011, and Black children were the most likely among racial and ethnic groups to be under the care of a grandparent.

In 2010, Camila Alire, president of the American Library Association, launched the Family Literacy Focus initiative aimed at encouraging families to read and learn together. The Black Caucus of the American Library Association (BCALA) chose to support and celebrate grandparents through Reading Is Grand!, a new intergenerational literacy program connecting grandparents with their grandchildren. BCALA wanted to highlight and celebrate the role that grandparents play in passing down the unique cultural and familial values that help children grow into valuable contributors to our global community.

In African American families, elders are often considered the family "linchpins," tasked with preserving and transmitting family legacy for continuity (Hunter and Taylor, 1998). They are commonly regarded as the "dominant family members" and can either be familial or "fictive kin," a voluntary relationship meant to replicate that of "biological kin" (Hunter and Taylor, 1998). Gatherings such as family reunions and venues that support other purposeful gathering "rituals" offer African American elders the continued opportunity to participate in "meaningful intergenerational communication" in which their knowledge and wisdom "are welcomed and heeded" (McCoy, 2011). From caregivers to teachers, the role of grandparents is valued, honored, and respected.

The Reading Is Grand! Program

Reading Is Grand! awards small grants to selected local libraries to implement programs that connect grandparents with children and young adults, share stories, and promote and celebrate African American culture and history. This type of intergenerational programming has been replicated in school and public libraries serving children and their families across the continental United States, and activities have ranged from collaborative storytelling to talks given by community elders who make history come alive. Fourteen programs have been funded since 2010 nationally, mostly in suburbs and small cities. BCALA awarded its 2019 grants based on a library's creativity, proposed involvement of grandparents in activities, and potential for community impact (Black Caucus of the American Library Association, 2019).

We share three important features of funded programs in the hope that more libraries will be inspired to take action. They are (1) recognizing literacy in its many forms, (2) extending the notion of "grandparent," and (3) connecting the disconnected.

Recognize literacy in its many forms: oral, written, and project based. The 2010 kickoff program for the Reading Is Grand! initiative occurred at the Whitney Young Branch of the Chicago Public Library. Program participants heard and exchanged stories, engaged in creative crafts, and met acclaimed author Irene Smalls. Ms. Smalls read from her books *My Nana and Me* and *My Pop Pop and Me* and discussed how sharing stories, both written and oral, fosters the development of literacy and lifelong learning.

The focus on celebrating "grandfamilies" was exemplified at the Quinby Street Resource Center, in Sharon, Pennsylvania. At its "Celebrating Grand-Families: Telling Stories of Our Royal Trees" event held on National Grandparents Day, grandparents were celebrated as "royalty," complete with palace decor and red carpet. Participating grandfamilies shared stories, created memory books, and learned about the importance of the oral tradition of storytelling for preserving cultural traditions.

Extend the notion of "grandparent." The concept of the African American elder as community linchpin was reinforced across the programs hosted by the grant-winning recipients of 2017 and 2018. Programs planned and implemented by the Quinby Street Resource Center, Broadview Public Library (Illinois), Carver Ranches Library (Broward County, Florida), and Middle College High School (Memphis, Tennessee) all extended the definitions of "grandparents" and "grandfamilies" to include nonkin community elders. Although these programs cast a much wider net in terms of the relationships between the participants, each highlighted and celebrated the role that "grandparents" play in passing down the unique cultural and familial values that help children grow into valuable contributors to our global community.

Connect the disconnected. Reading Is Grand! gives elders and youth the opportunity to communicate, listen, and participate in shared activities. Carver Ranches Library hosted four programs that brought together their large senior population who feel disconnected from the youth today, even if the youth in question are their grandchildren. The "Elders Share Their Stories: Intergenerational Storytelling" teen program epitomized the sharing of wisdom, as the participating teens learned a great deal about the history of their community and received sage advice on goal setting and striving for success on their own terms.

At Middle College High School in Memphis, librarian Alice Thompson organized a lecture with two elders who were eyewitnesses and participants in the Memphis Sanitation Strike of 1968. This was followed by a question-and-answer discussion facilitated by Memphis historian Johnnie Mosley.

Participation Challenges and Successes

Programs experienced varying degrees of success. Funding is needed as well as administrative support and commitment. In addition, libraries will need to consider logistical support such as transportation, scheduling, and refreshments when planning these programs.

Program participation depends on access and scheduling. We learned that one of the challenges among library grant recipients was arranging the appropriate time for seniors to participate. The librarian at the Broward County Library, in Florida, for example, reported that though the city has robust senior programming with transportation available for seniors from 8:00 a.m. to 12 noon, seniors had to arrange their own transportation after noon. This presented a challenge since the seniors, in many cases, could not commit to regular attendance at afternoon programs. The times of senior availability were incongruent with children's school schedules.

Participation also hinges on timing with relevant events. Librarians observed that programs held on, before, or after National Grandparents Day seemed to reach the intended audience. The growing recognition and promotion of National Grandparents Day also provide library staff with an additional vehicle for branding.

Reflections

Almost a decade of implementation of the Reading Is Grand! initiative has shown that successful programs were all based on relationships with their respective senior communities. While not all of the libraries were able to recruit and attract biologically based "grandfamilies," many of the libraries provided outreach to the seniors in their community and relied on their knowledge of African American heritage, history, and culture. Libraries may want to partner with churches and other organizations that have strong relationships with the elderly.

The libraries that have established, continuous relationships with grandparents, children, and the community at large were more successful than those libraries that hosted a one-time special program. If libraries wish to connect grandparents and young children, they may want to first establish relationships with them and then develop programs around their interests and needs.

References

Black Caucus of the American Library Association. "BCALA Announces Reading is Grant! Grant Winners." News release, June 24, 2019. https://www.bcala .org/press-releases/bcala-announces-reading-is-grand-grant-winners.

Hunter, Andrea G., and Robert J. Taylor. "Grandparenthood in African American Families." In *Handbook on Grandparenthood*, edited by Maximiliane E. Szinovacz. Westport, CT: Greenwood Press, 1998, 70–86.

Livingston, Gretchen. *At Grandmother's House We Stay: One-in-Ten Children Are Living with a Grandparent*. Washington, DC: Pew Research Center, 2013. https://www.pewsocialtrends.org/wp-content/uploads/sites/3/2013/09 /grandparents_report_final_2013.pdf.

McCoy, Renee. "African American Elders, Cultural Traditions, and the Family Reunion." *Journal of the American Society on Aging* 35, no. 3 (2011): 16–21. https://www.asaging.org/blog/african-american-elders-cultural -traditions-and-family-reunion.

PART 3

Building Partnerships

Introduction to Part 3

M. Elena Lopez, Bharat Mehra, and Margaret Caspe

Librarians develop partnerships with families to guide them in expanding children's learning opportunities and to support lifelong adult learning. Approaching them in a nonjudgmental manner and in ways that build on their strengths, interests, and cultures clears the path for trusting relationships. Having fun learning experiences, especially across different age groups of children, helps cement ties among families, community members, and librarians.

The chapters in this part all highlight different ways that librarians come to build partnerships with families. The key themes that emerge are these:

- Building partnerships is based on recognizing family strengths.
- Building partnerships involves supporting families as active learners and decision-makers.
- Building partnerships with families means fostering community (i.e., community of families as peers and community of libraries and families working together).

Families are diverse in their configuration (e.g., single-parent, LGBTQ, traditional, extended), social circumstances, and cultural backgrounds. Developing positive and trusting relationships across these different types of families is anchored on the principle that *families have strengths that can reinforce their learning and enrich library collections and programs.* In chapter 9, "Designing Learning Experiences with and for Families," Mega Subramaniam and Tamara Clegg lead us to explore design thinking as an approach that draws upon family knowledge and interests to cocreate family learning experiences. They walk us through the design-thinking processes of inspiration, ideation, and iteration with techniques that librarians can use to boost their services and programs.

Ricarose Roque and Sari Widman describe a university-library partnership in chapter 10, "Engaging Families in Computational Literacy Opportunities." They define computational literacy as "the ability to create, express, and invent with technology." Engaging parents and children as *active learners and decision-makers* is central to the success of developing computational literacy skills. Families learn to code and develop products that correspond to storytelling. They have fun learning experiences as they use their "funds of knowledge" to produce—and not just consume—digital content.

Building family partnerships is also about *fostering community*. In chapter 11, "Age Is But a Number: How to Create Multigenerational Family Programs in Your Public Library," Jessica Hilburn and Becky Stahl share how the Benson Memorial Library's adult and youth services departments collaborated to develop family programming. By designing programs involving mixed-age groups of children, they encouraged families to bond with one another and network with other families in the community. In addition, librarians interacted with a variety of family members and expanded their connections to the community.

In chapter 12, "We're Happy You're Here: Honoring Family Strengths to Build Relationships and Enhance Programming at the Denver Public Library," Sarah McNeil describes library efforts to create a strength-based foundation in its relationships with families. This approach asks librarians to consider what they can learn from families: what brings them to the library, how they support themselves and their peers, and how libraries can support families. A strengths-based approach has informed the library's services for children and families, from creating early childhood programs that build on parents' interest in child development to increasing access and to family learning experiences for Spanish-speaking community members.

Lisa Guernsey introduces the idea of librarians as "media mentors" who guide and serve as a resource for families' choices to tap into digital tools and content. In chapter 13, "Media Mentors Start by Listening to Parents," she provides examples of conversations with parents in an informal focus group and draws out lessons for how librarians can mentor families on choosing and using media that match their interests, needs, and home environments. Interestingly, what excites parents is not so much the technology but the experience of having fun while learning together with their children.

As director of the Cleveland Public Library, Felton Thomas Jr. makes sure that the library is open to all community members. This means removing barriers—small and big—to access and engage with library resources. In chapter 14, "Lending an Umbrella to the Community," Thomas and coauthor Laura Walter describe the steps their library is taking: training, because staff are the "heart and foundation" of the library; internal evaluation to learn what is working, what needs to be improved, and to plan future department services; and policy actions, such as the removal of fines and collaboration with community agencies that offer a wide range of family supports. They hope that by removing barriers, the library serves as an umbrella that "shelters the community through education, acceptance, and hope."

Together, the chapters show the important roles of librarians in creating an environment that welcomes families and creates pathways for learning through strengths-based and trusting relationships. Librarians are guides and mentors as well as learners and community builders.

Providing programs that are relevant and respond to the interests of families while treating them as equals goes a long way to building trust, the foundation of family-library partnerships.

CHAPTER NINE

Designing Learning Experiences with and for Families

Mega Subramaniam and Tamara Lynette Clegg

Engaging families in libraries means bringing together community members from multiple generations to promote rich and deeply engaging experiences for all involved (Urban Libraries Council, 2016; Weiss et al., 2016). However, creating experiences that are appealing and relevant for multiple generations, while also ensuring that each family member has an important role to play and can learn from other family members, can be a challenge. Design-thinking approaches have emerged as a structure to address these challenges by bringing library staff and family members together to plan, design, develop, implement, and evaluate family learning experiences.

This chapter considers and puts forth approaches for leveraging design thinking for creating innovative learning experiences with and for families in library contexts. Drawing on examples from our own work, we share participatory design (PD) techniques that engage families in the development of programs and services, paying particular attention to the roles that library staff can play in encouraging learning in such engagement.[1]

PD provides multiple techniques whereby adults and children can be involved as design partners by contributing insights, design ideas, and feedback (Fails, Guha, and Druin, 2012). Researchers have argued that children's ideas extend beyond those of adults because each generation of children has grown up in a unique context with technologies and social contexts distinct from those of other generations. Children's ideas are different from those of adults and should be included in the design process (Druin, 2002). Additionally, individuals who participate in PD bring content understandings that extend the range of designs beyond what technology or learning environment designers can conceive and imagine (Yip et al., 2013a). Hence engaging families in the design of experiences for families invites the perspective of those deeply and intimately familiar with family interactions (Yip et al., 2016)—a.k.a. the "experts" in family interactions.

The PD techniques that we share in this chapter leverage design thinking as a vehicle for *planning* innovative family learning experiences in libraries, *codesigning* these experiences, and *engaging* families in learning activities. We highlight the various roles that library staff can embrace to facilitate such learning experiences. We also highlight key challenges that library staff may face and offer ways to address them.

Design Thinking: A Quick Introduction

The shifting landscape of powerful new technologies (e.g., social media, ubiquitous computing, artificial intelligence) has led to the proliferation of a participatory culture. Previously, society emphasized a producer-and-consumer culture whereby experts produced new knowledge resources for consumption by the general public. In our current participatory culture, the general public (even young children) can draw upon new media to become producers, problem-solvers, and even experts themselves (Jenkins, 2009). With this culture shift, a movement called design thinking has emerged.

Design thinking is a people-focused approach to creating solutions to problems using the perspective of design (Coleman, 2016; IDEO, 2015). This movement toward broadening design thinking allows stakeholders to tackle complex problems by applying the processes and philosophies of designers (i.e., empathizing with stakeholders, inventing innovative prototypes, and iterating to produce new solutions). IDEO (2015) defines design thinking as occurring in three main stages—inspiration, ideation, and iteration—that leverage human-centered design principles of being iterative, empathetic, and intuitive throughout the problem-solving process. Design teams can be composed of researchers and practitioners, intergenerational members of adults and children, community members and service providers such as library staff and public servants, children of multiple age groups, and many more combinations of people with diverse roles and responsibilities.

Regardless of the composition of the design team, design thinking necessi-
tates an overarching disposition toward working in teams, exploration of
ideas, experimentation, a love of storytelling, thinking with one's hands,
receiving critique and providing constructive comments, and a value for
bridging the gap between thinking and solving problems to create a better
world (Brown, 2009; IDEO, 2015; Jenkins, 2009).

We have leveraged the design-thinking process in a range of research
projects with families and communities. As we describe the processes and
techniques involved in the design-thinking stages throughout this chapter,
we specifically reference two projects most relevant to working with libraries
and families: Science Everywhere and Safe Data Safe Families. Throughout
these two projects, we use design-thinking processes and PD with youth,
families, teachers, library staff, and community members.

Science Everywhere (https://hcil.umd.edu/science-everywhere/) is a six-
year project funded by the National Science Foundation and focused on the
design of a social media app and large, community touch-screen displays
where youth aged six to sixteen and community members (e.g., parents,
teachers, mentors, after-school coordinators) capture and share science experiences that youth are having throughout the community. The tools enable
youth and community members to encourage and build upon their experiences across neighborhood settings (e.g., home, school, community centers,
libraries) (Ahn et al., 2018; Ahn et al., 2016; Cabrera et al., 2018; Mills et al.,
2019). We partnered with two neighborhood communities in the United
States, one in the mid-Atlantic region and another in the Pacific Northwest.
Both partner neighborhoods include Title I schools (which most participating youth attended) that serve students from predominantly low-income
neighborhoods.

Safe Data Safe Families (https://safedata.umd.edu/) is a four-year design
project (currently in year four) focused on the design and development of
educational resources for low-socioeconomic-status families to reduce risky
behaviors online and enhance their overall privacy-related digital skills.
During the first year of this project, we conducted interviews with fifty-two
families (fifty-four adults and twenty-three children) and eleven focus groups
with thirty-six public library staff nationwide to learn about families' everyday digital practices and challenges. Thirteen participating families identified as Latinx. The families were recruited via four library branches in the
mid-Atlantic region that serve high-poverty communities and via a nonprofit
organization that works with Latinx families. We are in the process of using
what we have learned to collaboratively design the resources for and with
these families (Subramaniam et al., 2019; Vitak et al., 2018b).

Furthermore, our experiences with the design-thinking process and PD
methodology were honed through our early participation in the intergenerational Kidsteam design group at the University of Maryland (UMD). Kidsteam

is a design team of kids aged seven to eleven as well as adult designers, researchers, and developers that meet twice per week at the UMD to codesign technologies for a range of research projects and companies (Druin, 2002; Fails, Guha, and Druin, 2013; Walsh et al., 2013). We draw on selected examples from the two abovementioned projects and the Kidsteam codesign group throughout this chapter to describe the design-thinking process, PD techniques, and ways to harness benefits and mitigate challenges inherent in each.

Design-Thinking Stages: Inspiration, Ideation, Iteration

The first stage of design thinking, inspiration, focuses on how the design team is motivated to solve a problem or create something new to improve a situation. This results in a design challenge that they would like to pursue, and it is often framed as "I have a challenge" (IDEO, 2015, p. 9). For example, one challenge we have explored in the Science Everywhere project is, How might we help parents learn various skills from their children that can be used in everyday life activities? During this stage, the design team conducts interviews and observations to understand the context in which the eventual design is situated.

The second stage, ideation, focuses on brainstorming ideas to address the challenge. Brainstorming techniques guide design teams through developing concrete ideas based on what was learned during the inspiration stage, framed as "I've learned something" (IDEO, 2015, p. 9). For example, in the Science Everywhere project, in addressing how parents might learn skills from children, we learned in PD sessions with children that they needed ways to show their parents that their skills were indeed useful even for their parents. For example, youth wanted to teach their parents certain skills such as how to make evidence-based arguments and use new technologies (e.g., showing their parents how to use a new app). However, their parents' experience of their children exhibiting mastery of these skills was often not in ideal situations (e.g., arguing against their parents' rules, using technology when they are not supposed to), typically resulting in the children getting in trouble. The children therefore recognized that they needed to find methods that would allow them to reorient and demonstrate the use of these skills in the context of positive situations and outcomes. Their designs reflected this need and helped them to establish these skills as useful.

The last stage in design thinking, iteration, further refines the design ideas and helps reach a satisfactory resolution to the design problem; it is framed as "I have a prototype" (IDEO, 2015). In prototyping for the design challenge from the Science Everywhere project mentioned above, one child used a digital storytelling app to tell his parents the story of a football player being sued. His story included the use of argumentation skills, such as presenting evidence from investigations of the matter. Across these designs, we learned that children were especially keen for their parents to hear about the details of their skill/activity, to acknowledge them as skills, to proceed to the context in which that skill is experienced, and then to try it out themselves.

Techniques Library Staff Can Use in the Design-Thinking Stages

In this section, we describe a few techniques that can be used in the different stages of the design-thinking process. Each of the techniques are from the tradition of PD. We have specifically chosen to highlight PD techniques that we have personally implemented with families in each of the design-thinking stages. As we present each technique below, we also share examples on how we have utilized the approach with families that we have worked with. Although some of these examples are to engage families in nonlibrary settings, the techniques that we share can be adapted and extended to library programs. Our examples map each stage of the design-thinking process to specific PD techniques, but these techniques can be modified and adopted in other stages as needed. As you work with the families that you serve, you will also learn the PD techniques that work best for your community and the problem that the community is trying to solve.

Techniques for Inspiration

One of the major goals of the inspiration stage is to identify the problem and design a challenge statement. It can be helpful to be specific about the types of families your design focuses on, based on your observation of families in your library context as well as your library's and/or state's strategic goals. For example, you may specifically be focused on immigrant families, families who have children with autism spectrum disorder, or families that do not come to the library, among others. At the inspiration stage, defining the problem is necessary but with the caveat that it will shift and change as you inspire, ideate, and iterate together.

The Big Paper Technique. This two-dimensional brainstorming activity allows teams of families and other stakeholders to "collaboratively work on one idea" using a large piece of paper that is placed on the floor or on a table (Guha, Druin, and Fails, 2013, p. 15). The steps for facilitation are these:

- Use large sheets of paper to allow design participants to gather around one workspace (figure 9.1).
- Divide large sheets of paper into three sections: What, Why, How. (Guha, Druin, and Fails, 2013; Walsh et al., 2013)

Figure 9.1   Big Paper Technique. (Photo credit: Kidsteam, Human Computer Interaction Lab, University of Maryland)

Ask families to sketch out their questions, challenges, and design ideas on a specific topic based on the three sections. For example, in the Science Everywhere project, we posted three large sheets of big paper on the walls around the meeting room and modified the questions. Each sheet of paper had a concrete question for families to ponder and respond to:

- What would you like this program to be?
- How do you feel about science?
- What was the best science experiment that you did with your family?

Families used small sticky notes to respond to the questions. They wrote one idea per sticky note so that each idea could be easily grouped and arranged.

Sticky Noting. Families can use sticky noting to evaluate an existing family program or a program that is under development (Fails, Guha, and Druin, 2012). The steps for facilitation are these:

- Assemble a supply of pens/pencils and sticky notes.
- Ask family members to write their likes, dislikes, surprises, and design ideas about a program, on the sticky notes. Each like, dislike, surprise, or design idea is written on a separate sticky note.
- Use colored notes to differentiate ideas, such as blue sticky notes for likes, pink for dislikes, etc.
- Gather the notes and stick them on a large wall space or whiteboard (figure 9.2).
- Group the sticky notes into categories (likes, dislikes, surprises, design ideas) and subcategories (thematic elements that emerge within the larger categories, such as content, timing, and potential partners).

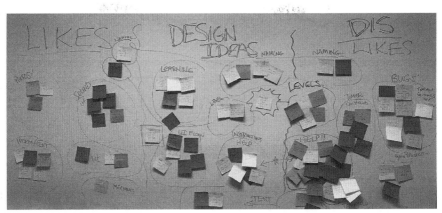

Figure 9.2   Sticky Notes Clustered into Themes on a Whiteboard. (Photo credit: Kidsteam, Human Computer Interaction Lab, University of Maryland)

• Discuss and review with families the themes that emerge. This results in an informal frequency analysis that points to the fertile direction of the next iteration of the program.

Techniques for Ideation

The main goal of the ideation stage is to begin considering possible solutions to the challenge in a tangible way. Families can come together to address a substantial portion of the challenge; each family can design a part of the larger challenge and then bring it together for a cohesive solution; or each family can work together to build on one another's solutions. This is where families' perspectives of the challenge will evolve and change, and they will gain insights into the problem and may discover more problems and challenges to solve. It may take multiple ideation sessions to come up with themes that will point to a tangible solution to a challenge statement, or a single session can provide multiple ideas and tangible pathways for family programming at your library. The number of sessions dedicated to ideation will depend on the time and the availability of the families to participate in the ideation process, and the timeline for the offering and implementation of the program.

The "Bags of Stuff" Technique. Families ideate together by using tangible objects to represent their ideas and solutions to design challenges. Facilitators pay attention to the conversations that happen among groups of families and take written notes to ensure that the discussions and elaboration of the solutions are not lost in the representation of the artifact or solution produced (Fails, Guha, and Druin, 2012). A facilitator can be designated to be a *floater* who moves from one group to another to obtain a sense of

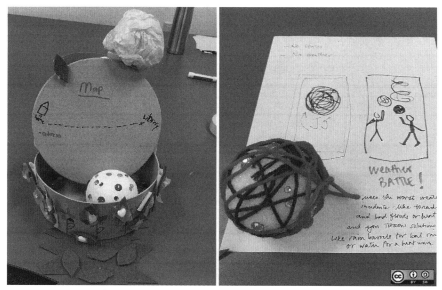

Figure 9.3   Artifacts Designed Using the "Bag of Stuff" Technique. (Source: Jennifer Hopwood)

direction of the conversations and solutions in all groups. Here are the steps for facilitation:

- Provide each design group with a bag that has "stuff" (figure 9.3), such as

    - arts and crafts materials: e.g., construction paper, crayons, glue, tape, scissors, yarn, and cotton balls.
    - "found objects": e.g., leftover Styrofoam packing, wine corks, old LEGO pieces, and small boxes.
    - appropriate three-dimensional materials that are core to the design problem: e.g., matchboxes to represent computers, if you are solving a tech challenge, or bells and noisemakers to represent auditory objects for an audio project (Druin, 2010).

- Create groups of families to brainstorm a solution to a problem and to design "low-tech" prototypes of their solutions by using the materials in the bag.
- Ask each group to present their ideas to one another after the low-tech prototypes are created.
- Take notes on a whiteboard, writing down the ideas that are surprising, that are most repeated among groups, or that receive the most reaction from the whole team.
- Discuss among facilitators the ideas, and decide which one(s) to pursue for further iteration (Chipman et al., 2006).

To illustrate, we used this technique in the Science Everywhere session in which children designed ways to teach their parents skills that they had. Children used small crafting items to build three-dimensional prototypes of their ideas, though one group member chose to use a storytelling app to "build" his idea of creating a skit for his parents.

The Mixing Ideas Technique. The mixing ideas method progresses across three stages of ideation, from individual generation of ideas to small groups mixing ideas together, to the final mixing with the goal of creating a single idea for the team (Guha et al., 2004). The steps for facilitation are these:

1. Generate ideas that address a particular challenge.

    - Children with the support of adult partners observe a situation where the challenge manifests itself.
    - Children document via writing or drawing how people are solving the challenge.
    - Adult partners support the children in terms of putting their ideas on paper (e.g., through writing the ideas down or helping draw them).

2. Reduce the number of ideas.

    - Children share and explain their ideas with other children.
    - Adults guide a whole group discussion on possible ideas to mix.
    - The process is repeated to combine the various ideas until a small number is generated.

3. Arrive at a single idea.

    - Adults take a larger role at this stage, including proposing possible road maps for combining ideas.
    - Mixing ideas includes all the children and adults involved.

To illustrate, in Science Everywhere, we created prototypes for the large touch screen displays that would be situated throughout the community. The displays would showcase the science posts learners were making to an existing social media app. We took the following steps:

- Generate initial designs. Children who were in an all-day summer program worked in groups using bags of stuff and big paper to develop prototypes of a large display system that would be placed throughout their community to showcase the science learning they were doing in their after-school program, at school, and at home in their daily lives.
- Condense prototypes. Children created various prototypes by mixing design ideas. One prototype was a Science Everywhere screen on a bicycle that children would ride and share their ideas with the community.

- Create the new idea. In one session, groups of parents and children took several of the prototypes and mixed them to create a new idea. Building on the previous idea, they envisioned a Science Everywhere blimp that would show their activities and posts more broadly to the world.

The Mission to Mars Technique. In "Mission to Mars," children interact with "Martians," that are adults. The steps for facilitation are these:

- Assign the "Martian" adults to a different room than the children.
- Use videoconferencing technology, such as Skype or Google Hangouts, to enable communication between adults and children (Subramaniam, 2016).
- Begin by having the Martian adult broadcast a message in the form of asking for a potential solution to a problem or by providing a prompt to the children. Then the Martian can opt to go offline or stay online.
- Have the children work in small groups on design solutions to the prompt or problem that the Martian has presented (Dindler et al., 2005).
- Plan the brainstorming time for the children depending on the nature of the problem presented to the children and the time that the children and adults can allocate to this technique.
- Complete the session by having each group of children present their ideas to the Martian. The approach of speaking to a Martian allows children to be more open, honest, and descriptive because they are creating an idea for a "Martian" rather than for a human adult.
- Take notes to amass the big ideas presented by the children (Dindler et al., 2005).

To illustrate, we adapted this technique in the Science Everywhere project by having an adult designer in a remote location join the team virtually to pose a design challenge to the codesign team. Parents and children separately used different design techniques to propose science learning and program activities. They then came together to share their ideas.

Techniques for Iteration

The main goal of the iteration stage is to further refine your ideas to ensure that a solution emerges. At this stage you may also need to go back to the ideation stage to continue the ideation of experiences and perspectives to further solidify your design. Rapid prototyping of your design takes place in the form of low-fidelity prototypes that often will move progressively toward high fidelity. Low-fidelity prototypes often are simple, quick, and easy to create; they take the form of sketches or mock-ups, with the goal of turning your ideas into tangible representation. High-fidelity prototypes are often functional, interactive, and closer to the final product. At this stage, your goal is toward creating the tangible solution that you want to implement or develop (IDEO, 2015).

The Layered Elaboration Technique. Researchers have discovered that young people are often uncomfortable messing with or ruining the work of other youth and adult design partners. "Even if the work in question is a low-tech, initial, brainstormed prototype, designers, especially youth design partners, can be sensitive to changing the work of others" (Fails, Guha, and Druin, 2012, pp. 137–38). Hence, the layered elaboration technique works well because it allows young people and adults to ideate by adding, changing, extending, and/or removing the ideas of others without eliminating the original ideas or ideas that were presented by others. The steps for facilitation are:

- Begin with forming groups that will each choose a unique color marker.
- Provide a base design for solving a problem to the whole group; alternatively, small groups can also design from scratch.
- Allow the entire group to come together so that each group briefly presents its ideas. The large group meeting allows elaboration on the designs so that the next iteration can occur.
- Use a clear overhead transparency to illustrate the first iteration of ideas from the large group meeting.
- Pass this transparency to one group, which will add ideas on top of the previous idea by drawing on the new transparency paper with its color marker.
- Repeat this process until each group has had an opportunity to include its design ideas. In this way, all changes are layered on transparency sheets and recognizable through the use of different colored markers. Elimination of ideas is indicated by crossing them out (Walsh et al., 2010).
- Identify "hot spots," or places in the sketches where there are many changes or crossing out of ideas as areas for further iteration or discussion.
- Conduct a final debrief meeting after all groups have had a chance to provide their design ideas. During the debriefing, a facilitator will capture the big ideas on a whiteboard or a large sheet of paper.

To illustrate, as we iterated on the design of the Science Everywhere social media app, we used the layered elaboration technique to solicit ideas from families on how we could design features in the app to help parents and children use the app together to share their family science experiences. Parents worked in groups with their children to design features on top of screenshots of the existing Science Everywhere app. During brief stand-up meetings, each family group shared the features of its design and then switched to another screenshot, designing ideas on top of the previous group's ideas (figure 9.4).

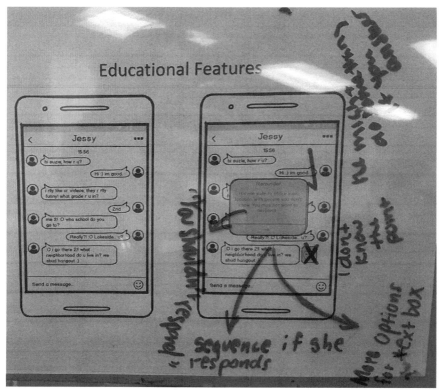

Figure 9.4 Layered Elaboration Technique. (Photo credit: Kidsteam, Human Computer Interaction Lab, University of Maryland)

Typical Challenges When We Design with Families

The design-thinking approach and PD techniques help families easily understand and engage in the design processes. They have many benefits that make them worthwhile particularly for library staff in terms of *planning* innovative family learning experiences in libraries, for *codesigning* these experiences, and for *engaging* families in learning activities. The approach and techniques facilitate the development of innovative programmatic ideas that include the voices of adults and children who will eventually participate in these experiences (Subramaniam, 2016), instead of library staff making determinations on what programs and services families will and should engage in. Additionally, they allow library staff to take the role as facilitators and mentors of learning and further facilitate families' deepened engagement with learning, instead of being experts on learning in libraries (Clegg and Subramaniam, 2019). Constant and sustained engagement through the design-thinking stages with families will also position library staff to better serve their communities based on real needs that these families have and will empower families to share their learning challenges with library staff.

However, introducing these processes to new audiences, particularly families, and helping them become fully engaged, freely offering their ideas and collaborating with others to do so, is a process, and there are often challenges along the way. We have identified four challenges from our own experiences designing with families in and out of library settings.

Challenge 1: Taking on the Role of Designer—Embracing Divergent Thinking

Design thinking emphasizes divergent thinking, or a disposition of generating creative ideas by exploring many possible solutions (Lieberman, 1965). Divergent thinking is often fostered in playful, spontaneous, joy-filled contexts (Lieberman, 1965) and can—in fact, should—be leveraged throughout the design process. Often, however, such divergent thinking interactions are not the norm, especially for adults in new social settings. Hence, when engaging new families in PD, it can be challenging to help them begin to feel comfortable sharing such wide-ranging ideas, especially as divergent thinking encourages wacky, off-the-wall, "bad" ideas during idea generation.

Young children, on the other hand, are often quite comfortable with such thinking processes (Lieberman, 1965). It can therefore be useful to encourage children's playful ideas as models for designing and design interactions. Additionally, creating a playful space can be quite important for fostering divergent thinking. This can be done with playful colors in the room, funny or inspirational quotes written or posted on walls/boards, and upbeat music played in the background. Facilitators play important roles highlighting participants' divergent ideas as models as they arise, generating their own wild and wacky ideas as groups are working, and creating prompts that inspire such playful ideation. For example, one prompt we often use is to ask participants to pretend they are Oprah, a superhero, or a used car salesperson and to generate ideas from those perspectives (Liedtka and Ogilvie, 2011). In Science Everywhere, we paid close attention to the setup of the meeting room for sessions, often using colorful tablecloths to add color and a sense of playfulness to the decor. We also wrote welcoming and playful notes on the board. Additionally, facilitators would encourage groups to pursue playful ideas (such as the Science Everywhere bicycle or blimp) that children suggested as they floated and helped specific groups.

Challenge 2: Countering Existing Power Norms

Within families, there are typically well-ingrained power norms between family members (e.g., children must obey parents, parents make decisions, etc.). While these norms are often necessary and positive, they can pose challenges to the design-thinking process. For example, in Science Everywhere we have found that during activities with their children, parents are often accustomed to taking on the role of behavior manager (Yip et al., 2016). This often means (1) parents are less engaged in the design activity and (2) they are overseeing their children's interactions, determining what is allowed and what is not. However, in going through the design-thinking stages with families, all members should be fully engaged in the design process, and all ideas should be heard, valued, and taken seriously. This can be particularly challenging for families from low-SES communities where authoritarian parenting styles have been found to be more common (Hoff, Laursen, and Tardif, 2002). We have therefore found it useful to have parents and children work in groups separate from their own family members so that all groups consist of parents and children from different families (Yip et al., 2016). Having such mixed groups can break down the parent-child power dynamics and facilitate new adult-child dynamics that are more conducive to design-thinking processes.

Challenge 3: Knowing Which Technique to Use

Figuring out which technique to use and when to use it is something all PD facilitators grapple with when they plan a design session. In the Safe Data Safe Families project, we unsuccessfully adapted the big-paper approach to obtain information about how low-socioeconomic-population families are currently identifying whether or not a website is safe for their children. We divided the big-paper technique into two sections. In section 1, we asked families to indicate websites that they would consider safe and would allow their child to share their information on that website. In section 2, we asked them to indicate what signals or features these websites had that indicated safety. Similarly, we had another poster where they did the same but for websites that they did not consider to be safe. Unfortunately, these families struggled to come up with the websites and to remember the features that signaled whether they were safe or unsafe. In hindsight, we think that showing them some examples of websites and then using the sticky-noting technique to indicate features that signal the safeness of the website would have worked much better. We could have adapted the sticky-noting technique by projecting the websites on a big screen and then asking them to place different color sticky notes, with a reason written on each sticky note, on features that signal either safety or unsafe conditions.

Over time, determining the appropriate PD techniques becomes less complex as the facilitator learns the ins and outs of each technique and garners a general framework for grouping the techniques by stage of design. There are no hard and fast rules, and rules are meant to be broken, but our description above of PD techniques provides pointers for facilitators to choose appropriate PD techniques to meet their design challenge.

Challenge 4: Understanding Equal Partnership and How It Works

This last challenge is important for PD facilitators and codesigners alike. There are some PD approaches in which participants or codesigners may just participate in a single session. On the other hand, the cooperative inquiry methodology (Druin, 2002) that we espouse specifically advocates for *design partnership*. That is, codesigners are engaged in the design of a prototype throughout the design process, from inspiration and initial ideation stages to the implementation of the final design (and often through multiple iterations of a design) (Druin, 2002). This approach to codesign is challenging in that it requires ongoing design sessions with codesigners, a significant time commitment for all involved. Yet this approach ensures that the resulting design is a product of all codesigners' ideas and not simply an implementer's overwriting of codesigned ideas. Such ongoing participation of codesigners, however, enables participants to become deeply involved in the PD practices and dispositions and to develop a more integrated group dynamic. Libraries are ideal spaces for this type of continued participation of families because of their consistent presence in communities, since they are spaces in which families regularly engage.

Conclusion

In this chapter, we presented design thinking as an approach to design families' library-based learning experiences, programs, and services with and for them. We also introduced selected PD techniques that allow librarians to inspire, ideate, and iterate with families in their communities. Mastery of the PD techniques requires familiarization with the techniques and potential challenges, and adaptability to the needs and comfort level of the families that librarians work with. Some means of achieving this include observing other educators who are utilizing the design-thinking approach and PD techniques with their community and/or working in partnerships with researchers who are well versed in these techniques (Coburn and Penuel, 2016). The design of family engagement programs via the design-thinking approach may initially take time to execute, but mastery of this approach and PD techniques will shape your mindset and that of the families you serve to see themselves as the designers of their own learning experiences.

Acknowledgments

Our heartiest gratitude goes to the Human-Computer Interaction Lab at the University of Maryland, particularly to Dr. Allison Druin (now at the Pratt Institute), who founded the Kidsteam PD program and who has inspired us to utilize these PD techniques in our own work. With her encouragement and mentorship, we are now able to share these techniques with library staff nationwide who can empower families to contribute to the design of programs and services at their library. We would also like to thank the families who were involved in the Science Everywhere and Safe Data Safe Families projects that have been mentioned in the chapter. The Science Everywhere and Safe Data Safe Families projects were generously funded, respectively, by the National Science Foundation (#1441523) and by the Institute of Museum and Library Services National Leadership Grant (LG-81-16-0154-16).

Note

1. For a more exhaustive description of PD techniques, we encourage the readers to refer to Fails, Guha, and Druin (2012) and the Design Thinking for Libraries website, http://designthinkingforlibraries.com.

References

Ahn, June, Tamara Clegg, Jason Yip, Elizabeth Bonsignore, Daniel Pauw, Lautaro Cabrera, Kenna Hernly, Caroline Pitt, Kelly Mills, Arturo Salazar, Diana Griffing, Jeff Rick, and Rachael Marr. "Science Everywhere: Designing Public, Tangible Displays to Connect Youth Learning Across Settings." *Proceedings of SIGCHI Human Factors in Computing Systems*, New York, April 2018. https://doi.org/10.1145/3173574.3173852.

Ahn, June, Tamara Clegg, Jason Yip, Elizabeth Bonsignore, Daniel Pauw, Michael Gubbels, Becky Lewittes, and Emily Rhodes. "Seeing the Unseen Learner: Designing and Using Social Media to Recognize Children's Science Dispositions in Action." *Learning Media and Technology* 41, no. 2 (2016): 252–82. https://doi.org/10.1080/17439884.2014.964254.

Brown, Tim, "The Making of a Design Thinker." *Metropolis*, October 1, 2009. https://www.metropolismag.com/ideas/the-making-of-a-design-thinker/.

Cabrera, Lautaro, June Ahn, Jason Yip, Tamara Clegg, Kenna Hernly, Elizabeth Bonsignore, Caroline Pitt, and Daniel Pauw. "Exploring Practices on the Move: Facilitating Learning Across a Neighborhood." *Proceedings of International Conference of the Learning Sciences*, London, June 2018. https://repository.isls.org//handle/1/487Chipman, Gene, Allison Druin, Dianne Beer, Jerry Alan Fails, Mona Leigh Guha, and Sante Simms. "A Case Study of Tangible Flags: A Collaborative Technology to Enhance Field Trips." *IDC '06: Proceedings of the 2006 Conference on Interaction Design and Children*, Tampere, Finland, June 2006. https://doi.org/10.1145/1139073.1139081.

Clegg, Tamara, and Mega Subramaniam. "Redefining Mentorship in Facilitating Interest-Driven Learning in Libraries." In *Reconceptualizing Libraries: Opportunities from the Learning and Information Sciences*, edited by Victor R. Lee and Abigail L. Phillips. Abingdon, UK: Routledge, 2019, 140–57.

Coburn, Cynthia, and William Penuel. "Research-Practice Partnerships in Education: Outcomes, Dynamics, and Open Questions." *Educational Researcher* 45, no. 1 (2016): 48–54. https://doi.org/10.3102/0013189X 16631750.

Coleman, Mary Catherine. "Design Thinking and the School Library." *Knowledge Quest* 44, no. 5 (2016): 62–68.

Dindler, Christian, Eva Eriksson, Ole Sejer Iversen, Andreas Lykke-Olesen, and Martin Ludvigsen. "Mission from Mars: A Method for Exploring User Requirements for Children in a Narrative Space." *IDC '05: Proceedings of the 2005 Conference on Interaction Design and Children: Toward a More Expansive View of Technology and Children's Activities*, Boulder, CO, 2005. https://doi.org/10.1145/1109540.1109546.

Druin, Allison. "Children as Codesigners of New Technologies: Valuing the Imagination to Transform What Is Possible." *New Directions for Youth Development* 128 (Winter 2010): 35–43. https://doi.org/10.1002/yd.373.

Druin, Allison. "The Role of Children in the Design of New Technology." *Behaviour and Information Technology* 21, no. 1 (2002): 1–25.

Fails, Jerry Alan, Mona Leigh Guha, and Allison Druin. "Methods and Techniques for Involving Children in the Design of New Technology for Children." *Foundations and Trends in Human-Computer Interaction* 6, no. 2 (2013): 85–166. https://doi.org/10.1561/1100000018.

Guha, Mona Leigh, Allison Druin, Gene Chipman, Jerry Alan Fails, Sante Simms, and Allison Farber. "Mixing Ideas: A New Technique for Working with Young Children as Design Partners." *IDC '04: Proceedings of the 2004 Conference on Interaction Design and Children: Building a Community*, Baltimore, MD, 2004. https://doi.org/10.1145/1017833.1017838.

Guha, Mona Leigh, Allison Druin, and Jerry Alan Fails. "Cooperative Inquiry Revisited: Reflections of the Past and Guidelines for the Future of Intergenerational Co-Design." *International Journal of Child-Computer Interaction* 1, no. 1 (2013): 14–23. https://doi.org/10.1016/j.ijcci.2012.08.003.

Hoff, Erika, Brett Laursen, and Twila Tardif. "Socioeconomic Status and Parenting." In *Handbook of Parenting Volume 2: Biology and Ecology of Parenting*, edited by Mark Bornstein. Mahwah, NJ: Lawrence Erlbaum Associates, 2002, 231–52.

IDEO. "Design Thinking for Libraries: A Toolkit for Patron-Centered Design." http://designthinkingforlibraries.com (accessed August 10, 2019).

Jenkins, Henry. *Confronting the Challenges of Participatory Culture: Media Education for the 21st Century*. Cambridge, MA: MIT Press, 2009.

Lieberman, J. N. Playfulness and Divergent Thinking: An Investigation of Their Relationship at the Kindergarten Level. *The Journal of Genetic Psychology* 107, no. 2 (1965): 219–24. https://doi.org/10.1080/00221325.1965.10533661.

Liedtka, J., and Ogilvie, T. *Designing for Growth: A Design Thinking Tool Kit for Managers*. New York, NY: Columbia University Press, 2011.

Mills, Kelly, Elizabeth Bonsignore, Tamara Clegg, June Ahn, Jason Yipp, Daniel Pauw, Lautaro Cabrera, Kenna Hernly, and Caroline Pitt. "Connecting

Children's Scientific Funds of Knowledge Shared on Social Media to Science Concepts." *International Journal of Child-Computer Interaction* 21 (2019): 54–64. https://doi.org/10.1016/j.ijcci.2019.04.003.

Subramaniam, Mega. "Designing the Library of the Future for and with Teens: Librarians as the 'Connector' in Connected Learning." *Journal of Research on Libraries and Young Adults* 7, no. 2 (2016). http://www.yalsa.ala.org /jrlya/wp- content/uploads/2011/02/Subramaniam_Designing-the -Library_Final.pdf.

Subramaniam, Mega, Priya Kumar, Shandra Morehouse, Yuting Liao, and Jessica Vitak. "Leveraging Funds of Knowledge to Manage Privacy Practices in Families." *Proceedings of the 82nd Annual American Society for Information Science & Technology Conference*, Melbourne, Australia, 2019. https://doi .org/10.1002/pra2.67.

Urban Libraries Council. *Leadership Brief: Libraries Supporting Family Learning.* Washington DC: Urban Libraries Council, 2016. https://www .urbanlibraries.org/assets/124-11_ULC_Leadership_Brief_Families _Learning_proof2.pdf.

Vitak, Jessica, Yuting Liao, Priya Kumar, and Mega Subramaniam. "Librarians as Information Intermediaries: Navigating Tensions between Being Helpful and Being Liable." *13th International Conference on Information, iConference*, Sheffield, UK. 2018a. https://doi.org/10.1007/978-3-319-78105-1_80.

Vitak, Jessica, Yuting Liao, Mega Subramaniam, Priya Kumar. "'I Knew It Was Too Good to Be True': The Challenges Economically Disadvantaged Internet Users Face in Assessing Trustworthiness, Avoiding Scams, and Developing Self-Efficacy Online." *Computer Supported Collaborative Work (CSCW) Conference*, article 176 (2018b): 1–25. https://doi.org/10.1145 /3274445.

Walsh, Greg, Allison Druin, Mona Leigh Guha, Elizabeth Foss, Evan Golub, Leshell Hatley, Elizabeth Bonsignore, and Sonia Franckel. "Layered Elaboration: A New Technique for Co-Design with Children." *CHI '10: Proceedings on the SIGCHI Conference on Human Factors in Computing System*, Atlanta, GA, 2010. https://doi.org/10.1145/1753326.1753512.

Walsh, Greg, Elizabeth Foss, Jason Yip, and Allison Druin. "FACIT PD: A Framework for Analysis and Creation of Intergenerational Techniques for Participatory Design." *Proceedings of the SIGCHI Conference on Human Factors in Computing Systems*, New York, 2013. https://doi.org/10.1145/2470654 .2481400.

Weiss, Heather, Margaret Caspe, M. Elena Lopez, and Lorette McWilliams. *IDEABOOK: Libraries for Families.* Cambridge, MA: Harvard Family Research Project, 2016. https://globalfrp.org/content/download/73/436/file/IdeaBook.pdf.

Yip, Jason, Tamara Clegg, June Ahn, Judith Odili Uchidiuno, Elizabeth Bonsignore, Austin Beck, Daniel Pauw, and Kelly Mills. "The Evolution of Engagements and Social Bonds during Child-Parent Co-Design." *Proceedings of the 2016 SIGCHI Conference on Human Factors in Computing Systems*, New York, 2016. https://doi.org/10.1145/2858036.2858380.

Yip, Jason, Tamara Clegg, Elizabeth Bonsignore, Helene Gelderblom, Emily Rhodes, and Allison Druin. "Brownies or Bags-of-Stuff?: Domain Expertise in Cooperative Inquiry with Children." *Proceedings of the 12th International Conference on Interaction Design and Children*, New York, 2013a. https://doi.org/10.1145/2485760.2485763.

Yip, Jason, Elizabeth Foss, Elizabeth Bonsignore, Mona Leigh Guha, Leyla Norooz, Emily Rhodes, Brenna McNally, Panagis Papadatos, Evan Golub, and Allison Druin. "Children Initiating and Leading Cooperative Inquiry Sessions." *Proceedings of the 12th International Conference on Interaction Design and Children*, New York, 2013b. https://doi.org/10.1145/2485760 .2485796.

Engaging Families in Computational Literacy Opportunities

Ricarose Roque and Sari A. Widman

In a library meeting room, families sat together in clusters, drawing, talking, laughing, swiping their fingers across tablet screens. Using a computer application called ScratchJr, the families programmed animated stories. One mother asked her two daughters if they would like to create a story about their camping trip. A brother and sister sat side by side, as the sister programmed their characters to move. Another mother recorded her voice saying, "Happy Birthday," to re-create her son's birthday party. A father and mother showed their daughter how to add new characters and program them to move; their daughter responded by exclaiming, "Let's make something fun!"

Since 2012 the Family Creative Learning (FCL) program has invited families to create and share stories using technologies such as ScratchJr featured in the vignette above. We have worked with community-based organizations, after-school programs, and libraries to engage nondominant[1] families in collaborative learning with new technologies. We seek to create an environment where families can build on their goals, roles, practices, and cultural resources, and support one another in the context of computing (Roque, Lin, and Liuzzi, 2016). Our team has worked within the New England, Southwest, and Mountain regions of the United States.

In this chapter, we describe the FCL program in public libraries. With the support of the Institute of Museum and Library Services (IMLS), we at the Creative Communities research group at the University of Colorado Boulder collaborated with the Denver and Boulder Public Library systems to engage families in computational literacy. We describe the ways we adapted the FCL model for public libraries and our exploration of new opportunities with storytelling and coding. Finally, we share the experiences of families and facilitators.

Computational Literacy

Learning to code or using computer programming can enable young people to create and express their ideas. As people learn to code, they engage in computational concepts and practices and creative thinking, and they develop problem-solving strategies (Wing, 2006). In the FCL project, we use the phrase "computational literacy" to refer to the ability to create, express, and invent with technology. We frame computational literacy across three dimensions: concepts (e.g., sequences, events, and loops), practices (e.g., experimenting, remixing, and debugging), and perspectives (seeing oneself as a creator and collaborator with computing) (Brennan and Resnick, 2012). We want people to become computational creators in addition to computational thinkers.

But what does computational literacy look like? Figure 10.1 shows the storyboard and ScratchJr screenshots from a family project about a visit to the San Diego Zoo. The family had to break down its story into multiple scenes. These scenes encapsulated different characters, objects, and actions. In one scene, the family was getting ready to move from the house to the car. The family members programmed this scene by having individual characters move across the screen. After the characters moved across the screen, the scene changed and showed the characters inside a moving car. To create these scenes and actions, family members engaged with the computational concepts of sequence and events to make characters move and change scenes. They also engaged in computational practices of experimenting to explore the ScratchJr code and debugging whenever they got stuck.

The FCL Model in Community Settings

From 2012 to 2015, we developed the FCL model through an iterative design process with staff and educators at community-based organizations such as "Computer Clubhouses" and community centers (Roque, 2016). The FCL focused on children aged eight to twelve who participated in a four- to six-week workshop series held once a week for two hours at a community site. The workshops are implemented by facilitators who welcome families and guide and support their interests rather than prescribe activities.

(A)

(B)

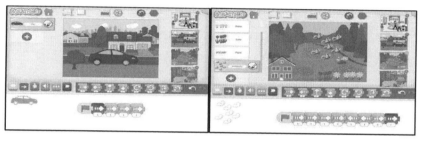

Figure 10.1 A Family Trip to San Diego Represented in a Storyboard (A) and in ScratchJr (B)

Facilitators include community center staff, local volunteers, and students from local high schools and universities.

The core design elements of the FCL model are as follows:

- Eat: Workshops begin with a shared meal from a local restaurant.
- Meet: Facilitators meet separately with parents and children to engage them in activities that prepare them for Make.
- Make: Parents and children engage in design-based activities using creative technologies such as the ScratchJr programming environment.
- Share: Families discuss their projects with each other and receive feedback and questions. Every workshop series culminates in a community showcase where families share their projects with other families, staff members, and community members.

Expanding FCL to Libraries

To adapt the FCL program in public libraries, we first took steps to know and understand those whom we were engaging. We had regular conversations with our library partners. We held focus groups with parents to understand the library and community context. These conversations helped us to reflect on the potential opportunities for families.

We regularly met with our library partners at Boulder and Denver Public Libraries to adapt and implement FCL into their settings. Our Denver library partners were in predominantly low-income areas of the city and served a diverse patron demographic, including African American and immigrant communities from Mexico and Vietnam. In contrast, Boulder is a largely affluent and predominantly white college town. However, the library had recently embarked on a new community outreach effort to engage a small but growing Latinx population in the city. Our partners' goals varied, from increasing family engagement to building stronger relationships with the Spanish-speaking community in their city and to increasing awareness of their technology tools and resources.

Prior to implementing FCL with our library partners, we held six 90-minute focus groups with twenty-two parents to increase our understanding of the local context and to gain insight into the needs of parents in the community (Widman and Roque, 2019). With the exception of one father, all were mothers who were primarily Latinx; some attendees were either Chinese or Turkish. We asked parents about their families' library use, access to resources in the broader community, and technology use, attitudes, and challenges. We were particularly interested in understanding the kinds of barriers families might face to access library resources or to attend a workshop series such as FCL.

Our focus groups included an icebreaker, a group activity to discuss conversation norms, and, in some cases, a walking tour of the library or trip to the makerspace. Visits to the makerspace and walking tours allowed us to introduce participants to resources, identify what parts of the space they used and were aware of, and hear their perspectives. Focus groups also included a resource-mapping exercise in order to get a sense of the community assets participants valued. To facilitate parents' participation, we provided food and childcare and a Spanish interpreter when needed.

Adapting FCL in Libraries

Considering our project goals as well as our conversations with families and meetings with library staff, we made several adaptations to FCL's model, which are described below.

Addressing Family Needs

We sought to address the needs that parents shared during the focus groups. Parents reported that access to childcare was their greatest barrier to participation. We provided dinner, childcare, interpreters, and translated materials to represent the languages spoken by families.

Parents also shared a desire for more activities designed for all-age participation that their whole family could attend. While we initially considered limiting participation to ages five to seven years, we opted to do away with any age limitations after hearing from parents. We encouraged older siblings to participate along with their younger siblings and provided childcare for very young children who might have trouble engaging in workshop activities. Because some parents described concerns about transportation, we also made bus passes available to participants who needed them.

Engaging in More Active Communication and Recruitment

Unsurprisingly, the parents we spoke to did strongly associate the library with books, but they were much less aware of the other resources the libraries offered, including makerspaces and STEAM (Science, Technology, Engineering, Arts, and Mathematics) programming. We worked with our library partners to more actively communicate and share resources with families. We encouraged our partners to go beyond passive communication strategies such as posting on social media or sending announcements through email newsletters. Instead, we persuaded them to reach out to organizations that already had relationships with families, such as local elementary schools. During the FCL workshops, we worked with our partners to incorporate exposure to other resources and upcoming events, such as holding the Make portion of FCL in the libraries' makerspaces when possible or alternately arranging makerspace tours.

We also started to host one-off events and workshops prior to the FCL workshop series in order to build relationships with community members and create more visibility for both FCL and other library opportunities to learn with technology. Additionally, in Boulder, we leveraged a partnership with an elementary school to host workshops that were cosponsored by the library in order to introduce families to library resources.

Enlisting Facilitators

Library staff members participated as facilitators during the workshops. Many of the library staff had some familiarity with coding with Scratch or ScratchJr, as many were either coordinators in the makerspace or were coordinating STEM programming for their library. We encouraged library staff members to build on practices already in use, such as building relationships with family members and learning side by side with participants.

In addition to library staff members, we invited other library community members such as "teen techs" or local high school interns and local professionals. We augmented library facilitators with undergraduate and graduate students from CU Boulder, who became members of our FCL team. We especially tried to recruit students who could speak the languages of families.

Combining Storytelling and Coding

Past FCL workshops engaged families with code through a variety of activities that included designing interactive animations, games, and stories. In adapting to the library setting, we increased our focus on storytelling. We hoped that integrating storytelling could better support younger learners, connect to the traditional literacy activities that already engaged children and families in their library, and recognize and value families' "funds of knowledge," or the cultural resources and backgrounds of families (González, Moll, and Amanti, 2005).

During the workshops, we asked families to share a favorite family story, memory, or vacation and asked them to program and animate their stories using the ScratchJr programming environment, which was designed for children aged five to seven (see figure 10.1B). In ScratchJr, children can program "sprites" or characters and objects on the screen by dragging, dropping, and connecting blocks with different commands. Children can program a range of actions that include movement, sound, appearance, and events. ScratchJr also includes various built-in images such as people, animals, vehicles, and background images that range from parks to outer space.

As we prepared activities for families and began to see them create and share their stories through code, we saw multiple parallels between computational literacy and storytelling, which we discuss further in the next section.

Implementing FCL in Libraries: Bringing Family Stories to Life with Code

The families who participated in FCL's various library implementations came in different configurations. Some came as a parent-child pair, while some brought the whole family. While we advertised FCL as being ideal for kids between five and seven years old, families came with a variety of ages. The youngest participant was three years old; she worked on a ScratchJr project with the support of her two parents.

Children engaged in a variety of storytelling activities during the Meet portions of the workshops to prepare them to engage in storytelling during Make with their parents. Multiple languages were spoken, with the most common languages being English and Spanish. During Make, families initially shared stories on paper storyboards to allow them to express and share a story. Afterward, they transformed their story into an animation by programming sprites and backgrounds with the ScratchJr programming environment.

As families engaged in telling stories with ScratchJr, they exhibited the components of computational literacy. They used code to express concepts, experimented with the coding blocks of ScratchJr, and recognized their creativity as a family. In some cases, families' stories stayed grounded in real-life events, as they moved from paper-based depictions on storyboards, to animations in ScratchJr. At times, family stories took on a different—even fantastical—turn as children were inspired by the built-in images and sounds in ScratchJr. For example, what started as a family trip to the beach turned into a new adventure into outer space after the family discovered a rocket ship image in ScratchJr. Another family took the prompt to tell your story of a family vacation in a silly direction, animating a family "vacation you *don't* want to go on," with one of the sons creating a story where he gets eaten by a shark but then the family gets ice cream in the end.

Each family had its own dynamic. Parents took on a variety of roles in response to their goals, past interactions, and children's needs at the time. Some parent-and-child pairs worked closely together, consulting each other as they worked on their projects. Other parents watched closely as their child worked on the project, occasionally asking questions. Some parents acted like project managers, keeping track of time, making sure their children took turns, or calling on facilitators whenever they needed help (Roque, Lin, and Liuzzi, 2016; Roque and Jain, 2018).

Conclusion

Through our work adapting FCL into their library contexts, librarians shared new insights about families and the uses of technology in literacy development. Library staff members expressed how much they valued the experience of connecting and developing relationships with the whole family. Typically, their patron interactions would involve just one member of a family. However, in FCL they were able to meet, interact, and collaborate with other family members. This experience helped them develop a fuller understanding of their patrons' goals, interests, and backgrounds. Additionally, seeing what they could do with tools like ScratchJr and activities that involved storytelling in meaningful ways gave them an expanded sense of possibilities with computing.

We have documented our model in a Facilitation Guide, available for free download and remixing under Creative Commons license (Family Creative Learning Website and Facilitator Guide, n.d.). We support and encourage other educators to adapt the model. We are currently documenting our work with our library partners into a set of new resources and an updated facilitation guide.

Inspired by our experiences adapting FCL with our library partners, we plan to explore new possibilities for engaging families in computing. Some of these explorations will involve new activities such as incorporating physical computing, or allowing families to connect their projects to the physical world. Other explorations will address persistent challenges that emerged from our implementations, such as recruiting families and building community relationships with organizations connected to families. As we engage in these explorations, we remain committed to engaging families, especially from nondominant groups, in meaningful ways with computing. We see libraries as important partners in supporting families to see themselves as creators and collaborators with computing.

Acknowledgments

This project was made possible in part by the Institute of Museum and Library Services (LG-96-17-0176-17). We want to thank our partners at Boulder Public Library and the ideaLAB makerspaces at Denver Public Library as well as the families that ate, met, made, and shared with us.

Note

1. When we use the term "nondominant," we refer to people who are disconnected from opportunity by reasons of race, ethnicity, immigration status, and socioeconomic status (Gutiérrez, Morales, and Martinez, 2009).

References

Brennan, Karen, and Mitchel Resnick. "New Frameworks for Studying and Assessing the Development of Computational Thinking." Paper presented at the American Education Researchers Association, Vancouver, Canada, April 2012.

Family Creative Learning Website and Facilitator Guide. n.d. http://familycreativelearning.org/guide (accessed April 16, 2021).

González, Norma, Luis C. Moll, and Cathy Amanti, eds. *Funds of Knowledge: Theorizing Practices in Households, Communities, and Classrooms.* Mahwah, NJ: Lawrence Erlbaum Associates, 2005.

Gutiérrez, Kris D., P. Zitlali Morales, and Danny C. Martinez. "Remediating Literacy: Culture, Difference, and Learning for Students from Nondominant Communities." *Review of Research in Education* 33, no. 1 (2009): 212–45. https://doi.org/10.3102/0091732X08328267.

Roque, Ricarose. "Family Creative Learning." In *Makeology: Makerspaces as Learning Environments*, edited by Kylie Peppler, Erica R. Halverson, and Yasmin B. Kafai. London: Routledge, 2016, 47–63.

Roque, Ricarose and Rupal Jain. "Becoming Facilitators of Creative Computing in Out-of-School Settings." In *Rethinking Learning in the Digital Age:*

Making the Learning Sciences Count, edited by Judy Kay and Rosemary Luckin. International Conference of the Learning Sciences (ICLS), volume 1. London: International Society of the Learning Sciences, 2018, 592–99. https://repository.isls.org//handle/1/908.

Roque, Ricarose, Karina Lin, and Richard Liuzzi. "'I'm Not Just a Mom': Parents Developing Multiple Roles in Creative Computing." In *Transforming Learning, Empowering Learners*, edited by Chee-Kit Looi, Joseph Polman, Ulrike Cress, and Peter Reimann. International Conference of the Learning Sciences, volume 2. Singapore: International Society of the Learning Sciences, 2016, 663–70. https://repository.isls.org/handle/1/177.

ScratchJr. n.d. https://www.scratchjr.org (accessed April 16, 2021).

Widman, Sari, and Ricarose Roque. "Parent Perspectives on Interfacing with Computing Opportunities in Library Settings." In *Proceedings of the 2019 Connected Learning Summit*, Irvine, CA, October 2019. https://2019.connectedlearningsummit.org/proceedings.

Wing, Jeannette M. "Computational Thinking." *Communications of the ACM* 49, no. 3 (2006): 33–35.

CHAPTER ELEVEN

Age Is But a Number: How to Create Multigenerational Family Programs in Your Public Library

Jessica Hilburn and Becky Stahl

For the greater part of the past ten years, libraries have been shifting their emphasis from a depository of books and information to centers of community life. Being a center or even *the* center of the community keeps the library relevant to residents throughout their lifetime. At Benson Memorial Library in Titusville, Pennsylvania, we have sought to be a relevant community institution through family programming. Family programming involves the whole family learning together and sharing experiences that are fun and entertaining while also developing knowledge and creativity. Libraries are one of the only public learning spaces that serve entire families, from young children to teens and adults. Schools and after-school programs are segmented by age, but libraries are different: they are able to serve all ages simultaneously. This chapter describes the benefits of creating family programs and the methods to overcome barriers through lessons learned by our library.

Why Focus on Multigenerational Family Programs?

Our efforts at family programming support what research has shown to be important for family well-being.

Strengthening the parent-child bond. Through offering all-ages programming at the library, families have an opportunity to bond with each other that might not be possible outside the library. Brain science has shown how from starting at birth, reciprocal parent-child interactions influence the neural connections that support learning (Hutton et al., 2015). And while most brain development takes place before age five or six, a second wave of development takes place during adolescence, in which brain science shows that strong, supportive relationships with family members can help youth learn how to make informed decisions, develop relationships with peers, and avoid impulsive and risky behaviors (Steinberg, 2014). When the library is able to offer fun, structured activities that parents and children want to attend, the result is enrichment for all ages while also taking away stress from caregivers by letting them take a step back from the role of activity planner and letting the staff handle the work.

Research also indicates that school-age children spend only about 20 percent of their waking time in school (Banks et al., 2007). All learners need diverse out-of-school opportunities to enhance their knowledge and personal development, and the participation of concerned adults—parents and other interested adults—is an important element in encouraging learning. Choosing to create programs with games and fun activities gets families to play together (see figure 11.1). The benefits of play for children are numerous: from problem-solving and conceptual knowledge to social understanding and social and emotional regulation (White, n.d.; Zosh et al., 2017). And by playing together, families become more supportive of one another and interested in each other's lives (Hartwell-Walker, 2018).

Promoting interfamily connections. It is often difficult for families with children to form social connections. Where to go, whom to trust, and how to form bonds are all challenges that families, especially those with young children, face in modern society. Technology can make us feel less alone, but it does not provide as intimate a human bonding opportunity as face-to-face interaction has for millennia. Interfamily bonding is challenging yet crucial for young families, and the library is the perfect incubator for its development.

In a study by researchers Ian Ruthven, Steven Buchanan, and Cara Jardine (2018), young mothers expressed a desire to socialize and meet other young mothers but did not know how to make those connections. Young families are particularly in need of interaction and of knowing where help and information can be found, and they desire a sense of belonging in their community (Strange et al., 2014). Having children can be an isolating life development when young people do not know how to locate and have no place to meet with other young families in similar life situations.

Australian researcher Tim Moore (2006, p. 13) studied the importance of families connecting with one another regularly and explained that "to facilitate such interactions, we need to ensure that all families have easy access to family-friendly settings where they can meet other families and also access the services they need." The library is the perfect conduit for such interactions and, because of its reputation, trustworthiness, and friendliness to families, can serve in such a capacity with relative ease. Parents and children who otherwise may never have met are brought together through the library and form lasting bonds that positively impact their lives for years to come.

Figure 11.1 Youth Services Librarian Becky Stahl versus a Young Participant in the Benson Memorial Library Hula Hoop Faceoff Family Program, July 2019. (Photo credit: Courtesy of Bruce Pratt, with permission from Becky Stahl)

How Family Programs Emerged

Benson Memorial Library is a public library with a service area of just under 15,000 people (State Library of Pennsylvania, 2015). It is situated in Titusville, Pennsylvania, and serves an area that is classified by the U.S. Census Bureau as an urban cluster (between 2,500 and 50,000 people) surrounded by rural countryside (fewer than 500 people per square mile) (U.S. Department of Agriculture Economic Research Service, 2019). The two counties primarily served by this library are home to only 87 people per square mile, far below the threshold of rurality (U.S. Census Bureau, 2010). The population of the service area is majority white (96.7%), with only 74 percent of people having access to broadband internet in their homes, compared to more than 80 percent nationally (U.S. Census Bureau, 2018a). Household income falls more than $26,000 below the national average, and the poverty rate is 26 percent as opposed to the national rate of 12 percent as of 2018 (U.S. Census Bureau, 2018b). The largest urban city of 100,000 or more people is almost fifty miles away.

With four full-time and five part-time staff members, all of the programming at Benson is handled by the adult services librarian and the youth services librarian. Before 2018, programming at the library was separated by age with very little overlap. Youth programs rarely involved adults, and adult programs were rarely child-friendly (Titusville Herald, 2008; Hill, 2014).

Family programs emerged to address the barriers parents faced with our age-segregated programming. Librarians noted that a few parents who were regular library patrons expressed confusion regarding the age limits on programs. For parents with multiple children, one child might fit into the age category for a program while the younger or older child was left out. Because both children could not attend the program, that left parents to decide whether to invest the time in bringing one child or keeping both children at home. The latter was usually easier.

Parents also struggled with age limits when children were functioning above or below their age level. Other parents commented that they, too, wished to get in on the fun during programs. Parents expressed interest in participating with their children and, in cases of families with older children, competing against them for fun. Taking all of this feedback into account, we decided to open up age categories during the next summer reading program.

This decision did not come without its own challenges for staff. Libraries are for everyone, but time and again it feels impossible to serve people of all ages through library programs with limited funds and even more limited budgets. Libraries—including our own—often employ professionals who specialize in different age groups and develop collections and programs within these boundaries. Crossing operational boundaries became a priority when we heard from our community. We have broken down the walls of youth and adult services to offer unique, collaborative, multigenerational programming for all ages, as illustrated in table 11.1.

Creating Family Programs

An easy place to start family-oriented library events is with passive programming. Activities such as sticker art, coloring pages, or scavenger hunts can be enjoyed by multiple age groups and require little preparation, expense, or supervision. Simple things such as coloring can be fun for all ages if they are provided with a range of complexity in pictures to color.

Table 11.1   Family programming at Benson Memorial Library, 2019

Month	Program
January	Winter Reading Program
	Book Bingo
February	Winter Reading Program
	Family Trivia Night
	Quilt Show & Presentation
March	Book Bingo
April	*Game of Thrones*–Inspired Trivia Night
May	Book Bingo
	War at Cemetery History Program
June	Family Craft Night (Succulents)
	Family Trivia Night
	Art Show
	Astronaut Training Camp
July	Art Show
	Hula Hoop Faceoff
	Book Bingo
	Library Scavenger Hunt
	Hula Hoop Faceoff
August	Family Trivia Night
September	Book Bingo
	Downton Abbey–Inspired Tea Party
October	Family Trivia Night
	Cemetery History Program
	Halloween Trivia Night
November	Book Bingo
	NaNoWriMo Writing Event
	Family Craft Night (Cardboard)
December	Holiday Trivia Night

Interactive programming requires preparation and guidance, but the rewards are worth the work. Events such as trivia nights (general trivia, holidays, themed trivia), bingo, winter reading programs, craft nights, and physical activity programs pay dividends in engagement and fun for everyone.

Our experience suggests taking the steps described below to implement family programming at your library.

When first starting interactive family programming, choose something relatively simple and applicable to families of multiple generations. Bingo is easy to set up and requires a one-time expense of bingo cards and a rudimentary ball tumbler. First, make sure that you are legally allowed to run bingo at your library, as some states label it gambling and require you to have a permit. At "Book Bingo" we offer advanced reader copies and book donations as prizes, which helps to keep costs low. Since the game is easy to learn for youngsters and familiar for older people, all age groups are able to participate. Trivia nights are simple to run, with prizes as easy as fun-sized or mini candies.

Consider summer as a time to begin family programming. Summer reading is the busiest time of the year at Benson Memorial Library. With heavy foot traffic and people of all ages coming through the doors regularly, summer is a perfect time to experiment with joint programs where age categories are fluid and people of all ages can find something to enjoy (see figure 11.2). Furthermore, we have found that families who enjoy multiage programming during the summer months are more likely to return to the library when those programs are consistently held during the rest of the year.

Offer multiple activities whenever possible. During summer reading 2019, we offered a space-themed family fun night that offered several station activities for families to explore and experience at their own pace. We have found that offering multiple activity stations during a program has worked for our family programs because it encourages attendees to move around the room from station to station, and staff can either supervise the entire room to see if

Figure 11.2 Part of the Benson Memorial Library Art Show, Featuring Pieces Created by Patrons of All Ages, Which Ran from June 2019 through July 2019. (Photo courtesy of Jessica Hilburn)

anyone needs extra assistance with a task or be present at a single station that needs an extra helping hand. If a family really enjoys a specific activity, stations give them the freedom to come back and do that activity again.

Schedule programs consistently. With time and date, consistency is key. We hold family programs on Tuesdays or Thursdays and always at 6:00 p.m. And for the sake of everyone's attention span, we limit programs to one hour. Before long, people will start planning their lives to include family night at the library, since they are assured something will be held during a certain day and time. Commit to showing up for your community and before you know it, families will be planning around coming to the library because family programming is such a good time!

Experiment with different times and days of the week to see what works best for your community. We have discovered that there is no "perfect" time to host a program, just the best day and time that works best for your library. Look at circulation statistics or foot traffic if you have a door counter and pick your second or third most popular day. If it does not work after a couple of tries, pick a new day or ask your community members which day might work for them. The same thing goes when it comes to time of day. Do you have mostly stay-at-home parents with children? Then daytime might work for you. Do you have more working parents or multigenerational families, such as grandparents raising grandchildren? Try an evening hour, such as 6:00 p.m.

Try not to assume you know what adults or children like. Until you try it, you really do not know for sure. Adults in our community really love to color. It is relaxing, easy, and can be stopped and resumed whenever time allows. Likewise, children in our community enjoy history and heritage. You may not think a group of tweens would have any interest in a quilt program, but when they are encouraged to explore, ask questions, and interact with older patrons, learning in unconventional areas is an exciting result.

Balance the high energy of children with the typically lower energy of adults. Children have to be kept occupied, and adults' interest needs to be sparked and sustained. If doing a physical activity program, structure so that adults are participating by doing more passive or supervisory activities while the kids burn off energy. If running a program that older kids will likely be more interested in than their younger siblings, pare down the activity to its most basic parts for the younger ones to simultaneously enjoy.

Take a breather when you are running low on ideas. Work with your fellow staff members and the families who attend your programs to brainstorm together. It is totally natural for the creativity well to run dry now and again. Check the Programming Librarian website of the American Library Association or Facebook groups such as the "Programming Librarian Interest Group" for ideas. You can always modify things you see to become a family program.

Remember that it is all right if something you try does not work out. Not everything is going to be a winner. Sometimes the programs you work the hardest on fail and the easiest ones are wild successes. If no one comes, pick yourself up, dust yourself off, and try again.

Focus on outcomes over numbers. Statistics are great and can tell us a great deal about success and failure. But they cannot tell us how something made you *feel*. Was a program only attended by a few people, but those people had the time of their life? Did only two families come, but is there now a bond and friendship developing between people who never would have had the chance to meet otherwise? Those are successes. Not everything is quantifiable. Wherever you collect statistics, add a line about the outcomes of each program. Small positive reminders will hearten you whenever you falter.

Since the implementation of family-oriented programs, we have witnessed more smiles as parents and their children get to spend quality time in each other's company while exploring new ideas (Ray, 2018). When grandparents get to bring their grandchildren along to these programs, they often get to share stories from their youth and connect with other families. Different families even get to discuss topics with each other and bond over shared experiences through these programs.

Library Support of Family Programming

When consulting with administrators about the possibility of instituting family or all-ages programming at the library, it is important to highlight the benefits of collaboration. The best administrators trust their staff members and give them the flexibility to be creative and experimental when trying something new.

Combining youth and adult services blends together the two largest programming departments in the library. Allowing youth-centered minds and adult-centered minds to feed off each other's creativity creates better rapport and a more symbiotic work environment. Through working together, staff members develop a vested interest in the success of each other's ideas, work, and programs. Staff can divide and conquer much bigger, more complex programs that they may not have the time or confidence to tackle alone. Creating connections between staff members and patrons of their nondominant age group makes the library more friendly, approachable, and welcoming to patrons of all ages. Encouraging staff to collaborate is a community-facing example that your library not only *believes* libraries are for everyone but *lives* it.

Libraries are for everyone, and by making them not only an essential informational hub but also a center of fun and excitement, the library becomes a place that people *want* to visit. Family programming has exponentially grown program participation at our library. In 2016, 950 adults attended programs over twelve months. By the end of 2019, adult and family program attendance included 2,320 participants (Benson Memorial Library, 2020). Every program presents an opportunity for interaction and community building that did not previously exist. The effect of these events is tangible and reportable, making viability both quantifiable and salient to administration and funders.

Conclusion

"I love coming to the library for family programs because it is a chance for me to spend time with the people I love without having to worry about cost," one of our longtime family event attendees recently told us after a program. Engaging every member of the family connects librarians and library workers more to individuals in the community and vice versa. Approachability is key to the success of any public space, and encouraging staff to interact with patrons in all age groups is essential in family programming. Listening to parents and getting to know how libraries can support their interests and needs opens new opportunities for library programming, as was the case with our family programs. Welcoming people into the library with their families in tow vests stakeholders' interest in the growth, development, and continuation of the public library in their community. As a result, family programming facilitates continued interest, lifelong learning, and social interaction for all ages.

From our experience, combining youth and adult services personnel, ideas, and goals makes the library a space of increased community-building, interfamily social networking, parent-child bonding, and fun for all ages. Literacy is always one of our primary focuses at the public library, but creating a sense of community excitement, fun, and possibility is also key. Mixing the creativity and ingenuity of youth and adult services makes for better programs and thus a more interactive library experience for the entire community. By implementing the strategies and ideas contained here, libraries will find success with family programming, the positive effects of implementing these kinds of programs, and how family programming can be easily integrated into existing programming routines in libraries everywhere.

People will never age in or age out of family programming. Programs should be applicable to as many age groups as possible. Having a little something for everyone allows people of different ages and walks of life to enjoy the library together, forming bonds that could potentially last a lifetime. Help make your library a center of your community, and ensure support through education, entertainment, and interaction for all ages. Your work matters.

References

Banks, James A., Kathryn H. Au, Ametha F. Ball, Philip Bell, Edmund W. Gordon, Kris D. Gutierrez, Shirley Brice Heath, et al. *Learning in and out of School in Diverse Environments*. Seattle, WA: The Life Center and the Center for Multicultural Education, University of Washington, 2007. http://life-slc.org/docs/Banks_etal-LIFE-Diversity-Report.pdf.

Benson Memorial Library. "2019 Year in Review." 2020. https://benson.ccfls.org
/about/2019yir.

Hartwell-Walker, Marie. "The Benefits of Play." *PsychCentral*, October 8, 2018.
https://psychcentral.com/lib/the-benefits-of-play.

Hill, Mary. "Library Gearing Up for Science-Themed Summer." *Titusville Herald*,
June 6, 2014. https://www.titusvilleherald.com/news/article_cd66d567
-7b0a-56bc-ac7c-4c0935245ce0.html.

Hutton, John S., Tzipi Horowitz-Kraus, Alan L. Mendelsohn, Tom DeWitt, Scott
K. Holland, and the C-MIND Authorship Consortium. "Home Reading
Environment and Brain Activation in Preschool Children Listening to
Stories," *Pediatrics* 136, no. 3 (2015): 466–78. https://doi.org/10.1542
/peds.2015-0359.

Moore, Tim. "Creating the Conditions to Support Positive Child Development
and Family Functioning: The Role of the Built Environment," Paper presented at ARACY/Griffith University Urban Research Program Creating
Child-Friendly Cities Second National Conference, Sydney, Australia,
October 30–31, 2006. https://www.researchgate.net/publication
/228728975_Creating_the_conditions_to_support_positive_child
_development_and_family_functioning_The_role_of_the_built
_environment.

Ray, Sean P. "Christmas Stories, Songs Fill Halls of Tarbell House," *Titusville Herald*, November 30, 2018. https://www.titusvilleherald.com/news/article
_bb09d3bc-f45d-11e8-90f9-afe8e2742adb.html.

Ruthven, Ian, Steven Buchanan, and Cara Jardine. "Relationships, Environment,
Health and Development: The Information Needs Expressed Online by
Young First-Time Mothers." *Journal of the Association for Information Sci-
ence and Technology* 69, no. 8 (2018): 985–95.

State Library of Pennsylvania. "PA Public Library Statistics." 2015. https://www
.statelibrary.pa.gov/Libraries/Statistics/Pages/default.aspx.

Steinberg, Laurence. *Age of Opportunity*. Boston: Houghton Mifflin Harcourt,
2014.

Strange, Cecily, Colleen Fisher, Peter Howat, and Lisa Wood. "The Essence of
Being Connected: The Lived Experience of Mothers with Young Children
in Newer Residential Areas." *Community Work and Family* 17, no. 4 (2014):
486–502. https://doi.org/10.1080/13668803.2014.935704.

Titusville Herald. "This Week's Summer Reading Schedule Set." July 21, 2008.
https://www.titusvilleherald.com/arts_and_entertainment/article
_99f40635-c4c6-57af-acc6-f3fcf2593754.html.

U.S. Census Bureau. "American Community Survey 5-Year Estimates." 2018a.
https://www.census.gov/quickfacts/fact/table/US,titusvillecitypennsylva
nia,crawfordcountypennsylvania/PST045219.

U.S. Census Bureau. "Census of Population and Housing." 2010. https://www
.census.gov/quickfacts/fact/table/US,titusvillecitypennsylvania,crawford
countypennsylvania/PST045219.

U.S. Census Bureau. "Small Area Income and Poverty Estimates." 2018b. https://www.census.gov/quickfacts/fact/table/US,titusvillecitypennsylvania,crawfordcountypennsylvania/PST045219.

U.S. Department of Agriculture Economic Research Service. "What Is Rural?" October 23, 2019. https://www.ers.usda.gov/topics/rural-economy-population/rural-classifications/what-is-rural.aspx.

White, Rachel E. *The Power of Play: A Research Summary on Play and Learning.* St. Paul, MN: Minnesota Children's Museum, n.d. https://www.childrensmuseums.org/images/MCMResearchSummary.pdf.

Zosh, Jennifer M., Emily J. Hopkins, Hanne Jensen, Claire Liu, David Nealse, Kathy Hirsch-Pasek, S. Lynette Solis, and David Whitebread. *Learning through Play: A Review of the Evidence.* Billund, Denmark: LEGO Foundation, 2017. https://www.legofoundation.com/media/1063/learning-through-play_web.pdf.

CHAPTER TWELVE

We're Happy You're Here: Honoring Family Strengths to Build Relationships and Enhance Programming at the Denver Public Library

Sarah McNeil

At the Denver Public Library (DPL) in Colorado, we serve families from many different avenues and walks of life. One thread ties our services and programs for families: we strive to create a strengths-based foundation for our relationships with families. Often families encounter a deficit-based mindset in their interactions with community institutions and their personnel (Montemayor, 2019). Well-intentioned questions such as, What do they *need?* and What are they *lacking* access to? imply that families are empty vessels into which outsiders need to pour resources in order to make them whole. These kinds of questions turn an organization into a giver and the family into a receiver, rather than turning the two into equal partners.

A strengths-based approach asks different questions: How are families already successful? What brings them here today? What can the library learn from them? How do families support themselves and their peers? This approach honors the fact that families are doing everything they can do to fill their own vessels. For DPL staff, the questions turn to, How can we support families in this effort? How can we be a partner? This mindset can be seen stretching across the family programming spectrum at DPL. It represents a shift in thinking in how to provide a program and what a successful program looks like. This approach fits into two of the newly delineated DPL values in action: welcoming everyone and strengthening connections. How this strengths-based approach is relevant to practice is the focus of this reflection.

Engaging parents and children in learning together. The Early Learning Department (ELD) is an outreach-based department of nine staff, the majority of whom are bilingual Spanish-English speakers. ELD works closely with families and other community organizations that serve families with young children and has, over the last decade, thought deeply on what it means to work with families from a strengths-based approach. This has resulted in practices that honor parents as curious learners and not just as recipients of information about their children and parenting (Denver Public Library, n.d.-a).

ELD served 2,300 adults in 80 Every Child Ready to Read programs in 2018 and 2,600 adults in 120 programs in 2019 (Pellicer Ferrando, 2020). Recognizing their popularity, the department decided to invest its resources in an additional suite of programming called Create to Learn. As one staff member asked, "Why are we asking parents to spend time away from their child to learn more about how to spend quality time with their child?" With this in mind, the team developed a handful of programs designed to engage both the adult and the child in a fun, playful activity that supports early learning such as yoga, art exploration, musical instrument exploration, and making books (Denver Public Library, n.d.-b). During these activities, staff provide some brief background on why they chose the activity and how it supports early learning; then, because most of these programs are self-paced, staff circulate during the program to connect individually with parents and caregivers. These one-on-one interactions allow staff to answer questions and connect in a more intentional and focused manner as opposed to requiring caregivers to speak up with questions and concerns in front of a group of their peers. It also supports deeper relationships as staff can interact with the family unit around the activity.

Building on parent interest to support child development. The Every Child Ready to Read program offers workshops for adults that begin with a grounding in brain science. We found that parents from all walks of life are fascinated by the neuroscience of development and how everyday activities positively impact this development. We established the LENA Start program to deepen the knowledge and skills that promote brain development and early learning. LENA Start is a behavioral change program for adults with children from birth to three years old that helps them support their children's language development (Ramirez et al., 2018). The program uses a ten-week curriculum to help parents understand how their child's brain develops, and it offers practical tools and tips to support that development. Parents use a little recorder, a "talk pedometer," as the LENA Foundation describes it, to record the language a child hears in one sixteen-hour day each week. This recording is completely confidential, cannot be accessed by staff, is erased as soon as it is uploaded, and generates a report for the parent that charts the number of adult words, child words, and conversational turns (the back-and-forth talk between the child and their adults) in the day. Parents can then see their progress week over week. Progress includes changes in the amount of language children hear, number of conversational turns, number of minutes a parent reads to a child, and exposure to electronic noise (e.g., television and digital screens).

What ELD has learned through this program is that parents are invested in helping their children succeed and that they are best motivated not through incentives or prizes but by the knowledge that they are developing skills to promote that success. Initially this program separated parents from their children during the session; however, after parents said they wanted more opportunities to practice these new language skills and interact with their cohort, subsequent cohorts now have an option for guided playtime after the session.

Creating a network of support. DPL's programs promote not only child but also adult development. By sharing their child-rearing experiences, parents learn and find support from their peers. They connect in ways that extend beyond participation in the LENA Start program. ELD is now exploring how to keep parents engaged with the library in a more structured way once the cohorts end. We have learned that addressing the concerns of families sparks conversations among them. By providing a physical space where they can relax and continue these conversations, parents feel less stressed with their parenting responsibilities. Parents have told us that several in their LENA Start cohort continue to meet as a group.

Making programming more equitable. DPL's Plaza program provides a safe space for immigrant and refugee adults to pursue a range of skills—English, citizenship, technology, and job seeking, among others—in order to thrive in Denver (Campbell, 2018). However, staff noted that there was no programming available for Spanish-speakers outside of Plaza and no opportunity for fun, engaging, and strengths-based experiences. A new suite of programs, "Diversión en español," was created simply, as the name translates, to have "fun in Spanish." During the pilot phase, three branch locations offered programs in Spanish that included dance, sugar skull painting, and a creature meet-and-greet with the local zoo.

Because of the overwhelming positive response from the community, DPL increased and diversified programming for Spanish speakers system-wide and published *Conexiones*, a Spanish-language companion to *Engage!*, the comprehensive DPL monthly programming publication. The push for additional programming from families and the larger community also prompted the creation of the Spanish Customer Experience team. Now staff from across the system, led by the immigrant services manager, focus on the experience of Spanish-speaking patrons of all ages and across all platforms—website, collection, and programming.

Expanding and connecting learning in the community. One of the important functions of DPL is to build bridges with community institutions and their resources. In this way library customers of all ages and entire families can explore and connect their interests. DPL is in the midst of a multiyear effort to make the Summer of Adventure program more culturally responsive and engaging for the entire family (Denver Public Library, n.d.-c). The Summer of Adventure coordinator organized excursions in 2019 for all patrons from different branch libraries around the city to different cultural institutions, such as the Denver Botanic Gardens and the Denver Art Museum. These excursions took place on Saturdays, included the entire family, were free, and included transportation, entry to the cultural institution, and a group meal afterward. Library patrons who were regular visitors to these cultural institutions and first-time visitors alike took advantage of this program, bringing together curious customers from all walks of life and encouraging them to learn something new and connect with each other.

By not only providing a pass to these cultural institutions but also the means to attend and enjoy the experience, DPL hopes to promote the use of these cultural gems among families who might otherwise feel intimidated, not welcome, or just generally uninterested or unaware of these opportunities in their community. By sharing a common community experience, staff who accompanied families on these excursions had a unique opportunity to deepen their interactions with participants. Likewise, library patrons, including families, made new connections.

DPL hopes to provide an oasis of fun, engagement, and connection where families can just be themselves. It creates welcoming spaces for families to visit DPL with their children and staff to connect with families to design and provide high-quality programming that supports the family as a unit. The library has moved away from a deficit-based model, asking what families and parents need, and toward a strengths-based model, asking how the library can provide experiences and learning opportunities for families to be their best selves. The message we are attempting to send to families is, "Come as you are. You're enough, and we're happy you're here."

References

Campbell, Ana. "Library's Plaza Program Brings Together Denver's Immigrants and Refugees." *Westword*, March 21, 2018. https://www.westword.com /news/denver-public-librarys-plaza-program-brings-together -immigrants-and-refugees-10104850.

Denver Public Library. "Activate Denver, Facilities Master Plan 2017–2027." n.d.-a. https://www.denverlibrary.org/sites/dplorg/files/2017/04/ActivateDenver _Facilities_Master_Plan_web_version.pdf (accessed February 18, 2020).

Denver Public Library. "Early Learning Fun in Our Community." n.d.-b. https:// www.denverlibrary.org/sites/dplorg/files/2016/08/Early_Learning _Training_Brochure.pdf (accessed February 18, 2020).

Denver Public Library. "Summer of Adventure." n.d.-c. https://denverlibrary adventures.org (accessed February 18, 2020).

Montemayor, Aurelio. *Family Engagement for School Reform.* San Antonio, TX: Intercultural Development Research Association, 2019. https://www .idraeacsouth.org/wp-content/uploads/2019/08/Lit-Review-Family -Engagement-for-School-Reform-IDRA.pdf.

Pellicer Ferrando, Alberto. "Google Chat message to Sarah McNeil." February 12, 2020.

Ramirez, Naja Ferjan, Sarah Roseberry Lytle, Melanie Fish, and Patricia K. Kuhl. "Parent Coaching at 6 and 10 Months Improves Language Outcomes at 14 Months: A Randomized Control Trial." *Developmental Science* 22, no. 3 (2018): e12762.

CHAPTER THIRTEEN

Media Mentors Start by Listening to Parents

Lisa Guernsey

It is a gray November day in Joppa, Maryland, but the mood inside the lobby of Magnolia Elementary School is bright. It is family day, and the sound of happy chatter fills the halls as parents emerge from classrooms and talk with teachers in the doorways.

A few parents are gathered by the school's front door, catching up with each other as they wait for school to let out. They do not know it yet, but in a few minutes, this group of parents—two Black fathers, one Black mother, two Latinx mothers, and one white mother—will be requested to participate in an informal focus group I am pulling together to help Harford County Library improve its services for families in digital media and technology. Within forty minutes, after these parents generously give their time and agree to answer a few questions, I hope to emerge from this school with insights for librarians who are coaching their peers on how to become media mentors, not only in Harford County but across the state (Harford County Public Library, n.d.).

Media mentorship is a concept that has grown over the past five years as librarians aim to help parents and educators to navigate the confusing world of digital media and determine the best media uses for young children, tweens, and teens (Haines and Campbell, 2016; Guernsey, 2018a, 2018b). To be a media mentor is to be a guide and resource to families, youth, and community members who have questions about choosing media of all kinds (books, apps, games, videos, and more) and who are seeking models for using technology and media in ways that promote learning and well-being (Guernsey and Levine, 2015). While the exact roles of media mentors will always morph as new possibilities (and concerns) become apparent, many librarians are keen to take on this role. Media mentorship was not only the topic of a book for librarians published in 2016 by the American Library Association (ALA) but also the subject of a white paper published by the Association of Library Service to Children (ALSC) and adopted by the ALSC board of directors the year before (Campbell et al., 2015). Media mentors can point parents and teachers to vetted resources and curated lists of media of all kinds, they can set up experiences for families to see models of what it looks like to use technology and media to spark learning and curiosity, and they can help build critical thinking skills for discerning quality and avoiding misleading claims or undesired data collection.

But before librarians can do any of this, they need to gain a deeper understanding of what the families in their specific communities need and want. They will need to find a way to learn from the growing diversity of parents with young children in their communities—including those who may not often set foot in their facilities.

This was the intent of this project in Maryland—to facilitate semistructured discussions with parents in the Harford County School District (north of Baltimore) who were not necessarily the usual attendee at storytimes. The project, Peer Coaching to Improve Technology, Information, and Digital Literacies for Families, was led by Conni Strittmatter, then director of Harford County Library's youth services (she is now with Baltimore County Public Library) and funded from 2017 to 2018 with a one-year $92,900 grant from the Maryland State Library system (Guernsey, 2018a, 2018b). While Harford County was the central site, Baltimore County and Carroll County libraries also participated, and at the conclusion, librarian leaders from eleven county libraries were involved.

Our Approach

To get started, we contacted leaders at three sites: an Early Head Start center; Magnolia Elementary School, which has an early learning center that is free to children in low-income families (this was the site of the gathering described above); and a public library hosting an afternoon storytime session. Leaders at these sites helped to "break the ice" and introduce me to parents. Each conversation was digitally recorded. Snack bags and drinks were provided for kids and parents in each session.

The interview style was casual and designed to help parents feel at ease. We did not ask for income or other demographic information. But in the course of conversation, the six parents at the sites cited their use of the Women, Infants, and Children (WIC) federal assistance program that provides supplemental nutrition to low-income families as well as their use of the early learning center. The ages of their children ranged from two to twelve years. One mother, who spoke Spanish and relied on another parent as a translator, was pregnant with her sixth child.

The conversation that afternoon focused on three topics: use of the library, use of technology and media, and use of the library to provide guidance on technology and media. For example, for library use we asked, "Have you been to your local public library since your daughter/son was born? If so, what brought you there?" For technology use and library guidance we asked, "Where do you go for support or advice when you have questions about using technology with your child?" and "Have you ever talked to a children's librarian about videos, apps, or e-books? What can you tell us about that interaction?" We would then ask follow-up questions dependent on the answers we heard. The library closest to the elementary school—the Edgewood branch—was named by three of the parents as the library they used most frequently, and they talked about checking out science kits and attending evening events. Here's a snapshot of the dialogue (in this and below, names have been changed):

> **Me: When you were going in [to the library], were you going in with kids? Or on your own?**
>
> *William*: Most of the time I did go in by myself. And when I did go in with my son, there's an area that is pretty entertaining for him.
>
> *Maria*: Oh yeah.
>
> *Angela (William's wife)*: Yeah, they've got the tablets in there.
>
> **Me: Oh, you mean the children's section?**
>
> *Maria*: Yeah, 'cause we come from New York, and they didn't have nothing like that. Not even down to—you know how you can take out the trucks and the science kits and stuff like that? We didn't have nothing like that in New York. They've got the little tablets table, the ABC station. I have a little magnifying glass [apparently provided at one of the libraries] that you can look through.
>
> **Me: Sounds like you definitely have gotten to know it then. How old is your son?**
>
> *Maria*: He's 5.
>
> **Me: 5? OK.**
>
> *Maria*: Because last year he couldn't attend school, so what we was doing is doing the library thing where they have LEGO nights. They even have family movie nights. They have so many events, you know.

Later in the conversation, we asked questions to learn more about how or if their children were using technology and media and how they felt about it. Here's one take, from Maria, a Latinx mother originally from New York:

Me: When it comes to technology at home or at the library, do you have any concerns? Do you put any limits on your kids?

> *Maria*: Everything. Everything. Because I'm very old school. Because now if you take the economy. If you go by what the economy does to you, not only does it take a toll on your pockets, but kids are learning things that they shouldn't be learning. And I appreciate that there is a gray level to everything they do put out there, but sometimes even I look at things and I'm like, hmm, no. I'm very skeptical about this. Now my husband thinks there is no age [limit] in things of him learning things. So he goes on things, I'll admit that, they do. And the other one, the shooting-focused video game and he is trying to tell me, imagine if he wants to go into the Army and stuff like that, and it's not like he is going to go outside with a gun or anything.
>
> But they were talking about the economy even in church, and he wasn't going on with everything. The iphone is coming out every . . . year and my kid wants an iphone and he is 5! And I'm like, What do you know about iphones? It's because technology is taking over our kids. And then they will have a book on a tablet, and you don't have enough money to buy a tablet and so what happens? My kid lacks from reading because everything is technology?

In this monologue, Maria's frustration comes through (particularly the pressure to buy the latest devices), as does the sense that she and her husband have different points of view. Yet what is also helpful here is that we can glean some differentiation in where she is feeling the most frustration. Here Maria is naming video games and smartphones, whereas earlier in the conversation, when she mentioned family movies and LEGO nights, which also include the use of technology and media, she sounded appreciative and hopeful.

Three Takeaways

My forty minutes with these parents was eye-opening and informed an analysis we wrote after reviewing transcripts from the three sessions.

Variation in parent attitudes. One obvious takeaway was the wide variation in parents' attitudes toward media and technology. For example, one parent asked if the library could help introduce her child to more than Disney cartoons, asking for "more showcase cinema." Another parent wanted bigger touch screens on library computers so her nearly five-year-old could use the online catalog herself, clicking on images of what she is interested in. And another said she tries to keep her child away from screens entirely and does not even check out movies. This finding led us to build peer-coaching tools that remind librarians that their interactions with customers should be neutral and avoid preaching one way or another.

The importance of family context. Another key finding is that families' own experiences and their personal context play a big role in their use of and attitudes about technology. Maria's reference to her church and her feelings about the economy are one example. Or consider the insights from a focus group session at an Early Head Start center, where one mother talked about how much her toddler daughter loved the "how-to" videos on YouTube about making slime. She showed pride that her daughter could find these videos on her own, but she also said she was worried about how slime making would lead to a mess that she would have to clean up, as keeping a tidy household was important to her. These takeaways led us to recognize in our workshop materials that librarians cannot possibly know the context in which media and technology might be used at home. That means that the focus in media mentoring should be on first asking questions and listening to parents' specific needs.

Importance of fun in learning. Lastly, what came through in these conversations is that what excites parents most is not the technology per se; it is the learning, exploration, and fun experiences that they want to give their children. No matter what demographic we were talking to, this focus on fun and learning was front and center. As library programs continue to move into media mentorship, reaching families will require creating exciting opportunities for families to learn new things using a variety of media. It is then, in those learning moments, that librarians become better positioned to mentor families on using and choosing media that match their values and needs.

Conclusion[1]

Today's families are awash with digital media and technology, and it is not uncommon for parents to feel overwhelmed, confused, and frustrated as they try to determine the best approach for their children. Few parents have time to sort through all the claims about what is harmful or helpful, keep up with the research and decipher the sensationalized headlines about "screen time," and figure out which apps, games, or books to use at what time and in which ways. Media mentors are a key part of the solution, answering questions and giving parents a chance to learn new tools and strategies for helping their children. But media mentors cannot assume that parents and other family members will automatically come to them. Media mentors and other librarians have a responsibility to first listen to family and community members to learn and get a deeper sense of their needs, their worries, and their dreams for their kids. That very act of listening and learning to families can become an important sign that libraries and librarians are committed to doing everything they can to help navigate this new digital world.

Note

1. Editors' Note: The Maryland project on media mentorship was adapted in Illinois during the COVID-19 pandemic, a time when schools and libraries turned virtual. The author published a brief in 2021 that highlighted the importance of library outreach to parents to meet their digital needs and to inform them of library resources (Guernsey, 2021).

References

Campbell, Cen, Claudia Haines, Amy Koester, and Dorothy Stoltz. "Media Mentorship in Libraries Serving Youth." White Paper published by the Association for Library Service to Children, 2015. http://www.ala.org/alsc/sites/ala.org.alsc/files/content/2015%20ALSC%20White%20Paper_FINAL.pdf.

Guernsey, Lisa. "Lessons from the Illinois Media Mentor Project." *New America*, April 14, 2021. https://www.newamerica.org/education-policy/reports/lessons-from-the-illinois-media-mentor-project/.

Guernsey, Lisa. "Ask the Parents: Gathering Perspectives on Libraries, Media, and Technology." *New America*, September 28, 2018a. https://www.newamerica.org/education-policy/edcentral/ask-parents-gathering-perspectives-libraries-media-and-technology.

Guernsey, Lisa. "Maryland Libraries Build a Peer-Coaching Program to Train Media Mentors." *New America*, July 11, 2018b. https://www.newamerica.org/education-policy/edcentral/maryland-libraries-build-peer-coaching-program-train-media-mentors.

Guernsey, Lisa, and Michael H. Levine. *Tap, Click, Read: Growing Readers in a World of Screens.* New York: Jossey-Bass, 2015.

Haines, Claudia and Cen Campbell. *Becoming a Media Mentor: A Guide for Working with Families.* Chicago: American Libraries Association, 2016.

Harford County Public Library. "Peer Coaching Media Mentorship Toolkit: Parent Discussion Groups." n.d. https://sites.google.com/view/hcpl-media-mentorship-toolkit/parent-discussion-groups (accessed January 10, 2020).

CHAPTER FOURTEEN

Lending an Umbrella to the Community

Felton Thomas Jr. and Laura Walter

At Cleveland Public Library, we understand that removing barriers for our patrons can be life-changing—even when the barrier is as small as an umbrella.

Let me explain. We operate Kindergarten Clubs (K-Clubs). This program ensures that four- to six-year-old children are prepared to enter kindergarten and is generously funded by PNC Bank and Starting Point, a northeast Ohio childcare and early education resource agency. What makes this program unique is that it serves the entire family, not just children. Families arrive, enjoy a meal together, and then children gather with a librarian for their programming while parents meet separately with a parent educator. Children and their families attend K-Club once a week for a nine-week period in the summer leading up to the school year. Each week has a theme, and children receive a free book and activities at every session. We consider K-Club a vital part of our early literacy programming and are proud to host it in several branch libraries each year.

In the summer of 2018, our K-Clubs were in full swing, and one little boy was particularly enthusiastic about the program. When he missed K-Club one week, his grandmother called Rhonda Pai, our early childhood and literacy coordinator, to apologize for their absence and to express just how disappointed her grandson had been to miss K-Club. Rhonda assured the grandmother that missing a session was fine and that her grandson could still receive the book he'd missed when he returned for the next session. But when the grandmother shared why they hadn't been able to attend, Rhonda was caught off guard.

"She mentioned how badly it had been raining that week," Rhonda recalls. "She explained that they had to take two buses to reach the Kindergarten Club, and she didn't want her young grandson out in the rain. I told her I understood—it really had rained a lot that week!—but then she shared something else. They would have attended even in the rain, she told me, but one thing held them back: they didn't own an umbrella. If they owned an umbrella, they would have been there."

When Rhonda first shared this story, it affected me deeply. Sometimes, we get so caught up in looking at the big-picture ways we can transform our communities that we risk losing sight of the smaller details that can nonetheless have a huge impact on the lives of our patrons. In this case, a simple umbrella is what prevented a young boy and his family from attending a program designed to help enrich his educational opportunities.

This led me to contemplate how we could address barriers of all sizes for our patrons. What can we do to ensure our patrons receive the tools, materials, education, understanding, and empathy they need to find success? As with so many other aspects of our work here at the library, it all starts with the heart and foundation of our organization: the staff.

Fortunately, a Bruening Foundation grant for early literacy training went into effect around this time. This grant specifically focused on training our staff to better assist families with children aged zero to three. Along with experts from Ohio State University, we created a curriculum and trained key staff members as facilitators to administer special early literacy training. Through this training, we set out to help our staff understand how to work with families who have children in this age range, how to communicate effectively with parents, and how to give parents and caregivers the tools they need to help enrich their children's educational experiences. This training was made available to all public services staff members throughout our library system.

This early literacy training is meaningful because it helps our frontline staff develop a deeper understanding surrounding families' needs and how early developmental stages affect children's behavior and learning. Above all, the training helped prepare our staff with appropriate solutions when addressing the challenges, questions, and concerns these families may face.

A second component of this grant utilized Ohio State University's Early Literacy Library Programming Assessment (ELLPA). System-wide, our youth services staff evaluated their children's departments to determine what was working, what could be improved, how to work together more effectively as a team, and how to implement a growth plan for their departments or collections. This type of assessment might entail ensuring board books are located on lower shelves, within the reach of young children, as well as developing appropriate collections and organizing the collection to allow patrons to more easily locate materials.

The ELLPA assessment particularly emphasized the importance of parent resource centers and writing centers within youth departments. For example, creating a writing center within a branch entails providing a dedicated space where young children can access paper, crayons, and other writing utensils, while parent resource centers offer the space, interactive toys, and clear direction to help caregivers engage with their children. As a result of these initiatives, our public services staff have a stronger grasp of what information parents need and how to provide them with necessary resources.

Our staff can always learn more and do more for our communities. As Rhonda explains, we are a vital point of contact for our patrons. Parents turn to local library branches for direction, materials, and assistance when they want to help their children thrive. Our libraries are where parents come to find books on the ABCs, the 1-2-3s, and shapes and colors—as well as other resources that offer support beyond the preschool environment. But I also firmly believe we can be more for families and their young children.

To that end, we continue to look for additional ways to remove barriers to library resources and learning. In 2019, we launched our fine-free initiative to restore access to library patrons whose accounts were blocked due to overdue fines (see Jones, chapter 18). In 2018, thanks to a grant from the Cleveland Foundation, we began offering mobile hot spots, portable devices that provide internet access patrons may check out for free, to help bridge the digital divide in our neighborhoods. Finally, our successful, longstanding partnership with the Greater Cleveland Food Bank ensures thousands of children in our community receive healthy meals year-round, which provides them with the nutrition they need to learn, grow, and play.

Cleveland Public Library celebrated its 150th anniversary in 2019. Since 1869, we've established a proud tradition of breaking down barriers both big and small while also ensuring our youngest patrons have a strong start in life. In this way, I hope our library system serves as an umbrella for our patrons—an overarching symbol that shelters the community through education, acceptance, and hope.

PART 4

Leading for Impact

Introduction to Part 4

M. Elena Lopez, Bharat Mehra,
and Margaret Caspe

Leading for impact comes from nurturing positive change in family engagement. Through their work philosophies, values, outlooks, approaches, strategies, and practices, libraries in the twenty-first century develop new ways of engaging families. They seek continued external support from governing agencies and professional bodies as well as internal constituents at various levels for effective implementation of leadership. Top-down and bottom-up leadership in engaging families in learning is significant to generate multimodal outcomes and meaningful impacts. The key themes that emerge from this part are

- Library leadership can and does further social justice in underserved communities.
- Leadership in family engagement through national library networks and initiatives results in positive gains for children and families as well as public libraries.
- Leadership at the regional and state levels removes barriers to family engagement and also creates possibility for programs and services uniquely tailored to a state and community contexts.

Relevant to the contemporary public library is a shift in family engagement practices toward a *social justice and advocacy role* beyond their neutral stance as passive bystanders as was witnessed in the past. Proactive leadership programs in public libraries to address the goals and needs of historically underserved communities make the world a better place to further fairness, justice, and equity for all, including those on the margins of society.

In chapter 15, "'Un-level' the Playing Field to Give Every Child a Chance," Donna Celano and Susan Neuman address policy and program initiatives to give *all* children a chance to succeed and pursue their dreams. Their call for shaping programming embraces a more expansive view of how literacy provides impetus to public libraries. Their libraries of today integrate social justice and advocacy by promoting inclusivity of participation from underserved users in efforts to adapt library spaces and librarian roles to foster parent engagement, provide digital resources and training, and fill community gaps to serve as many as possible.

Continuing this theme of social justice and advocacy, Olivia Forehand addresses the issues of homelessness as a barrier to family engagement in learning. Chapter 16, "Homelessness as a Barrier to Family Engagement in Learning," examines the ways the Nashville Public Library in Tennessee takes on the challenge and discusses library efforts to support and work with families experiencing homelessness. These include provision and access to social workers and associated services, development of community partnerships, growth of outreach initiatives, a deliberate and systematic focus on learning, and effective staff training.

Leadership through national library networks and initiatives contributes to recognized family learning models, emergence of best practices, and documented evidence of success. Chapter 17, "Family Place Libraries: A Place for Families to Learn and Grow," describes a comprehensive framework for family support within the public library. Kristen Todd-Wurm introduces us to the innovative early learning practices and family engagement at Family Place Libraries, a national model with an extensive library network that helps families recognize their full potential.

Leadership change at the *regional (i.e., local city or county) and state levels* is instrumental to overcome barriers to library access and participation. In chapter 18, "Removing Barriers for Youth and Families through Elimination of Fines," Misty Jones highlights the case of the San Diego Public Library, in California, and its efforts to remove barriers for youth and families through fine elimination in their strategic planning process. The chapter identifies lessons learned in removing barriers to learning for children and families.

The reflections in this part underscore that leadership at all levels must join forces to elevate the roles of libraries in promoting family engagement in learning. The goal of equitable access and participation depends on the incentives of federal agencies, the vision of state and regional libraries, and the knowledge creation by universities or research organizations and their library partners. Together, they push forward new possibilities for library practice that benefits children and families.

In chapter 19, "Talking, Thinking, Making: How IMLS Grants Help Libraries Facilitate Family Literacy and Learning," Sandra Toro describes federal initiatives that support research and development to improve library services for children and families. Through these initiatives, libraries—often in partnership with universities—innovate learning strategies, discover and disseminate promising practices, and promote equity. The chapter spotlights successful projects such as harnessing technology in family-centered learning, strengthening youth digital engagement, discovering promising family-oriented STEM efforts, and developing inclusivity of underserved families and communities.

Bharat Mehra and Scott Sikes focus their attention on rural families' information needs that, from a social justice perspective, stay unmet and underserved. In chapter 20, "Information Needs of Rural Families: A Social Justice Imperative," they share valuable examples of their involvement in grants funded by the Institute of Museum and Library Services. This involvement and other activities have been directed to build capacity of leadership among rural librarians, support family economic well-being and engagement, serve neglected community members, and raise visibility of family and community voices.

In chapter 21, "Six Ways to Build a State Library Platform for Family Engagement," Mark Smith describes a state library platform for creating new possibilities for family engagement, especially among the state's diverse families. Efforts include support of family engagement in young children's literacy and learning, summer reading programs, innovative programs that provide a safe space for children to learn and celebrate cultural heritage, lifelong learning literacy among children and families, and digital-based learning for young people and their families.

The devastating coronavirus pandemic of 2020 transformed public libraries and once again mobilized their leadership to serve communities in challenging times. In chapter 22, "Public Libraries Adapt to Connect with Families in Times of Crisis," Ashley J. Brown describes the different steps several public libraries took to keep their communities safe and informed and also connected to education, entertainment, and to one another.

Chapters in this part provide leadership directions so that public libraries engaging families in learning might generate maximum impact. The collection helps to build on positive efforts to move forward toward a future of hope and progressive change.

CHAPTER FIFTEEN

"Un-level" the Playing Field to Give Every Child a Chance

Donna C. Celano and Susan B. Neuman

Having studied libraries for many years, we have grown to cherish the important role they play in many communities. Committed to social justice as well as free and equal access for all, the library is one of the few institutions that has historically focused on breaking down social, economic, and educational barriers (Mehra, 2015). We have witnessed this commitment firsthand as a result of our work with two policy initiatives, a William Penn Foundation drive to equalize resources in neighborhood libraries and the Public Libraries Association's Every Child Ready to Read program, a research-based model for all communities to foster family engagement. As we illustrate on the following pages, public libraries serve as the heart and hub of many neighborhoods, offering promise and opportunities to our nation's neediest children for equity and inclusion.

As we have found, public libraries are especially crucial for helping children in underserved communities develop the skills they will need to achieve in school and beyond (Neuman and Celano, 2012). Children in neighborhoods of poverty have less access to books, computers, and other informational material than do their wealthier peers. In our 2001 study, we found that only one book title was available for every twenty children living in neighborhoods of poverty in Philadelphia; children in a more affluent neighborhood of the city had thirteen titles for every child (Neuman and Celano, 2001). Fast-forward eighteen years, and we are finding that the digital age has only exasperated these disparities. A follow-up study found that in one high-poverty neighborhood in Washington, DC, 830 children must share one book (Neuman and Moland, 2019). Without access to these resources, children living in underresourced communities face challenges developing the informational capital they will need to be successful in today's knowledge-based economy.

Public libraries often "level the playing field" for children in underserved communities by offering them access to books, computers and other informational materials they need to develop information capital. Despite libraries' best efforts to provide resources to all, children living in poverty are still less likely than their wealthier peers to achieve academic success. In our ten-year study of two libraries in different urban neighborhoods of Philadelphia, one in poverty and one in affluence, we examined the patterns in library usage that lead to disparities in children's learning (Neuman and Celano, 2012). While these differences include discrepancies in children's access to print resources, it also relates to their unequal use of books and technology. For example, in observations in the two libraries, we saw that children spend the same amount of time reading—about ten minutes—in each library visit. On closer look, we noticed that children in neighborhoods of poverty read at their age level about 58 percent of the time; 42 percent of the time was spent reading below their age level. We might see, for example, twelve-year-olds reading *Highlights* magazines or board books. In the more affluent neighborhood, students read at their age level 93 percent of the time with a small percentage (7 percent) reading above-level materials. While parents in wealthier neighborhoods were available to assist children in selecting reading materials, children in underserved areas had few adults accompanying them on library visits. These differences in children's book use point to the need for additional training and resources for librarians to work with families in neighborhoods of poverty.

We saw the same discrepancies with technology use. In 24 hours of observation in each neighborhood, we found different patterns of computer use. In the low-income neighborhood, children (ages ten to twelve years) averaged 14 minutes on entertainment activities and 4.6 minutes on information-gathering activities. In contrast, the children in the more affluent community averaged 4 minutes on entertainment and 24 minutes on activities that provide information.

Still, we believe libraries are the perfect place to address this growing polarization in children's achievement. Located in about every community in the country, many operate five to seven days a week. Just as important, their services are free. The key is that libraries must do more than just level the playing field for all children by providing resources. Instead, they need to "tip" their assets toward children living in poverty in ways that will help them expand their knowledge.

Sure, we can hear many librarians say, "How can we possibly do more?" Budget woes and staffing cuts still plague many libraries (Institute of Museum and Library Services, 2018). How, then, can libraries devote more resources to help children in the poorest of neighborhoods?

We recently had the opportunity to visit scores of libraries throughout the country in many types of communities (Neuman, Moland, and Celano, 2017). In our three-year study, we observed storytime programming, interviewed librarians, and collected survey data in sixty libraries across fifteen states. Whether they were in large urban centers, sprawling suburbs, or sleepy rural areas, we have seen library practices and programs break down barriers to children's success by incorporating a more expansive definition of "resources." Instead of relying on extra funding, they draw on what the Aspen Institute's Report, *Rising to the Challenge: Re-Envisioning Public Libraries*, says are three assets that all libraries have: people, place, and platform (Garmer, 2014). They focus on reimagining librarians' roles, enhancing library as a community space, and acting as a platform to connect families to resources. In our suggestions below, we outline how a strategic use of people, place, and platform can help libraries emerge as needed community leaders in helping children develop information capital.

Shape Programming to Embrace a More Expansive View of How Literacy Develops

For centuries, libraries have served as a valuable resource in any community to promote reading skills and educational gains (Kevane and Sundstrom, 2014). Filled with books and led by trained librarians, they have long viewed their mission as fostering a love for reading. For years, libraries have supported young children's early literacy by holding storytimes and helping children select appropriate books (Albright, Delicki, and Hinkle, 2009). In order to help our neediest children, however, public libraries must refocus and "amp up" their resources to promote a more expansive view of literacy development.

This renewed view means that libraries are focusing not only on reading books but on the other activities in which children learn vocabulary and other early literacy skills. The times that children play, talk, sing, and write also figure very prominently in a child's early learning (Weisleder and Fernald, 2013; Weigel, Martin, and Bennett, 2006). Since early literacy starts in infancy, libraries must offer developmentally appropriate programming that accommodates children from their earliest years.

To promote this more expansive view of literacy development, libraries are revamping a resource they already have: the weekly storytime. Many are changing traditional storytime programs for toddlers and preschool-age children to incorporate more playing, singing, and talking (Celano, Knapczyk, and Neuman, 2018). For example, we are seeing more programs with titles such as "Parachute Play for Toddlers," "Funs for Ones," and "Books, Blocks, and Tots," an indication that librarians are focusing on developmentally appropriate activities for children of different ages. Other programs are incorporating STEM/STEAM with activities such as "Preschool STEAM" or "Playdough Lab." These offerings provide children with opportunities to hear novel words and explore new concepts in a play context, thus helping to build children's vocabulary and knowledge stores. Finally, many libraries are embracing bilingual families' needs by offering bilingual storytimes, such as "Amigos and Libros," an effort that helps to boost the vocabulary of dual-language learners, who often enter school with smaller English vocabularies than their English-only classmates.

While we applaud these changes, libraries can do more with programming to promote children's early literacy. In our observations, for example, we saw plenty of storytimes with playing and singing, but we rarely, if ever, found any attention to writing activities. Writing represents an important literacy skill, but in most cases, we found that storybook-reading sessions were followed with arts and crafts. Simple activities such as asking children to "drite" (draw and write) might be a better source of learning about writing than the arts and crafts-related activities.

In addition, we saw many content-rich opportunities for young children to develop knowledge. For example, we saw a fair number of storytime programs focusing on science, such as "Color Science," "Space Day," and "Water Science." Fewer opportunities were available for older children, such as a "Family LEGO Night" operating in an urban Texas library. In our experience, students from neighborhoods of poverty are eager to learn and develop greater expertise if given opportunities to do so. Unfortunately, it is rare that such opportunities are offered to them. Public libraries need to focus attention on providing programs that help all children develop the rich knowledge base they will need to develop information capital.

Adapt Library Spaces and Librarian Roles to Foster Parent[1] Engagement

Hand in hand with embracing a more expansive view of how literacy develops is libraries' emergence as community leaders in another key factor in children's school success: parent engagement. Libraries have long focused on family literacy since the late 1980s, following the publication of *A Nation at Risk* (National Commission on Excellence in Education, 1983). Since then, librarians have always encouraged families to read and learn together, through formal programming and informal interactions. More recently, librarians have been strategically focusing on the important role that parents play in their children's education and literacy development. Spurred by programs such as the Every Child Ready to Read initiative, a joint effort by the Public Library Association and Association for Library Services to Children, librarians encourage parents to engage with their children during routine activities such as playing, singing, talking, reading, and writing (Celano and Neuman, 2015).

This focus on parent engagement is rooted in a wealth of research showing that parent-child interactions are crucial factors in children's cognitive and social development (Neuman and Roskos, 2007). Not all parents, however, have the time, resources, or support to engage in the types of interactions that research has shown to be predictive of children's outcomes. In our experience, parents from underserved neighborhoods want to provide a good start to learning, but they often do not know what they could do to help. As we heard in librarian interviews, families in under-resourced neighborhoods face challenges in raising their children because they have little access to community supports such as educational opportunities, medical care, and community programs, which are abundant in wealthier communities. Helping parents realize their value as their children's first and best teacher is the first step in helping children build information capital.

Libraries' focus on parent engagement is evident on many levels. First, many libraries are remodeling children's areas to foster family interaction. A typical space includes a play area with toys, technology for children and comfortable seating that promotes caregiver-child interactions. Many libraries are now community destinations for families to come play, featuring décor reflecting local customs and culture. In a Missouri suburb, for example, we found a children's area with a play cabin called the Friendly Book Inn. Stacks of LEGOs, child-sized shopping carts, plastic food and containers, and a wooden railroad set beckoned children and caregivers to come and play. Nearby, brochures, signs, and posters also offered information about parents' roles in early childhood literacy.

Coinciding with remodeled children's spaces are new policies on food. Many libraries now welcome families to bring food into the libraries, while others offer cafés or coffee shops. While some librarians register complaints about crumbs in the keyboards or spills on books, a growing number of librarians recognize that relaxing policies about food encourages families to come and stay longer. In the Mission branch library in San Francisco, we saw caregivers and their charges first take part in a lively, bilingual storytime. After the program wrapped up, the entire group spread out a picnic lunch on library tables to continue the conversation and community.

A related shift is a move to revise policies on noise. With children's areas now designed to encourage parent-child conversations, libraries are far from the hushed chambers of previous years. "The shushing years are over," many librarians told us. The new policies, they say, make young children more comfortable and encourage teens to hang around. By providing play spaces as well as new policies on food and noise, librarians hope parents and children feel welcome even if they do make noise and leave a little mess.

In addition to providing a welcoming space, another notable adjustment is in librarian's roles. Today, many librarians see themselves as educators, both of children and their parents. Before the push for parent engagement, parents typically dropped off children at storytime, leaving them in the care of the librarian. The parents who did stay sat quietly in the back while the librarian conducted storytime (Albright, Delicki, and Hinkle, 2009). In today's storytime, the librarian's focus is not only on the children but also on their parents and caregivers (Celano and Neuman, 2015). As one librarian explained, "The librarians' role has been transformed. I don't just do storytimes for the kids. I do parent education through the use of storytimes. I insist that a parent or caregiver attend and be a participant, not just a spectator. If I set up a partnership with the parent or caregiver, the child will ultimately benefit."

In our observations, we see that parents are often encouraged to stay for storytimes, sit on the floor, and participate in singing, playing, and reading with their children. Some librarians address parents and caregivers directly, offering insights of how they can expand children's literacy skills. For example, one Chicago librarian explained to caregivers that songs and chants will be repeated twice "because repetition is the key to building early literacy with our little ones." If not addressing parents directly, librarians model storybook-reading strategies and other ways for parents to engage with their children.

Many libraries are also increasingly augmenting parent engagement efforts by offering programming solely for parents. While children play with library staff in a different room, librarians offer advice and suggestions on how parents can play with their children in ways to promote vocabulary development. At one Maryland library in a small town, a librarian offered several suggestions during a parent-only session:

"Talk every day to your child. Let him respond."

"When you hear music at home, sing along with your child."

"Pretend play is important. Pretend you and your child are the characters in a book."

The focus on parent engagement, while inspiring, is not without challenges. Even with redesigned spaces, many libraries struggle to attract parents in under-resourced communities to attend programming and other events. Work schedules, transportation issues, language barriers, and an unfamiliarity with library services detract many families who could benefit most from attending. In addition, not all librarians are comfortable with addressing parents. While many model ways for caregivers to engage with their children is quite common, few librarians have mastered how to speak directly to parents during programming. What's interesting is that those who do incorporate what we term "asides" seem to draw large numbers of families. Still, it seems that many librarians could benefit from additional training in early literacy development, including learning some simple, effective routines that parents can use at home.

Provide Digital Resources and Training

As our work has shown, public libraries are an important resource for children living in poverty to access information technology, such as computers, tablets, and e-readers. We have seen that children from urban neighborhoods of poverty often have access to technology during the school day, but their access is limited once they leave school (Celano and Neuman, 2010). This lack of access during out-of-school time is of increasing importance in this digital age. Much like reading, children must use their after-school and holiday time to become proficient with digital resources.

Although most families in low-income areas are accessing the internet by means of a smartphone, we do not see this access making up the difference. Families in high-poverty areas are not using technology in ways that would help close the knowledge gap between their children and those from more affluent families. Research shows that 96 percent of low-income families access the internet by means of a smartphone, but fewer have a tablet, computer, or high-speed internet in the home, technologies that would help their children gain more information (Common Sense Media, 2017). In addition, low-income families are less likely to download e-books or use educational apps on a smartphone, two other important ways that would help children use technology in more efficient ways (Vaala, 2013). What's more, many families in underserved areas report internet connection issues such as slow service or outdated devices. Many also report having to share devices (Rideout and Katz, 2016).

In addition to seeing that children in poverty lack access to certain digital resources, children living in low-income neighborhoods also lack capable adults to help them become proficient users of technology (Katz, Moran, and Gonzalez, 2018). For example, we have observed that children in one urban area of high poverty start using computers at a later age (around age seven), compared to children in wealthier neighborhoods, who, with adults to guide them, began using computers at age three (Neuman and Celano, 2012).

In our research, we found that libraries are emerging as leaders in helping families in underserved areas to use technology more efficiently. They provide space and resources for families to interact using digital resources, such as computers, tablets, e-readers, and video games. To accommodate parents who often must use library time to pay bills, apply for jobs, or keep in touch with families, some libraries place adult computers in or near the children's area, so that the adults can keep an eye on children while they finish their task at hand. In addition to providing access to technology in the physical space of the library, many libraries are beefing up online children's resources, such as e-books, games, and apps for families to use together.

While providing resources fills a growing need for many families in low-income areas, we find that some librarians are taking bigger steps and emerging as "media mentors" who guide low-income families to help their children use information technology in more efficient ways (Haines and Campbell, 2016; see Guernsey, chapter 13). In our experience, we have seen librarians incorporate technology use during storytime programming, thus sending a message to parents that technology and interactive media are valuable for early learning. For example, a librarian might encourage families to read e-book stories or use educational apps on a tablet. We have also observed librarians giving tips to parents on how they could use technology with their children in ways to promote learning. To a lesser extent, we have observed libraries offer parent-only programs to encourage parents to interact with their children using technology. In these programs, libraries offer suggestions to parents on how to download songs or audiobooks to engage with their children. Others give information on educational apps and games, along with the reason to use them. For example, one librarian suggested, "There are a few simple apps that promote talking, such as Touch the Sound." Another said, "One of the best book series is Bob Books. The app will help children to become prereaders."

Without a doubt, technology use by children and parents is mushrooming in libraries throughout the country. Once at home, families can continue to use the many resources available on library websites. Although libraries provide technology and families certainly use it, many librarians shy away from families' growing technology use. Only a few librarians incorporated technology use during storytimes. In even rarer instances, librarians spoke to parents directly about how to use technology in ways to promote learning.

While we applaud these efforts, we think libraries have much to do to tap their potential in this digital age. Certainly, libraries promote that families "unplug" and interact through toys and books. Digital resources offer a vast amount of knowledge, and both parents and children use technology frequently. We encourage libraries to seize the opportunity to promote technology use in ways that would help the neediest children learn valuable information-gathering skills.

Fill in Community Gaps

Although family relationships are critical to children's school success, parents who live in resource-poor areas face extreme difficulties in raising their children. As mentioned previously, families living in affluent or middle-class neighborhoods will have access to many educational, medical, and community supports; families living in poverty often see little of these. To fill in the gaps in these communities, local organizations, such as childcare centers and churches often step up to help connect families to government agencies, nonprofits, and other organizations that provide information and social services. Increasingly, local libraries are also stepping up to serve as resource brokers for children's early literacy development.

Libraries serve community needs in two ways. First, they provide a community space where people can gather. The need for a gathering space is particularly important in urban areas of poverty, where families often live in crowded conditions with few resources in the home. In addition, resource-poor areas often lack parks, recreation centers, and other community areas where families might gather and hang out. Many families see the library as a haven, cool in the summer and warm in the winter, filled with toys, books, and areas for parents and children to relax.

Certain design features in these spaces support the notion of community space for families. Libraries that display elements of local culture and bilingual signage treat patrons as integral members of the community, a feeling missing in many neighborhoods of poverty. For example, in a Farmington (New Mexico) library located not far from a Navajo reservation, wall art reflects local Native American beliefs in the cyclical nature of life. Libraries' strategic decision to include toys, blocks, and puzzles along with books sends important messages about early literacy: imaginative play and parent-child interactions help children learn. Some libraries also feature interactive video game areas, which offer families an area to dance and socialize. By offering spaces to play, read, watch, and do, libraries become community centers that help families counter the social isolation that may hinder their ability to raise young readers.

In addition to the passive role of providing space, libraries are filling community needs by serving as active resource brokers, reaching parents through direct connections with social services and early childhood programs. The most common connection is with preschools, day cares, and Head Start programs. During outreach visits, librarians bring books, library card applications, and information about upcoming events. Librarians model read-aloud practices to staff and encourage ongoing visits to the library.

Other librarians have made deeper inroads in the community. Some supply bookcases and books to Women, Infants, and Children (WIC) centers, housing offices, and wellness centers. Others have taught classes about the importance of early literacy to a nonprofit that provides food and shelter to pregnant women. Still others take books and conduct sessions about the importance of the library in a center serving immigrants and refugees.

One of the most interesting new ways that librarians are reaching families is by visiting literacy play centers that are springing up in the local laundromats throughout the country (Celano and Neuman, 2019). Although the idea of a laundromat serving as a literacy space may seem improbable, research shows that in many communities, a family's weekly trip to the laundromat is an ideal time to reach families. A study of three laundromats in Bronx, New York, found that when librarians led weekly storytimes in laundromats, children were engaged in forty-seven minutes of sustained literacy activity. The children in a control setting, a laundromat with no literacy center, had virtually no literacy activity. In these settings, children used the time instead to watch videos or stare into space.

Libraries also connect families to other organizations that could provide essential services. For example, one library offers families a free lunch program at the library as well as helping them connect to a food bank. Other librarians link families to local institutions that provide resources and services to refugees. In many libraries, families find brochures, flyers, and handouts about various family services, such as local doctors and dentists.

As we see it, libraries play an important role in many neighborhoods as community centers. In neighborhoods with limited resources, however, the significance of their role is magnified many times over. They serve as resource brokers, proving a passive space where families come to gather, but also serve as an active force, delivering messages of early literacy that will enable children to prosper. At the same time, they connect families with needed local services. To us, they are unsung heroes in many areas, not only filling a gap in social services but also supporting communities in need.

The extent to which libraries can fill community gaps certainly varies. Some libraries, equipped with large outreach staffs, conduct dozens of programs per month. Other librarians barely have time to leave the building even once over many months, thanks to funding cuts and staff shortages. In many areas with high immigrant populations, librarians struggle to entice families to visit, wary as they are of government entities. Still, we think the trend for libraries to fill in community gaps will continue to grow over time, as libraries emerge as leaders in helping families in poor communities to prepare their children for school.

Serving Many

Libraries are important community institutions serving many goals. As we spoke to librarians in many communities, we heard many talk about their "passion" for their "mission." One explained that her choice to pursue library work derived from her love of helping people in the community; her love of books came second.

As we traveled to libraries in many locations, we became keenly aware of how this view can reap benefits for one community group: young children living in areas of poverty. With revamped efforts, libraries can help these children develop the information capital they will need to succeed in life. In programming, they can embrace a more expansive view of how literacy develops and offer opportunities for children to grow vocabulary. By redesigning children's areas, they can provide a welcome space for families in areas of poverty to gather and socialize. By refocusing their roles, librarians can serve as educators to children as well as to their parents. They can provide space and resources for families to interact using digital technology, but they can also serve as "media mentors," guiding parents to help children use technology to gain more information. Finally, they can serve as "brokers," connecting families in underserved communities with the services and resources they will need to raise their children successfully.

While libraries face challenges in living up to these demands, we have seen what they are capable of doing for our nation's children who are living in need. With libraries' leadership, children in poverty will have a fighting chance to develop the information capital they richly deserve to participate in today's knowledge economy. As one librarian told us, "I can't think of a more democratic institution than the library." We could not agree more.

Note

1. The term "parents" also includes other adults who raise children, including grandparents, caregivers, and other family members.

References

Albright, Meaghan, Kevin Delicki, and Sarah Hinkle. "The Evolution of Early Literacy: A History of Best Practices in Story Times." *Children and Libraries* 7, no. 1 (2009): 13–18.

Celano, Donna C., Jillian Knapczyk, and Susan B. Neuman. "Public Libraries Harness the Power of Play." *Young Children* 73, no. 3 (2018): 68–74.

Celano, Donna C., and Susan B. Neuman. "Libraries Emerging as Leaders in Parent Engagement." *Phi Delta Kappan* 96, no. 7 (2015): 30–35.

Celano, Donna C., and Susan B. Neuman. "A Matter of Computer Time." *Phi Delta Kappan* 92, no. 2 (2010): 68–71.

Celano, Donna C., and Susan B. Neuman. "Using the Village to Raise a Reader." *Teaching Young Children* 13, no. 1 (2019): 30–34.

Common Sense Media. *Common Sense Census: Media Use by Kids Age Zero to Eight.* 2017. https://www.commonsensemedia.org/research/the-common-sense -census-media-use-by-kids-age-zero-to-eight-2017.

Garmer, Amy. *Rising to the Challenge: Re-Envisioning Public Libraries.* Washington, DC: Aspen Institute, 2014.

Haines, Claudia, and Cen Campbell. *Becoming a Media Mentor: A Guide for Working with Children and Families.* Chicago: American Library Association, 2016.

Institute of Museum and Library Services. *Public Libraries in the United States Fiscal Year 2015.* Washington, DC: The Institute, 2018.

Katz, Vikki S., Meghan B. Moran, and Carmen Gonzalez. "Connecting with Technology in Lower-income US Families." *New Media & Society* 20, no. 7 (2018): 2509–33. https://doi.org/10.1177/1461444817726319.

Kevane, Michael, and William A. Sundstrom. "The Development of Public Libraries in the United States, 1870–1930: A Quantitative Assessment." *Information & Culture: A Journal of History* 49, no. 2 (2014): 117–44.

Mehra, Bharat. "Introduction." *Library Trends* 64, no. 2 (2015): 179–97.

National Commission on Excellence in Education. *A Nation at Risk: The Imperative for Education Reform.* 1983. https://www2.ed.gov/pubs/NatAtRisk/risk.html.

Neuman, Susan B., and Donna C. Celano. "Access to Print in Low-Income and Middle-Income Communities: An Ecological Study of Four Neighborhoods." *Reading Research Quarterly* 36, no. 1 (2001): 8–26.

Neuman, Susan B., and Donna C. Celano. *Giving Our Children a Fighting Chance: Poverty, Literacy, and the Development of Information Capital.* New York: Teachers College Press, 2012.

Neuman, Susan B., and Naomi Moland. "Books Deserts: The Consequences of Income Segregation on Children's Access to Print." *Urban Education* 54, no. 1 (2019): 126–47.

Neuman, Susan B., Naomi Moland, and Donna C. Celano. *Bringing Literacy Home: An Evaluation of the Child Ready to Read Program.* Chicago: Association for Library Service to Children and the Public Library Association, 2017.

Neuman, Susan. B. and Kathy Roskos. *Nurturing Knowledge: Building a Foundation for School Success by Linking Early Literacy to Math, Science, Art, and Social Studies.* New York: Scholastic, 2007.

Rideout, Vicky, and Vikki Katz. *Opportunity for All? Technology and Learning in Lower-Income Families.* New York: Joan Ganz Cooney Center at Sesame Workshop, 2016.

Weigel, Daniel J., Sally S. Martin, and Kymberley K. Bennett. "Contributions of the Home Literacy Environment to Preschool-Aged Children's Emerging Literacy and Language Skills." *Early Childhood Development and Care* 176, no. 3–4 (2006): 357–78.

Weisleder, Adriana, and Anne Fernald. "Talking to Children Matters: Early Language Experience Strengthens Processing and Builds Vocabulary." *Psychological Science* 24, no. 11 (2013): 2143–52. https://doi.org/10.1177/0956797613488145.

Vaala, Sarah E. *Aprendiendo Juntos (Learning Together): Synthesis of a Cross-Sectorial Convening on Hispanic-Latino Families and Digital Technologies.* New York: Joan Ganz Cooney Center at Sesame Workshop, 2013.

CHAPTER SIXTEEN

Homelessness as a Barrier to Family Engagement in Learning

Olivia Forehand

The numbers are staggering. In the United States in 2018, more than 550,000 people experienced homelessness on any single night, with families with children constituting 33 percent of this total (National Alliance to End Homelessness, n.d.). The term "homeless" refers to a person "who lacks a fixed, regular, and adequate nighttime residence" (U.S. Interagency Council on Homelessness, 2018). This can include situations where someone is sleeping in places not designed for human habitation, such as cars, parks, or train stations, or can include anyone who is permanently living in a shelter that was designed to be a temporary living arrangement (U.S. Interagency Council on Homelessness, 2018). Because public libraries have increasingly become places of refuge for people experiencing homelessness, librarians are expanding their services and programs for these patrons (American Library Association, n.d.). In this chapter we will explore how the Nashville Public Library has taken on this challenge and highlight ways its staff members have supported and worked with families experiencing homelessness.

In the 2016–2017 school year, an estimated 15,404 public school students in Tennessee experienced homelessness over the course of the year (U.S. Interagency Council on Homelessness, n.d.). In Nashville, it is estimated that there are more than 20,000 people experiencing homelessness, and that about 8,000 of these individuals are children (Open Table Nashville, 2018).

Poverty and homelessness affect both children's education and the ways that their caregivers are able to be involved in that education. Children's academic achievement can often be linked to their family's housing status and poverty level. Students who are experiencing homelessness do less well academically than their housed peers, with lower standardized testing scores and lower high school graduation rates (Shimberg Center for Housing Studies, 2019). These students also miss more days of school than their peers and are more likely to be subject to disciplinary action at school (How Housing Matters, 2018). In the article "Lived Experience of Homeless Youth," four young people experiencing homelessness speak about their experiences, and each faced stigmatizing social perceptions of homeless youth as "unmotivated," "drug dealers," "unruly," or "broken" (Hammack and Toolis, 2015). Many of our society's narratives surrounding youth homelessness frame the children as predominantly criminals who are "at fault" or clients who are "at risk" (Hammack and Toolis, 2015). It may be that these negative perceptions account for the disciplinary action these children face at school and why they may choose not to attend school at all.

In families who are experiencing homelessness or poverty, parents are less likely to be active participants in their children's education (Child Trends, 2013). But this difference does not mean that parents of children who are experiencing homelessness care less about their children's education; many low-income parents wish to be engaged but face additional barriers that parents of a higher socioeconomic status do not experience (Lechuga-Peña and Brisson, 2018). One of these barriers is simply that low-income workers' schedules are less flexible, which makes it difficult for them to participate in their children's schools or attend school functions (Child Trends, 2013). Additionally, homelessness causes mental stress in parents; inadequate or unstable housing leads to "symptoms of depression and anxiety, and to less stable family routines . . . a home lacking some of the most basic elements of comfort may exacerbate other pressures that poor parents face" (Coley et al., 2013, 2). Homelessness causes a unique set of obstacles that parents must overcome in order to fully be engaged in their children's learning.

Public Libraries Serving the Homeless

To aid those experiencing homelessness, libraries have developed new programs and resources, often in conjunction with community organizations and local government entities. One of these libraries is the Nashville Public Library (NPL). It has expanded its efforts to reach and assist people who are experiencing homelessness; it has done so since 2012, when a new library director came on board and was approached by the head of the Adult Services and Reference Department to talk about how the library could better serve this community. The efforts to focus on the homeless have largely been spearheaded by library administration and staff with support from the library board (Liz Coleman, email interview, February 18, 2020). Staff observations and citywide efforts combined to improve these services; at the time, the mayor was also holding meetings with staff from agencies across the Nashville Metro government to look at how to try to end homelessness in Nashville (Liz Coleman, email interview, February 18, 2020).

Patrons are in support of these efforts as well. Librarian Liz Coleman mainly hears supportive comments from patrons who "appreciate that the library offers a safe place for people to get in out of the weather, have internet and restroom access, etc. As long as everyone seems to be getting the same resources, service, use of space, etc., people seem to be pretty good" (Liz Coleman, email interview, February 18, 2020). There has been some backlash, namely from an article in 2016 from a local publication criticizing the main library and the patrons there who are experiencing homelessness. But according to Coleman, the article seemed to mainly create even more support for the library's services in the long run.

Five Ways NPL Meets the Needs of Families Experiencing Homelessness

1. Social Workers

NPL hosts Metro Social Services that involves social workers and other outreach workers from local agencies serving people experiencing poverty and homelessness, such as the Mental Health Cooperative and agencies serving veterans. Social workers, who have experience working both with families and individuals who are experiencing homelessness, come to the main branch of the library twice a month to offer assistance and resources to the patrons who need those services. The library also hosts a weekly peer support group for people who are experiencing homelessness and offers legal assistance on a monthly basis (Liz Coleman, email interview, October 2, 2019).

2. Community Partnerships

The library now hosts Coordinated Entry System (CES) office hours, which allow people who are experiencing homelessness easy access to government services (Liz Coleman, email interview, October 2, 2019). The Nashville-Davidson County CES is a process through which people who are experiencing homelessness "can access the crisis response system in a streamlined way, have their strengths and needs quickly assessed, and quickly connect to the appropriate housing and mainstream services within the community." (Metropolitan Development and Housing Agency Community Development Department, 2018).

3. Youth Outreach

For youth services specifically, the library maintains connections with a local youth organization called the Oasis Center. Oasis is an organization that provides outreach and assistance to teens facing a variety of challenges "from crisis intervention to youth leadership and community engagement to college and career access" (Oasis Center, n.d.). One such resource is the Youth Homelessness Demonstration Project, which comprises two grant-funded projects. The first aims to house teens who are currently experiencing homelessness, and the second aims to identify and help young people experiencing housing crises whose situations would otherwise end in homelessness (Marshall, 2019). NPL's close relationship with the Oasis Center ensures that any teens or young people who are experiencing homelessness can be connected to resources and professionals who can best help them.

4. Focus on Learning

NPL has developed a program called Bringing Books to Life, which emphasizes the importance of early childhood literacy. This program provides both educators and parents with the tools to engage with their children's learning from a young age and welcomes all families to participate (Nashville Public Library, n.d.-a). As part of the preschool literacy program, families are invited to a branch library for dinner and a family-oriented storytime given by Bringing Books to Life staff. Each family receives free books and information on the importance of reading aloud to children. (Nashville Public Library, n.d.-b). The accessibility of this program allows families who are experiencing homelessness to fully participate in and receive the benefits of the education being provided by the library.

5. Staff Training

The Tennessee State Library and Archives subscribed to Ryan Dowd's "Librarian's Guide to Homelessness," an online course that provided training for library staff members to better interact with patrons who were experiencing homelessness. This training was available to all Tennessee libraries for the period from July 2019 to June 2020, so the staff of NPL had been encouraged to take advantage of this opportunity. They have since applied several lessons learnt in strengthening their ties and services to the homeless community. Coleman also states that in the past, the staff of Open Table, a Nashville organization dedicated to serving those who are experiencing homelessness, has offered trauma-informed training on de-escalation techniques to the staff of the library (Liz Coleman, email interview, February 24, 2020).

Trends beyond Nashville

NPL offers many resources to families who are experiencing homelessness, but there are additional services that other libraries are offering that NPL could adopt as well. Liz Coleman, a librarian at NPL, believes that having a social worker on staff full time, or at least on-site several times a week, would be even more effective due to the relationships that person could build with library patrons (Liz Coleman, email interview, October 2, 2019). This is becoming a more common practice in large libraries; for example, the San Francisco Public Library hosts a team of social workers and "health and safety associates" on-site. Librarians can refer patrons to this team, who conduct assessments and offer resources for the services that they need (Esguerra, 2019). These social workers also keep binders of paper copies of relevant resources, which "spare patrons the time to go from one agency to another to find the information that can readily be provided to them during their visit at the library" (Esguerra, 2019). Having a social worker on staff full time allows libraries to serve families who are experiencing homelessness to the fullest extent possible.

Closing Thoughts

For families who are experiencing homelessness, increasing their engagement in their children's education begins with ending their struggles caused by homelessness. Homelessness causes students to do less well academically and puts stress on both parents and families (Shimberg Center for Housing Studies, 2019; Coley et al., 2013). Many low-income parents wish to be engaged in their children's education but face many barriers to doing so (Lechuga-Peña and Brisson, 2018). Public libraries such as NPL are meeting these challenges by providing resources and assistance to families who are experiencing homelessness in order to improve their lives and engage more fully in their children's learning.

References

American Library Association. "Poor and/or Homeless Library Patrons." n.d. http://www.ala.org/tools/atoz/poor-andor-homeless-library-patrons (accessed October 25, 2019).

Child Trends. "Parental Involvement in Schools." 2013. https://www.childtrends
.org/?indicators=parental-involvement-in-schools.

Coley, Rebekah Levine, Tama Leventhal, Alicia Doyle Lynch, and Melissa Kull.
*Poor Quality Housing Is Tied to Children's Emotional and Behavioral Prob-
lems.* How Housing Matters Policy Brief. Chicago: MacArthur Foundation, 2013. https://www.macfound.org/press/grantee-publications/poor
-housing-tied-childrens-emotional-and-behavioral-problems#:~:text=Li
vinginunsafeorunsanitary,detrimentaltochildren'swell-being.

Esguerra, Leah. "Providing Social Service Resources in a Library Setting." *Public
Libraries Online*, January 4, 2019. http://publiclibrariesonline.org/2019/01
/providing-social-service-resources-in-a-library-setting.

Hammack, Phillip L., and Erin E. Toolis. "The Lived Experience of Homeless
Youth: A Narrative Approach." *Qualitative Psychology* 2, no. 1 (2015):
50–68. https://doi.org/10.1037/qup0000019.

How Housing Matters. "How Does Homelessness Affect Educational Outcomes
of Children in Florida?" March 14, 2018. https://howhousingmatters.org
/articles/housing-instability-can-detrimental-effects-floridas-youth
-strategies-help.

Lechuga-Peña, Stephanie, and Daniel Brisson. "Barriers to School-Based Parent
Involvement While Living in Public Housing: A Mother's Perspective."
Qualitative Report 23, no. 5 (2018): 1176–87. https://nsuworks.nova.edu
/cgi/viewcontent.cgi?article=3062&context=tqr.

Marshall, Brandon. "Oasis Center Rolls Out Two New Programs to Prevent
Youth Homelessness." News Channel 5 Nashville, August 13, 2019.
https://www.newschannel5.com/news/oasis-center-rolls-out-two-new
-programs-to-prevent-youth-homelessness.

Metropolitan Development and Housing Agency Community Development
Department (MDHACDD). *Nashville-Davidson County Coordinated Entry
System Policy and Procedures Manual.* Nashville, TN: MDHACDD, 2018.
http://www.nashville-mdha.org/wp-content/uploads/2016/07/CES
-Policies-and-Procedures-Manual-_June-18-2018.pdf.

Nashville Public Library. "Bringing Books to Life." n.d.-a. https://nashvillepublic
library.org/bringingbookstolife (accessed October 5, 2019).

Nashville Public Library. "Preschool Literacy Program." n.d.-b. https://
nashvillepubliclibrary.org/bringingbookstolife/preschool-literacy
-program (accessed February 2, 2019).

National Alliance to End Homelessness. "State of Homelessness." n.d. https://
endhomelessness.org/homelessness-in-america/homelessness-statistics
/state-of-homelessness-report (accessed August 28, 2019).

Oasis Center. "About." https://oasiscenter.org/about (accessed September 10,
2019).

Open Table Nashville. "Statistics on Homelessness." 2018. http://opentablenas
hville.org/wp-content/uploads/2018/04/Fact-Sheet.pdf.

Shimberg Center for Housing Studies. "Students Experiencing Homelessness in Florida: Updates and Solutions." August 2019. http://www.shimberg.ufl.edu /publications/Students_Experiencing_Homelessness_2019_update.pdf.

U.S. Interagency Council on Homelessness. "Key Federal Terms and Definitions of Homelessness Among Youth." February 2018. https://www.usich.gov /resources/uploads/asset_library/Federal-Definitions-of-Youth -Homelessness.pdf.

U.S. Interagency Council on Homelessness. "Tennessee Homelessness Statistics." https://www.usich.gov/homelessness-statistics/tn. n.d. (accessed August 28, 2019).

CHAPTER SEVENTEEN

Family Place Libraries: A Place for Families to Learn and Grow

Kristen Todd-Wurm

A young child is setting the table of a play kitchen with plastic plates, spoons, forks, and cups while her mother sits awaiting the pretend lunch that is about to be served.

Across the room, a father plays trains with his eighteen-month-old daughter as they sit on the floor and chant, "Choo . . . choo." Nearby, a grandmother watches her grandson build a cardboard block tower that is taller than he is as he counts each block with delight; only to turn around and use his entire body to knock it back down again.

Next to the grandmother sit two mothers holding newborns and immersed in a conversation about parenting and the struggles of going from one child to two, as they watch their toddlers joyfully play together.

A youth services librarian, engaged in a conversation with a parent who is concerned about her child's development, is actively providing referral information to local community agencies.

These are scenes you are likely to see every day in a Family Place Library. Family Place Libraries, a nationwide network of librarians who are trained in the Family Place Library approach, builds on the knowledge that good health, early learning, parental involvement, and supportive communities play a critical role in young children's growth and development (Family Place Libraries, n.d.). To become a designated Family Place Library, staff from the designated library must participate in a national comprehensive training institute and receive posttraining support in implementing and sustaining the core components of the initiative.

Currently in more than five hundred libraries in thirty-two states, Family Place Libraries provide rich, engaging opportunities for anytime, anywhere learning for very young children and their parents and caregivers. Family Place provides children and families an enjoyable place to learn and to connect with the community (Kropp, 2015).

The Family Place model includes five main components (Maughan, 2015). While each of these components is important on its own, the Family Place Libraries model strives to weave them together to create a comprehensive framework for family support within the public library.

- *Specialized collections.* The libraries offer a wide variety of books, open-ended toys, music, and multimedia materials for babies, toddlers, parents, and service providers. These collections of books, media, toys, and manipulatives are specialized in that they are aimed specifically at supporting young children and their families as well as professionals who are working with young children and families.

- *Coalition building and outreach.* Partnerships between the library and community agencies that serve families and young children are crucial in order to connect parents to community resources and develop library programs and services that are tailored to meet the needs of the local community. Outreach is two-pronged within this initiative, as librarians conduct outreach to connect with local agencies but also work to identify underserved audiences and/or nontraditional library users in order to expand the reach of services.

- *Early childhood space.* A specially designed, welcoming space within the children's area for families with young children is open and available all hours that the library is open. This space includes an array of developmentally appropriate toys and books for children aged birth to five years. Toys and board books are housed on low shelves, allowing even the youngest child to crawl over and self-select items to explore. The space encourages open-ended play and exploration in a family-friendly environment that is free and accessible to any family. Comfortable seating for parents and caregivers enables them to observe and participate in children's play, make friends with and share parenting experiences and concerns with other families, and conveniently browse the parenting materials in the space (figure 17.1).

- *The Parent-Child Workshop.* A five-week program involves toddlers and their parents and caregivers, emphasizing the role of parent as the child's first teacher. Each week a local professional, one who specializes in child development, nutrition, speech/hearing and language development, movement and play, or early literacy, talks individually with parents, answering specific

Figure 17.1   Workshop Space. (Source: Middle County Library, Selden, New York)

questions and concerns as the parents play with their children. This workshop series is offered two or more times per year at all Family Place Libraries throughout the country. Libraries report that it is one of their most popular programs and that it often results in two very specific outcomes. First, parents whose child may be experiencing a developmental delay of some sort are often connected with some form of early intervention services through the resource professionals available within the workshops. Second, parental isolation is decreased as many connections and lifelong friendships are built.

- *Programming for parents and children together.* Family Place Libraries offer developmentally appropriate and specialized programs for parents and children that include but are not limited to the traditional storytime. Programs are designed to be open-ended and exploratory as well as educational, and librarians are often the facilitators of the parent-child interactions.

Family Place Libraries: Engaging Underserved Families and Communities

Successful Family Place Libraries can be found in a variety of communities across the country, from the smallest rural town to densely populated suburban or urban cities. The model can be successful in any community because it provides library staff with the tools necessary to help parents and caregivers develop knowledge in child development and parenting as well as appropriately connects these adults to community resources. Below we highlight a few examples.

Whitehall Public Library (Pittsburgh, Pennsylvania): Reaching Refugee Families

Whitehall Public Library serves a population of around fourteen thousand people. There is a significant immigrant community within the service area, and most were not utilizing any services at the library (Whitehall Public Library, n.d.). Many of these families had very limited opportunities to engage within the community at large, and most had no experience with any library. Library director Paula Kelly knew that these families would benefit greatly from what the Family Place initiative had to offer, but she knew that it would be difficult to get these families into the building.

In partnership with the Greater Pittsburgh Literacy Council and South Hills Interfaith Movement, the library was able to identify and learn about the needs of resettled refugee families in large apartment complexes. Through this partnership and a grant from the Pittsburgh Indian Community & Friends, refugee families with young children were transported to the library for a five-week Library Learners program, a version of the Parent-Child Workshop, including local resource professionals who converse one-on-one with families through translators on topics such as nutrition, child development, speech and language, health, and early literacy.

Families from Nepal, Bhutan, Burma, Afghanistan, Turkey, Morocco, Burkina Faso, and Thailand were present and enjoyed not only the connections made with other families but also the information received from experts in varying fields. The library is now viewed as a trusted institution of knowledge and also a community hub where families can go to connect. Families who may have feared the library and looked at it as a government institution that would not necessarily be welcoming of refugee families quickly came to view it as a safe haven; that was true especially among those who needed it most. The Family Place initiative allows libraries to build relationships with families and outside agencies that broaden the traditional scope of library services.

York County Libraries (York, Pennsylvania): Supporting Families with an Incarcerated Loved One

The Family Place Libraries model strives to support libraries in their role of working with families who are nontraditional library users in order to diversify the library service population. York County Libraries is another example of a Family Place Library that brings basic collaboration to the next level in order to better serve at-risk families (York County Libraries, n.d.).

York County Libraries partnered with the York County Prison System to implement a program titled Beyond Our Walls, a four-week early literacy experience for parents that culminates with the parents recording themselves reading a book to their children. The recording, along with the book and library resources are then mailed to the child(ren), allowing all to have the experience of listening to their parent read a story. Librarians Felicia Gettle and Lisa Schmittle work with the inmates, teach the importance of early literacy skills and child brain development, and provide an introduction to both community and library resources that will assist in the reentry process. Every incarcerated parent that participates in the Beyond Our Walls program is given a library card to use upon release from prison. If the parent had a library card prior to incarceration, all fines incurred for the parent and/or child are forgiven, and a clean slate is set up for each family.

Lisa Schmittle states, "This program fulfills our missions as a Family Place Library by encouraging incarcerated parents to view our fourteen library locations as community hubs for healthy family development, parent and community involvement, and lifelong learning." Library staff reports that participants in the program feel comfortable coming to the library upon release and often trust staff to assist them with additional needed resources such as referrals for career improvement, childcare subsidies, and other basic needs. A high number of library cards issued through the program have been utilized (206 of 261), with 723 items circulated to date. This program won the Pennsylvania Library Association's 2019 Best Practices Award for Family/Multi-Generational Programming and is a shining example of using collaboration to engage all families on an equitable level.

Texas State Libraries and Archive Commission: A Statewide Approach

The Texas State Libraries and Archive Commission chose to allocate funding for a statewide expansion of Family Place, resulting in over ninety libraries in the state implementing the initiative in 2019. Bethany Wilson, youth services consultant for the state of Texas, shared that the libraries in Texas reported an increase in program participation among families with young children, resulting in increased program offerings to meet community needs. Librarians frequently see parents and caregivers meeting one another and forging relationships while utilizing the Family Place space within the library. The early childhood area in the library is now a destination for many young families, and a visit to the library has become an integral part of their week.

As the word about the Family Place initiative and its effectiveness spread throughout the state of Texas, it became evident that more rural libraries needed this service (Texas State Library, n.d.). There are very few, if any, services directly aimed at the education and development of young children and their parents/caregivers in the rural areas of Texas. The initiative is now expanding to work with rural communities so that Family Place will position the library as an anchor location dedicated to providing early learning and developmental experiences for children birth to five.

Understanding Family Place Libraries' Impact

A handful of evaluations have shown the benefits of Family Place Libraries for libraries, library staff, and families. For example, an interim report of a large-scale study showed that 95 percent of Family Place librarians felt more secure in their ability to identify community resources to assist parents. More than 80 percent of parents report that the library has supported them in their role as parents, and 65 percent report that staff at the library talked with them about child development (Nagle, Licke, and Griffiths, 2012).

In an evaluation conducted as part of a three-year National Leadership Grant from the Institute for Museum and Library Services, 88 percent of directors reported that the Family Place Libraries initiative had exceeded their expectations (Nagle et al., 2016). In the words of one director, "Family Place brings together the critical elements for families—reading and learning, a relationship with a knowledgeable staff equipped with tools to support families, an opportunity to discover family learning in a new way, a place to meet others in the community and form strong cohort relationships."

In the same study, librarians reported feeling more knowledgeable and skilled in their work with families. One librarian said, "We think less about fixed and rigid programming and more about a rich experience every time they [families] come. As a result, we have liberated staff from the routines of the role so that the everyday interactions are a program in and of themselves."

And parents reported feeling more connected to the library. As one parent shared, "The library has been a place for me to connect with other moms who have children in the same age range and value education/literacy. What have I learned? I'm not alone."

Conclusion

We believe that the power of Family Place lies in its potential to help families and libraries realize their full potential. Libraries become community hubs for healthy child and family development, parent and community involvement, and lifelong learning beginning at birth. Moreover, the library is often positioned as a key institution within the community for early childhood and parental support. This new role allows libraries to be "at the table" with other community stakeholders and often allows libraries to grow their services through innovative partnerships with outside agencies. Many of our Family Place libraries continuously grow the initiative by taking on additional roles in family engagement. The Family Place Libraries initiative strives to be a model for family engagement and parent support where the library is the golden thread in the fabric of community support.

References

Family Place Libraries. n.d. https://www.familyplacelibraries.org (accessed December 19, 2019).

Kropp, Lisa. "Family Place Libraries Recast the Librarian's Role in Early Learning." *School Library Journal*, June 8, 2015. https://www.slj.com/?detailStory =family-place-libraries-recasts-the-librarians-role-in-early-learning.

Maughan, Shannon. "All in the Family: A Look at How the "Family Place" Library Program Is Transforming Libraries." *Publishers Weekly*, June 12, 2015. https://www.publishersweekly.com/pw/by-topic/industry-news/trade -shows-events/article/67126-ala-2015-all-in-the-family.html.

Nagle, Ami, Mariel Beasley, Sarah Griffiths, Catherine Jahnes, and Sabine Schoenbach. *Family Place Libraries™ Model: Final Evaluation Report.* Durham, NC: Nagle & Associates, 2016. http://www.familyplacelibraries.org /sites/default/files/family_place_evaluation_report_2-1-16_0.pdf.

Nagle, Ami, Gillian Licke, and Sarah Griffiths. *Family Place Libraries™ Model: Interim Evaluation Report.* Durham, NC: Nagle & Associates, 2012.

Texas State Library. "Family Place Libraries Project." n.d. https://www.tsl.texas .gov/ldn/familyplace (accessed December 19, 2019).

Whitehall Public Library. n.d. https://www.whitehallpl.org (accessed December 19, 2019).

York County Libraries. "For Families." n.d. https://www.yorklibraries.org/library -services-programs/families (accessed December 19, 2019).

CHAPTER EIGHTEEN

Removing Barriers for Youth and Families through Elimination of Fines

Misty Jones

In 2016, the San Diego Public Library embarked on a strategic planning process that involved analysis of policies and procedures with an emphasis on developing a more equitable approach to services. The purpose of this review was to make sure we were providing a positive user experience and employing best practices for serving patrons of all abilities. The policy of charging overdue fines for late return of materials was part of this review, and the findings challenged us to rethink this longstanding library practice and look for a solution that better aligned with our mission and vision. We found that fines do not serve as a deterrent for returning books late, but they do serve as a deterrent for many families to participate in programs and services offered by the library. By charging fines, we created a barrier to information and learning for youth and families. This one policy undermined our objective of developing an equitable approach to library services.

Because fines were considered by city officials as a source of revenue for the Library Department, simply proposing to eliminate fines because they no longer fit our mission would have been an insufficient argument. We needed to develop a proposal that looked at many different angles and addressed issues and concerns from a variety of stakeholders. It was a lengthy and tedious process that proved successful for San Diego Public Library and could be successful for other libraries as well. In this chapter, we present several different questions you can ask to make the case for going fine-free and lessons we've learned in our journey along the way.

Question 1: Why Charge Fines?

It is important to look at your policies, determine why your library charges fines in the first place, and then determine whether you are achieving the intended purpose.

For most libraries, fines are issued as a type of deterrent, a way to make sure patrons return their books on time so that others can check them out. San Diego is no different. According to City of San Diego Council Policies, library overdue fines are a type of user fee that falls into the category of penalties, fines, or deterrents to the public. Other fees in this category are parking tickets or noise ordinance violations. Policy also states that user fees shall be reviewed annually relative to the reasonableness of the fee and the fiscal effect as it relates to deterrence. It is probably safe to say that this policy was never fully reviewed. It was assumed to be effective.

However, a more in-depth analysis proved this was not the case. In reviewing the effectiveness of library fines as a deterrent, studies have shown that fines are not the best way to motivate patrons to return materials. One of the biggest indicators of this is the fact that there were thousands of dollars of fines accrued each year. If fines are such a deterrent, why do patrons still return their items late? Kathy Dulac of the Milton Public Library, in Vermont, reported that after eliminating fines, more patrons returned items on time and also stated they felt more welcome in the library (Dixon, 2017). The Vernon Public Library, in Illinois, eliminated adult overdue fines and found that books and other library materials were returned, on average, eight days earlier than before the policy shift. Additionally, the number of new cardholders increased 8 percent, and checkouts increased 1 percent within three months (Pyatetsky, 2015). The Columbus Metropolitan Library, in Ohio, eliminated all overdue fines in January 2017. The decision was made when the board realized that fines not only were not encouraging the timely return of materials but were actively working against the library's very reason for existence. "We've shut off access to the library when one of our staunchest principles is trying to provide the widest access to materials that we can," the system's CEO, Patrick Losinski, said. "We just felt fines ultimately were counter to the overall purpose and vision of our library" (Graham, 2017). This is consistent with what we discovered at San Diego Public Library. Overdue fines were clearly not serving as a deterrent and were creating more barriers to service, barriers we were working very hard to eliminate.

Question 2: What Impact Do Fines Have on Service Patrons?

In reviewing any policy or procedure, it is crucial to assess the impact to patrons.

Fines have been a consistently negative theme in interactions with patrons. Staff often have uncomfortable interactions with patrons who are upset or angry over fines. These patrons leave the library with a negative image and many times we lose not only those patrons but their entire families. There have been many stories of parents not allowing their children to check out books because they cannot afford the fines or of children being afraid of the library because of the threat of fines. This is in direct conflict with the image we want to present and with the initiative of providing a positive user experience. We want our community to think of education, literacy, culture, and technology when libraries are mentioned. When their first thought is fines, it diminishes the positive and transformative work we are doing.

At San Diego Public Library, we looked at feedback from staff and patrons to gauge opinions on fines. The majority of staff felt that collecting fines was one of the most difficult and unsatisfying parts of their job. Patrons often reported feeling embarrassed and sometimes even ashamed when notified of fines. Some even thought they could not come back to the library because they had not paid their fine. Libraries should solicit this feedback and determine whether the amount of fine money collected outweighs bad publicity and the potential loss of support.

Question 3: Are Fines Disproportionately Impacting Patrons of Differing Socioeconomic Statuses?

In order to completely understand the impact of fines on your community, it is essential to look at fines through an equity lens.

For many libraries, including San Diego Public Library, there is an intense focus on making sure we are serving everyone in our community and creating an environment of inclusion. By providing free access to information, libraries serve as the great equalizer in our society. Charging overdue fines contradicts that message and creates unintentional barriers to service.

According to the U.S. Census (n.d.), the median income for San Diego is $75,456 (in 2018 dollars) with 13.8 percent of the population in poverty. In the San Diego region, 21 percent of adults lack basic literacy skills (NCES, 2017), and nearly 60 percent of children in economically disadvantaged areas do not meet standards in English language arts (Kidsdata.org, 2020).

An analysis of overdue fines by zip codes showed lower socioeconomic communities also owed the most in overdue fines. Many of our residents, the people we serve, are on limited incomes or living in poverty, and the impact of library fines on their ability to use library services is real. To assess the impact of fines on the different communities we serve, we looked at the number of bills, amount of unpaid balance, and total number of patrons with bills by branch library. We then created a map that showed unpaid fines by zip code. Comparing this map with statistical data of household income by zip code, we immediately saw that the majority of unpaid fines were in households in lower income areas.

In "Save the Libraries!" Neuman and Celano (2004) explain, "It is important to understand that incurring library fines does not always, or even often, mean a disregard for library materials or disrespect for other library patrons." There are many conditions such as lack of education, physical or mental disabilities, chronic unemployment or debilitating disease that can affect a person's ability to return library materials on time and the accumulation of fines that can be impossible to pay off with a limited income. This accumulation of fines from overdue materials often leads to people no longer using the library. Under the previous San Diego Public Library policy, any patron who reached a ten-dollar threshold on fines was then blocked from borrowing any further materials. Patrons who reached an amount of fifty dollars in fines were barred not only from borrowing but from all library services, such as computer use and online resources. In order to determine how these policies were affecting individual communities, we looked at median household income and percentage of patrons with no borrowing privileges by library service area. This analysis showed most patrons with blocked accounts were in underserved communities (see figure 18.1).

In fact, nearly 23 percent of San Diego Public Library patrons have lost access to the library due to fines, with some of the lowest socioeconomic

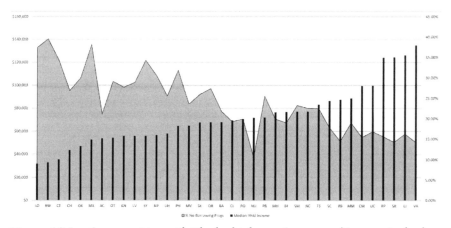

Figure 18.1   Communities with Blocked Library Accounts. (Source: Author)

areas showing nearly 40 percent of their patrons with blocked accounts. Looking at total numbers, we discovered eliminating fines would reinstate 128,032 more patrons, 13,268 of which were children or teens. This argument proved especially effective for elected officials who represented underserved communities. One city councilmember championed our effort early on because he was very concerned about the number of people, particularly juveniles, who no longer had access to the library.

Eliminating overdue fines removes a barrier to library services for those who need the library the most. Furthermore, it is in line with the American Library Association's Policy Statement on Library Services to the Poor (2012), which promotes "the removal of all barriers to library and information services, particularly fees and overdue charges."

Question 4: Are Fines Yielding the Financial Revenue You Hope to Achieve?

To convince key stakeholders, you can also make an argument that evaluates fines from a financial perspective.

For many libraries, fines are an important source of revenue and account for a portion of their funding each year. This can make eliminating fines a difficult decision. It can also mean that proposing the elimination of fines will likely come with opposition from city managers, boards, or other governing entities. In San Diego, we faced scrutiny from the city's financial team and the more fiscally conservative members of City Council regarding the potential loss of revenue.

Historically, the average amount of overdue fines collected every year at San Diego Public Library was approximately $675,000. This accounted for 0.05 percent of General Fund revenue and 1.25 percent of the library's operating budget. Upon analysis, we saw that it cost the library more in staff time and resources to collect overdue fines. To calculate this, we looked at how many fines were paid each year and what staff work was associated with the payment of those fines. Using the average number of daily register transactions, we determined that between 2014 and 2016, there was an average of 399,386 overdue fines paid in person (see figure 18.2).

If each payment took one minute, this would equate to 6,656 hours. Each library location must also prepare a daily deposit, which takes a staff member approximately 30 minutes with an additional 10 minutes for a second person to verify, for a total of 8,034 hours. Additionally, there is one account clerk in the library's business office who spends the entire workday preparing daily deposit uploads, and another account clerk who spends half of the workday reconciling and preparing bank and upload corrections. Using the fiscal year 2017 average hourly salary rate of a library clerk at $18.20/hour and including fringe benefits costs and supplies, the calculated cost of collecting overdue fines is $1,054,576 per year (figure 18.3).

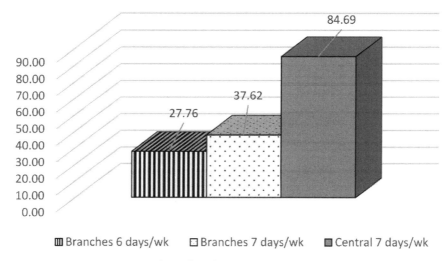

Figure 18.2   Average Number of Daily Register Transactions. (Source: Author)

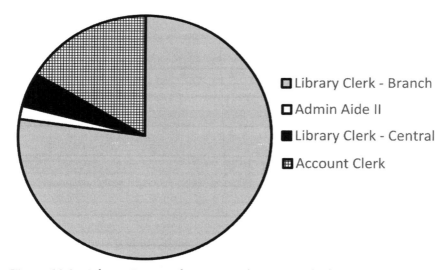

Figure 18.3   Library Personnel Expenses. (Source: Author)

This is a conservative estimate, as often the staff member collecting fines is of a higher classification than library clerk, and the amount of time spent per transaction can be far more than the estimated one minute. We all have stories of spending thirty minutes to an hour with patrons who are unhappy about a one-dollar fine. Furthermore, the library implemented automatic renewal in 2017, which resulted in the average amount of fines collected yearly to decrease significantly to approximately $300,000. From a strict cost-recovery perspective, the cost of collecting fines far surpasses the amount collected.

Putting It All Together: Creating a New Policy

Once you've assessed fees, socioeconomic, financial impact, and other factors, you are then ready to use the information you've collected to make a policy.

The ultimate goals for the San Diego Public Library were to eliminate barriers to usage for all patrons, increase access to materials, and increase circulation of materials. However, we still needed to make sure we had a sufficient policy for recovering materials, and we addressed those stakeholders concerned about loss of materials. We chose to implement a materials recovery policy that focuses on the return of items without the penalty for not returning items on time. This new policy provides a generous amount of time for patrons to return their items yet establishes a consequence for items not returned. New policies will differ by library but in developing new policy, it is advisable to consult with all stakeholders, including library staff, and to think the policy through. How will you handle existing fines? Are your loan periods the same? What about lost or damaged items? Will you refer patrons to collections for unreturned items? Regardless of your policy, it is imperative that it is easily understood by both staff and patrons.

Lessons Learned: Removing Barriers to Learning for Children and Families

When we first began our analysis of fines, we were shocked to learn that those affected by our current policies were largely low-income residents— the children, youth, and families who stood to gain the most educational benefit from our collections and services—who were deterred from library benefits because of fines. The elimination of fines was a multiyear process for the San Diego Public Library that involved developing a proposal addressing many different issues and concerns from a variety of stakeholders. Throughout the process, we learned a number of lessons that can help you achieve the goal of a fine-free library for your community:

1. *Know your stakeholders.* It is crucial to know ahead of time who will be in support and who will be in opposition. For supporters, provide talking points so they can advocate on your behalf. As for those in opposition, it is just as important to know their viewpoint and address their concerns. One of the most frequent arguments we received was that library fines taught children to be responsible and the elimination of fines would teach them the opposite. First, it is highly unlikely that any library job description includes the duty of teaching children to be responsible. That

is solidly the job of a parent or guardian. Second, isn't it a much better lesson to teach a child to return a book so that someone else can enjoy it rather than because otherwise, the library will charge you a fee and take away your privileges?

2. *Use solid data.* Gather statistics that reflect your community and your library service area and are important to your stakeholders. It's hard to argue with data, so find the data that supports your position. The San Diego City Council is very concerned about ensuring all San Diego citizens are receiving equitable services. Several of the councilmembers represent communities with low median household incomes. Because of this, we stressed the inequity of fines in our proposal by showing different sets of data that emphasized this point. One of the more fiscally conservative councilmembers has a special interest in literacy and education, so we also focused on literacy rates in economically disadvantaged areas and the real impact for those patrons if they lose access to the library.

3. *Know the financial impact.* Are fines a major source of revenue for your library? What percentage of your budget is that revenue? Do you have a proposal for replacing that revenue? For some fortunate libraries, this is not a concern, but this was not the case for San Diego Public Library. Fines made up a very small percentage of the budget, but $675,000 is still a substantial amount of revenue, and it was a budget reduction year. We had to plan to mitigate that loss. Fortunately, we had several hourly positions that we had been unable to fill for a couple of years, so we eliminated them. We also made the argument that we could provide new services and programs by reallocating rather than hiring new staff. The service to patrons should far outweigh any loss of dollars, but you need to be prepared in case you also need to mitigate the loss.

4. *Find a champion.* A champion can come from a variety of places. It could be an elected official, a major donor, or a partner organization. Having a strong, outspoken supporter can make all the difference in your success. One San Diego city councilmember embraced our proposal early in the process. He not only provided his support to the library, but he also did his own interviews with media outlets promoting the benefits of eliminating fines. He made sure the proposal did not get sidetracked by other priorities. After we eliminated the charging of fines, he went one step further to eliminate all outstanding fines.

5. *Educate your patrons and your staff.* When your proposal for fine elimination is approved, you want to make sure they know the library no longer charges fines, but you also need to make sure they understand the new policy. This task will fall largely on your staff, so make sure they understand the new policy and that they have talking points on the policy and the decision to eliminate fines.

The elimination of fines has already accomplished what we hoped. We have seen an increase in library card applications and circulation. The elimination of outstanding fines reinstated library privileges for over seventy-five thousand patrons, thirteen thousand of whom were youth. We have not seen an increase in lost materials, as many people feared we would, proving again that the threat of fines is not what causes people to return their books on time. The statistics, however, do not effectively convey the impact of fine elimination. The week after fine elimination was implemented, a young mother came into the library with her three children. The youth services librarian asked the children if they had library cards, and the mother immediately spoke up to say there was no way they would get cards because she was afraid she would not be able to keep up with the materials and she could not afford to pay library fines. The librarian told her that we no longer charged overdue fines, and all three children left the library that day with their own library cards. That is the impact of fine elimination.

References

American Library Association. *Extending Our Reach: Reducing Homelessness through Library Engagement.* Chicago: American Library Association, 2012. http://www.ala.org/aboutala/sites/ala.org.aboutala/files/content/olos/toolkits/poorhomeless_FINAL.pdf.

Dixon, Jennifer A. "Doing Fine(s)?" *Library Journal* (2017): 40–44. https://www.libraryjournal.com/?detailStory=doing-fines-fines-fees.

Graham, Ruth. "Long Overdue: Why Public Libraries are Finally Eliminating the Late-Return Fine." *Slate*, February 6, 2017. http://www.slate.com/articles/arts/culturebox/2017/02/librarians_are_realizing_that_overdue_fines_undercut_libraries_missions.html.

Kidsdata.org. "Students Meeting or Exceeding Grade-Level Standard in English Language Arts (CAASPP), by Socioeconomic Status 2016." 2020. https://www.kidsdata.org/topic/130/readingproficiency-income/trend#fmt=134&loc=2&tf=84,88&ch=231&pdist=94.

NCES (National Center for Education Statistics). "State and County Estimates of Low Literacy, California, San Diego County 2003." 2017. https://nces.ed.gov/naal/estimates/StateEstimates.aspx.

Neuman, Susan B., and Donna C. Celano. "Save the Libraries!" *Educational Leadership* 61, no. 6 (2004): 82–85.

Pyatetsky, Julia. "The End of Overdue Fines?" *Public Libraries Online*, November 15, 2015. http://publiclibrariesonline.org//the-end-of-overdue-fines.

U.S. Census. "Quick Facts, San Diego County, California." n.d. https://www.census.gov/quickfacts/fact/table/sandiegocountycalifornia/INC110218 (accessed June 28, 2020).

CHAPTER NINETEEN

Talking, Thinking, Making: How IMLS Grants Help Libraries Facilitate Family Literacy and Learning

Sandra Toro

Through grant making, the Institute of Museum and Library Services (IMLS) supports over seventeen thousand public libraries across the United States. It is in these libraries where lifelong learners, including families, can choose what and how they learn. Families can access computers and the internet; participate in programs that support social, emotional, and cognitive learning and development; and increase critical thinking, problem-solving, design thinking, and other skills. Over the seven years I worked at IMLS, I saw how grant programs encouraged public libraries to take leadership in investigating and improving family learning. By "learning," I mean the process of acquiring skills, knowledge, and/or behaviors. And "family learning" activities and opportunities are those designed to involve both youth and their parents or caregivers and to "contribute to a culture of learning in the family"

(Learning and Work Institute, n.d.). Through the IMLS grants, libraries facilitate family learning, innovate learning strategies, discover promising practices, and promote equity.

1. *Grants enable libraries to facilitate learning among family members and harness technology in family-centered learning initiatives.* Grants to States (G2S) projects support the purposes and priorities outlined in the Library Services and Technology Act. One exemplary G2S project is Indiana's Closing the 30 Million Word Gap: Using Technology to Educate Parents on Engaging with Their Children, a ten-month project funded in fiscal year 2017. The Mishawaka-Penn-Harris Public Library in Indiana developed a six-week early literacy program for lower-income families that incorporated a device that counted all the words a young child heard with the Every Child Ready to Read curriculum (IMLS, n.d.; Every Child Ready to Read, n.d.). The library partnered with Hannah's House, a local maternity home shelter, and mothers learned to measure the number of words they spoke to their children daily. By combining this technology with education programming, the library helped mothers increase verbal interactions with their young children. The library found the greatest outcome was increased awareness of parents regarding the number of words spoken with children. Seventy-five percent of the mothers reported that their experience with the counters made them change their behavior and engage with their children more frequently.

2. *Grants support innovative ways to understand and strengthen youth learning.* National Leadership Grants for Libraries (NLG) fund projects that enhance the quality of library and archive services nationwide by advancing theory and practice. Supporting Intergenerational Participatory Design Groups for Librarians and Youth for Design Thinking around Digital Learning is a three-year NLG project funded in fiscal year 2018. The project benefits working families through after-school programs in libraries that provide youth with engaging digital learning activities in a free and safe space (Afterschool Alliance, n.d.).

For this grant, the Information School at the University of Washington, the School of Education at California State University San Marcos, the Seattle Public Library, and the San Diego Public Library are supporting intergenerational participatory design (PD) groups through a communities of practice model. PD employs a collaborative relationship between users of digital-based products and their designers in the process of creating new technologies (Yip et al., 2017; see also Subramaniam and Clegg, chapter 9).

To date, the project team members have developed a theoretical model about adult-child roles and analyzed thirty-six codesign sessions during which participants worked on research projects, created branding, and engaged in exploratory design practice. In their analyses, the project team focused on how adults and children facilitated, socialized, designed, and elaborated together. The outcomes of the project will be used to create a process in which local libraries can engage in PD independently; provide a central training hub; and create materials, workshops, seminars, and presentations to help other librarian professionals engage in PD. So far, this project team has found that power dynamics can shift between adults and children and that building trust is key as librarians manage and negotiate tensions between group members. Librarians must also be willing to give up some of their power when engaging in codesigning to develop the "right" learning activities that afford both structure and freedom at the same time for learners (Yip, Lee, and Lee, 2019).

3. *Grants help researchers and practitioners discover promising practices to engage families in STEM that are shared with many other libraries and museums.* STEM Expert Facilitation of Family Learning in Libraries and Museums (STEMeX) was a special, one-time funding opportunity for research on informal educational approaches that leveraged community science, technology, engineering, and math (STEM) professionals in the broadest sense. It supported four separate grants for researchers to investigate the role of oral narratives delivered by STEM experts—scientists, engineers, and related technical practitioners—to children aged six to ten as well as to their families as part of object-based science inquiry in both museums and libraries. The grantees were the High Desert Museum, George Mason University, Loyola University of Chicago, and Pennsylvania State University. Their two-year grants were awarded in September 2016, and the Maine Mathematics and Science Alliance has evaluated work across the four projects.

Since the evaluators and researchers have identified practices that will be relevant for most libraries and museums. Here are their findings:

- Explicit narratives lead to more engineering talk among families.
- Investing in a diverse group of experts positively impacts families, as does the use of personal and professional stories by STEM experts.
- The process of creating written narratives helps families reflect and integrate their learning.
- Parents play a key role in engaging youth, particularly through scaffolding and questioning.
- Personal relevance provides connections for parents to work with their children.
- Parents use a variety of facilitation strategies with their children.
- Parents' assessments of their children's interest in STEM contains several dimensions (Zimmerman, Mcclain, and Crowl, 2019).

4. *Grants promote equity by specifically focusing on underserved families and communities.* Native American Library Services Enhancement Grants advance the programs and services of eligible Native American libraries in the areas

of preservation and revitalization, educational programming, and digital services. Two grants awarded in 2016 and 2018 have helped the Menominee Indian Tribe facilitate library makerspace-based participatory learning in response to an assessment of patron statistics, which indicated that only 350 resident children (23 percent of the youth population) used the library. Through the Menominee Makerspace Movement, the library staff has enabled families to bring their children to the library to access services while spending time together. An unexpected outcome of an increased focus on digital media over two years was excitement among parent and caregiver participants, who showed off their own accomplishments during making workshops through a variety of social media outlets.

Native Hawaiian Library Services Grants fund activities that enhance existing library services or implement new library services. Papahana Kuaola, an organization that promotes learning focused on Hawaiian Indigenous knowledge and based on its cultural and natural resources, used these grants between 2015 and 2017 to increase cultural knowledge of Hawaiian traditions and practices and help families contribute to the perpetuation of Hawaiian traditions and practices. The 2017 project, which occurred from October 2017 to September 2018, *Māka'ika'i Mele a Mo'olelo*—Song and Story Tour, focused on traditional Hawaiian literature. Sixty families on O'ahu, Moloka'i, and Lāna'i participated in literacy workshops incorporating history, story, and oral traditions in both Hawaiian and English through the use of oration, *mele* (words, chants, and poems), and performing arts. Although the project team initially planned to separate activities for children and adults, they learned that families preferred to stay together. Parents did not want to be separated from their children; they also wanted more quality time without electronic devices and to help their children understand their history and appreciate where they live.

Conclusion

Overall, as demonstrated through this sampling of family and youth learning projects, IMLS funding has helped learning sciences and other researchers and library-based practitioners investigate and refine daily practice as well as inform sociocultural and other theories about what family and youth learning looks like and how it happens (see textbox). We know lifelong learners, such as families, seek flexible, customizable, and personalized learning opportunities, and library professionals provide expertise, support, and resources in person and online (Toro and Thomas, 2018). As understandings about the process and products of learning become less constrained, additional IMLS-funded work will keep informing what we know about learning, how to build capacity, and how to facilitate access to information, ideas, and networks.

PROMISING FAMILY LEARNING PRACTICES FOR LIBRARIES

- Understand parents' perspectives on factors that affect learning experiences (e.g., quality time with their children, use of digital media, and transmission of language and culture.)
- Share decision-making with families to codesign meaningful learning experiences.
- Design learning experiences that combine structure and freedom to innovate.
- Create activities for both parent and child to learn together.
- Connect with families in ways that are personally relevant for them (e.g., personal narratives).

References

Afterschool Alliance. "This Is After School." n.d. http://afterschoolalliance.org/documents/factsResearch/This_Is_Afterschool_2018.pdf (accessed January 29, 2020).

Every Child Ready to Read. n.d. http://everychildreadytoread.org/about (accessed January 29, 2020).

Institute of Museum and Library Services. "Closing the 30 Million Word Gap: Using Technology to Educate Parents on Engaging with Their Children." n.d. https://imls-spr.imls.gov/Public/Details/80241 (accessed January 29, 2020).

Learning and Work Institute. "Family Learning." n.d. https://learningandwork.org.uk/what-we-do/lifelong-learning/learning-in-communities/family-learning (accessed January 29, 2020).

Toro, Sandra A., and Charles Thomas. "Preface: Innovations in Library Practice and Information Research." *International Journal on Innovations in Online Education* 2, no. 4 (2018). http://onlineinnovationsjournal.com/streams/adaptive-and-personalized-learning-online/4a9d08257c8d57b8.html.

Yip, Jason C., Kung J. Lee, and Jin H. Lee. "Design Partnerships for Participatory Librarianship: A Conceptual Model for Understanding Librarians Co Designing with Digital Youth." *Journal of the Association for Information Science and Technology* (2019): 1–15. https://doi.org/10.1002/asi.24320.

Yip, Jason C., Kiley Sobel, Caroline Pitt, Kung Jin Lee, Sijin Chen, Kari Nasu, and Laura R. Pina. "Examining Adult-Child Interactions in Intergenerational Participatory Design." *Proceedings of the 2017 CHI Conference on*

Human Factors in Computing Systems. Association for Computing Machinery, Denver, CO, 2017: 5742–54. https://doi.org/10.1145/3025453.3025787.

Zimmerman, Heather T., Lucy R. McClain, and Michele Crowl. "Leveraging Families' Shared Experiences to Connect to Disciplinary Content in Ecology: Preliminary Results from the STEM Pillars Museum-Library-University Partnership." In *Homeostasis and Novelty in Science Education*, edited by Phyllis Katz and Lucy Avraamidou. Boston: Brill, 2019, 41–60.

CHAPTER TWENTY

Information Needs of Rural Families: A Social Justice Imperative

Bharat Mehra and Scott Sikes

A majority of traditional public library research has historically spotlighted metropolitan and semiurban public libraries and excluded rural libraries (American Library Association, 2020; Mehra, 2019). Such a biased viewpoint and limited representation contributes to a marginalization of rural public libraries. It sends a message that rural libraries have no positive contributions or strengths to offer. It also upholds a perception that rural families and communities are a homogeneous group, with limited acknowledgment of the differences in their histories and life experiences (Mehra, Bishop, and Partee II, 2017a; Mehra, Sikes, and Singh, 2019a). Moreover, until very recently, several professional library organizations have been interested only in recording national trends in public library development without showcasing local and regional differences, especially in rural settings.

This chapter seeks to address the neglect of rural library research. It provides a glimpse of our activities with families and communities in rural libraries, reviews key scholarship related to their information needs, and shares insights from a social justice imperative in proposing an action-oriented, asset-framed approach. Some of the intertwining needs, wants, and expectations of rural families are obviously relevant to public library users as a whole and in a range of geographically varied settings.

Information Needs of Rural Families

In general, families who live in rural areas served by public libraries are commonly scattered over larger, more widely spread regions (Boyce and Boyce, 2000; Mehra, 2017). Furthermore, rural areas face specific socioeconomic challenges of lower educational attainment, shortage of economic opportunities, lack of broadband internet access, limited public transportation, outmigration, and aging populations (Hildreth, 2007; Real, Bertot, and Jaeger, 2014; Mehra, Bishop, and Partee II, 2017b). Each of these factors is important to any consideration of the information needs of rural families and children growing up in these environments. Simply put, and for many reasons, accurate and relevant information is more difficult to come by for families in rural areas, all the more for children and teenagers, the elderly, and those from low-income backgrounds (Mehra, Sikes, and Singh, 2020).

Insufficient technological access to broadband internet connection, in addition to isolation and lack of transportation, means rural families are more physically and socially distant from information resources such as public libraries and the programming and activities these agencies offer (Bertot, McClure, and Jaeger, 2008; Jaeger and Bertot, 2010; Strover, 2014). In 2018 a Microsoft study found 162.8 million people predominantly from rural and low-income communities not using the internet at broadband speeds. According to the American Library Association (n.d.), approximately 66 million users have low levels of digital readiness. Adrianne Furniss (2016), the executive director of the Benton Institute of Broadband & Society, empathized with children from rural farming communities, coining the term "digital deserts" to represent the areas where there is marginal availability of broadband services.

A Social Justice Imperative

This chapter recognizes the importance of representing the social justice principles of fairness and justice in all aspects of information-related work with families and communities in rural areas (Mehra and Rioux, 2016). Social equity in rural librarianship goes beyond treating everyone the same. It is about acknowledging and addressing the unique historical, political, economic, social, cultural, and/or biological differences that unfairly impact all individuals uniquely and shape their experiences and realities (Jardine and Zerhusen, 2015).

The action-related dimension of social justice librarianship prioritizes what can and should be done via information-related work, to change imbalanced power differentials between the haves and the have-nots and to make the world a better place for all. Action-oriented efforts to further social justice in rural libraries call for developing intentional, deliberate, systematic, and rigorous models, frameworks, theories, methods, and approaches to further social justice and inclusion advocacy (Bernier, 2019; Jaeger et al., 2014; Mehra, Elmborg, and Sweeney, 2019).

Our research and professional development projects have sought to address four main social justice imperatives in rural libraries: (1) building the capacity for leadership among rural librarians, (2) supporting family economic wellbeing and engagement, (3) serving neglected community members, and (4) raising up family voices. All of these projects are guided by an asset-based approach while collaborating with rural communities, and we share four examples.

Building the Capacity for Leadership among Rural Librarians

Different types of libraries need different types of librarians. For example, in the Southern and Central Appalachian (SCA) region, librarians need to take leadership in community efforts to address poverty and unemployment, economic challenges, low levels of information literacy and educational attainment, and a lack of access and use of information technology. Library professionals who are embedded in their communities are in a strong position to help address and develop meaningful solutions to these issues.

Through two grants awarded by the Institute of Museum and Library Services (IMLS) a team of faculty from the University of Tennessee, including the first author, partnered with four library systems in Tennessee—the Clinch River Regional Library (Clinton), Holston River Regional Library (Johnson City), Ocoee River Regional Library (Athens), and the Sevier County Public Library System (Sevierville)—to build the competence of librarians in the SCA region to better serve families and communities.[1] We trained rural library paraprofessionals to complete their master's degree at the University of Tennessee School of Information Sciences' distance education program. A requirement for enrollment was that librarians had to be local residents in the SCA region. In this way the librarians served as embedded change agents in traditionally underserved and underrepresented geographical regions (Mehra et al., 2011; Mehra et al., 2017). The librarians developed rural management and information technology competencies and course deliverables that were directly tailored to their rural settings, thereby affecting families' access and participation in the libraries' educational programs and services (Mehra and Singh, 2017). Today, the emerging programs for children and families in these libraries include NASA Stem Kits, Beginning Coding Club, Story Walks, and homework assistance for school-age children.

Supporting Family Economic Well-Being and Engagement

In our research we found that rural public libraries in the Appalachian region support small business development through access to the internet, provision of meeting space and educational resources, and the use of office equipment to support marketing, to name a few areas (Bishop, Mehra, and Partee II, 2016). Based on these findings, we developed collaborations between rural libraries and small businesses in a mid-southern state to create tangible products (i.e., blueprint design of a public library small business toolkit, a strategic plan for the community-focused services) that would support economic growth and family economic well-being (Mehra, Bishop, and Partee II, 2017b). An IMLS-funded planning grant[2] helped libraries address the needs of rural families and contribute to a possible practical solution to economic growth. The informational services provided by these libraries to restaurants, childcare centers, tutoring services, lawn services, and other small businesses directly helped families engaged in these businesses but also helped the broader community who relied on these services for their daily needs.

For instance, the Blount County Public Library in Maryville, Tennessee, provided a wide variety of programming for adults in workforce development training while partnering with family enterprises, the local department of labor career coach, and small businesses in the region. It also hosted a Small Business Community Information Exchange to facilitate conversations with thirty small business entrepreneurs, local families, public officials, and library representatives about implementing the library's small-business toolkit (Office of Community Engagement and Outreach, 2018).

Serving Neglected Community Members

Public libraries play a crucial role in reaching elderly users. A study conducted in a library system in Washington County (Virginia) by this chapter's second author found that in addition to meeting key information needs related to entertainment and intellectual stimulation, programming offered at rural locations beyond the primary library hub helped to mitigate challenges of transportation and limited access to technology and internet services. For example, on a weekly basis, librarians visited both assisted-living facilities and meetings of seniors held at community centers throughout the library service area to deliver reading materials, audiobooks, and other resources as well as to offer informational programs related to health, nutrition, and other needs specific to older populations. Such services provide vital social and community connections and serve as a key link for elder users to an institution that is central to the life of the larger community (Sikes, 2019). The library offered similar programming specific to young children and families at additional locations throughout the community, with possibilities for cross-generational activities and programming.

Raising Family and Community Voices

One of us (Sikes) is overseeing efforts to digitize and preserve the Appalachian Oral History Project, an initiative that collected oral histories throughout the Central Appalachian Region in the 1970s. Such a collection finds its primary value in making the material as widely accessible, searchable, and findable as possible. Providing access to this material benefits a host of users, from faculty and staff to community members to scholars and the public in the wider region and world. Through this collection, there exists enormous potential for both student research and projects and for more widespread scholarly work across a host of disciplines. Sikes has explored the role of digital archives in providing access to community history and created project-based learning opportunities for undergraduate students at Emory & Henry College. Students interview community members and learn about social inequality while also collecting historical information for use by social scientists, folklorists, and musicians. Many of the interviews illuminate the lives of families and the circumstances that have divided as well as brought together communities (Sikes, 2020; Sikes and Castillo, 2019).

A Word for Library Researchers

Our goal is to address the disparities in the knowledge that we have of rural librarianship. Rural libraries provide much needed information to address the unique circumstances of their communities. All of the above practice examples have been documented and published in library journals in our effort to engage in social justice scholarship.

Our research on community engagement activities of rural libraries, including their initiatives with small businesses, highlights work overlooked in representations of the region. It was important to tell stories of how libraries were making the most of limited resources available to help families and communities overcome their challenging conditions (Mehra, Sikes, and Singh, 2020). The stories provide a constructive picture of engagement and local capacity building, and they serve as counternarratives to past, solely deficit notions about the rural belt (Center for Regional and Economic Competitiveness and West Virginia University, 2015; Cooper and Terrill, 2009; Mehra, 2017). Work in progress includes a prototype geographic information system that can showcase positive case stories in an interactive multimedia map of SCA rural libraries' present and future community-engaged collaborations (Mehra, Bishop, and Partee II, 2018; Mehra, Sikes, and Singh, 2019b).

Our research on services to the elderly adds to the stories about community engagement work on the part of rural public libraries and offers for practitioners an example of effective and vital services that may be offered beyond the physical walls of the library (Sikes, 2019). Such services focus not only on the specific information needs of elder users but also on the role of rural public libraries as central to the vibrant civic life of a rural community. They also illuminate the possibilities of collaborative efforts among public libraries, local government agencies, and private entities. Furthermore, Sikes's work on Appalachian oral history fills the missing pieces of a dominant historical narrative that has long neglected to provide a complete picture of the diversity that is to be found in rural places.

A Word for Practicing Librarians

Information is power. The development of information resources that are relevant to the education and economic well-being of rural families and communities can potentially address and rectify historically imbalanced social, cultural, political, and economic inequities in our global networked information society. Rural libraries' efforts toward progressive community-wide changes can make a real difference in the lives of underserved people on society's margins. The few examples we have offered provide a glimpse into the conceptualization and implementation of social justice agendas in rural communities. They might inspire library professionals to keep informed of ways in which they can apply social justice as a tool to develop meaningful information-related products that are useful to rural and other marginalized communities. Effective collaborations with rural families and external stakeholders are key toward ensuring that local and regional communities are involved significantly in such programs so as to generate meaningful and valuable impacts.

Acknowledgments

The authors thank the Institute of Museum and Library Services for its support of rural libraries in the three grants mentioned in the chapter. We also acknowledge Baheya Jaber for her bibliographic skills.

Notes

1. https://sis.utk.edu/rural-librarianship and https://sis.utk.edu/itrl2-application-information.

2. https://sis.utk.edu/2014/09/18/ut-receives-imls-planning-grant-to-research-role-of-rural-public-libraries-in-economic-development.

References

American Library Association (ALA). "Broadband." n.d. http://www.ala.org /advocacy/broadband (accessed December 10, 2019).

American Library Association (ALA). *Library Technology Reports* 56, no. 1 (2020). https://journals.ala.org/index.php/ltr/issue/view/748.

Bernier, Anthony. "Isn't It Time for Youth Services Instruction to Grow Up? From Superstition to Scholarship." *Journal of Education for Library and Information Science* 60, no. 2 (2019): 118–38.

Bertot, John Carlo, Charles McClure, and Paul T. Jaeger. "The Impacts of Free Public Internet Access on Public Library Patrons and Communities." *Library Quarterly: Information, Community, Policy* 78, no. 3 (2008): 285–301.

Bishop, Bradley Wade, Bharat Mehra, and Robert P. Partee II. "The Role of Rural Public Libraries in Small Business Development." *Public Library Quarterly* 35, no. 1 (2016): 37–48.

Boyce, Judith I., and Bert R. Boyce. "Far from the Library: A Special Set of Challenges." *American Libraries* 31, no. 5 (2000): 50–52.

Center for Regional and Economic Competitiveness and West Virginia University. *Appalachia Then and Now: Examining Changes to the Appalachian Region Since 1965*. Washington, DC: Appalachian Regional Commission, 2015. https://www.arc.gov/assets/research_reports/AppalachiaThenAndNowCompiledReports.pdf.

Cooper, William J., Jr., and Tom E. Terrill. *The American South: A History*. 4th ed., vol. 2. Lanham, MD: Rowman & Littlefield, 2009.

Furniss, Adrianne B. "Happy 20th Anniversary, Telecommunications Act: A Day to Recommit to Universal Broadband Access." Benton Institute for Broadband & Society, February 5, 2016. https://www.benton.org/blog/happy-20th-anniversary-telecommunications-act.

Hildreth, Susan. "Rural Libraries: The Heart of Our Communities." *Public Libraries* 46, no. 2 (2007): 7–11.

Jaeger, Paul T., and John Carlo Bertot. "Transparency and Technological Change: Ensuring Equal and Sustained Public Access to Government Information." *Government Information Quarterly* 27, no. 4 (2010): 371–76.

Jaeger, Paul T., Ursula Gorham, Natalie Greene Taylor, and Karen Kettnich. "Library Research and What Libraries Actually Do Now: Education, Inclusion, Social Services, Public Spaces, Digital Literacy, Social Justice, Human Rights, and Other Community Needs." *Library Quarterly: Information, Community, Policy* 84, no. 4 (2014): 491–93.

Jardine, Fiona M., and Erin K. Zerhusen. "Charting the Course of Equity and Inclusion in LIS through iDiversity." *Library Quarterly: Information, Community, Policy* 85, no. 2 (2015): 185–92.

Mehra, Bharat. "Information ACTism in 'Trumping' the Contemporary Fake News Phenomenon in Rural Libraries." *Open Information Science* 3, no. 1 (2019): 181–96.

Mehra, Bharat. "Mobilization of Rural Libraries toward Political and Economic Change in the Aftermath of the 2016 Presidential Election." *Library Quarterly: Information, Community, Policy* 87, no. 4 (2017): 369–90.

Mehra, Bharat, Bradley Wade Bishop, and Robert P. Partee II. "A Case Methodology of Action Research to Promote Economic Development: Implications for LIS Education." *Journal of Education for Library and Information Science* 59, no. 1–2 (2018): 48–65.

Mehra, Bharat, Bradley Wade Bishop, and Robert P. Partee II. "How Do Public Libraries Assist Small Businesses in Rural Communities? An Exploratory Qualitative Study in Tennessee." *Libri International Journal of Libraries and Information Studies* 67, no. 4 (2017a): 245–60.

Mehra, Bharat, Bradley Wade Bishop, and Robert P. Partee II. "Small Business Perspectives on the Role of Rural Libraries in Economic Development." *Library Quarterly* 87, no. 1 (2017b): 17–35.

Mehra, Bharat, Kimberly Black, Vandana Singh, and Jenna Nolt. "Collaboration between LIS Education and Rural Libraries in the Southern and Central Appalachia: Improving Librarian Technology Literacy and Management Training." *Journal of Education for Library and Information Science* 52, no. 3 (2011): 238–47.

Mehra, Bharat, Jim Elmborg, and Miriam Sweeney. "A Curricular Model in a 'Social Justice and Inclusion Advocacy' Doctoral Concentration: Global Implications for LIS." Paper presented at the Association for Library and Information Science Education (ALISE) Annual Conference: Exploring Learning in a Global Information Context, Knoxville, TN, September 24–26, 2019.

Mehra, Bharat, and Kevin Rioux, eds. *Progressive Community Action: Critical Theory and Social Justice in Library and Information Science.* Sacramento, CA: Library Juice Press, 2016.

Mehra, Bharat, Everette Scott Sikes, and Vandana Singh. "Scenarios of Health Engagement Experiences and Health Justice in Rural Libraries." *International Journal of Information, Diversity, and Inclusion* 3, no. 3 (2019a): 56–87.

Mehra, Bharat, Everette Scott Sikes, and Vandana Singh. "An Exploratory GIS Prototype to Map Community Engagement in the Southern and Central Appalachian Rural Libraries." Poster paper presented at the Association for Information Science and Technology ASIS&T 82nd Annual Meeting, October 19–23, 2019b, Melbourne, Australia.

Mehra, Bharat, Everette Scott Sikes, and Vandana Singh. "Scenarios of Technology Use to Promote Community Engagement: Overcoming Marginalization and Bridging Digital Divides in the Southern and Central Appalachian Rural Libraries." *Information Processing and Management* 57, no. 3 (May 2020). https://doi.org/10.1016/j.ipm.2019.102129.

Mehra, Bharat and Vandana Singh. "Library Leadership-in-Training as Embedded Change Agents to Further Social Justice in Rural Communities:

Teaching of Library Management Subjects in the ITRL and ITRL2." In *Teaching for Justice: Implementing Social Justice in the LIS Classroom*, edited by Nicole A. Cooke and Miriam E. Sweeney. Sacramento, CA: Library Juice Press, 2017, 247–86.

Mehra, Bharat, Vandana Singh, Natasha Hollenbach, and Robert P. Partee II. "Rural Librarians as Change Agents in the 21st Century: Applying Community Informatics in the Southern and Central Appalachian Region to Further ICT Literacy Training." In *Rural and Small Public Libraries: Challenges and Opportunities*, edited by Brian Real. Bingley, UK: Emerald Group Publishing, 2017, 123–54.

Microsoft. *An Update on Connecting Rural America: The 2018 Microsoft Airband Initiative*. n.d. https://blogs.microsoft.com/uploads/prod/sites/5/2018/12/MSFT-Airband_InteractivePDF_Final_12.3.18.pdf (Accessed December 10, 2019).

Office of Community Engagement and Outreach. "Community Information Exchange Helps Library, Small Businesses in Blount County." *IMPACT: A Monthly Newsletter from the Office of Community Engagement & Outreach, a Unit of the Office of Research and Engagement*, University of Tennessee, February 16, 2018. https://engagement.utk.edu/blog/2018/community-information-exchange-helps-small-businesses-and-rural-libraries.

Real, Brian, John Carlo Bertot, and Paul T. Jaeger. "Rural Public Libraries and Digital Inclusion: Issues and Challenges." *Information Technology and Libraries* 33, no. 1 (2014): 6–24.

Sikes, Everette Scott. "A Conversation across Time: Reclaiming the Appalachian Oral History Project." Paper presented at the Appalachian Studies Association Annual Conference: "Appalachian Understories," Lexington, KY, March 12–15, 2020.

Sikes, Everette Scott. "Rural Public Library Outreach Services and Elder Users: A Case Study of the Washington County (VA) Public Library." *Public Library Quarterly* 39, no. 4 (2019): 366–88. https://doi.org/10.1080/01616846.2019.1659070.

Sikes, Everette Scott, and Ruth Castillo. "Cross-Campus Collaboration in the Digital Humanities: A Pedagogical Perspective." Paper presented at the Association for Library & Information Science Education (ALISE) Annual Conference: Exploring Learning in a Global Information Context, Knoxville, TN, September 24–26, 2019.

Strover, Sharon. "The US Digital Divide: A Call for a New Philosophy." *Critical Studies in Media Communication* 31, no. 2 (2014): 1–9.

CHAPTER TWENTY-ONE

Six Ways to Build a State Library Platform for Family Engagement

Mark Smith

Literally, the number-one operational goal of the Texas State Library and Archives Commission (TSLAC) is to "articulate and advance the value of Texas libraries as essential to our communities and state" (TSLAC, n.d.-a). Other operational goals speak to "supporting efforts to ensure digital inclusion" and to respond to the "informational needs of the increasingly diverse Texas population." And while TSLAC serves all types of libraries, capacity building in public libraries has been a central and motivating concern of the Texas State Library since its founding in 1909.

TSLAC pursues many strategies to promote and grow the role of Texas public libraries as platforms for education, lifelong learning, technology access, economic growth, cultural enrichment, and community engagement. Using a combination of state and federal funds, TSLAC provides a wide array of programs to the nearly 550 public libraries across the state of Texas.

Following are a few of the most successful youth and family programs and services offered by TSLAC.

1. *TSLAC supports family engagement in young children's literacy and learning.* Since 2015, TSLAC has supported the participation of seventy-nine Texas public libraries in the Family Place Libraries™ program, a training institute operated at

the Middle Country Public Library in Centereach, New York (see Todd-Wurm, chapter 17). To date, these Texas Family Place library locations have brought back to their communities a full range of best practices in creating a holistic approach to youth services, from a grounding in the science of brain development to furnishings, programming, family learning, and collections designed to help children use the library as a platform for success in school and later life.

2. *TSLAC supports summer reading programs that enable families to bond together through books.* Texas participates in a consortium of all fifty states working together to provide high-quality summer reading materials to children and youth of all ages. Each year TSLAC sends out the Collaborative Summer Reading Program manual to all main and branch public libraries in Texas. Nearly five hundred libraries participate each year by ordering materials through TSLAC to create fun and exciting programs. They keep children engaged in learning throughout summer months when they could get easily distracted and fall behind in their reading, which can negatively impact their success in school. Besides being a leading predictor of student achievement, reading is a fun activity for children and a way for families to bond both in trips to the library and in sharing their reading experiences.

3. *TSLAC's grants support innovative programs that provide a safe space for children to learn and for families to celebrate cultural heritage.* Each year, TSLAC provides between $1.5 and $2 million in competitive grants, most to public libraries, ranging from under $5,000 to $75,000 for a wide variety of projects (TSLAC, n.d.-b). Many successful grants target educational and learning opportunities in libraries. In 2020, fourteen public libraries received Texas Reads grants encouraging projects such as Arlington Public Library's El Día de los Niños and El Día de los Muertos programs promoting multicultural literacy celebrations in the library. Both TSLAC and the Texas Library Association have supported Día celebrations in local communities. Many libraries have used TSLAC grants to address science, technology, engineering, and math (STEM) projects in their libraries, such as the Andrews County Library, which received its first TSLAC grant ever to create a makerspace in the library to encourage STEM learning, and another first-time grantee, the Centennial Memorial Library in Eastland, which got funding to introduce an after-school robotics class.

4. *TSLAC fosters lifelong literacy among children and families in the library and in the community.* Our Texas Center for the Book encourages literacy and a love of libraries, books, and reading for Texans of all ages through a variety of projects. The Letters about Literature program encourages students in grades four to twelve across Texas to write letters to authors, living or dead, telling how their books have changed their lives. The letters are often inspirational, sometimes heartbreaking, but always a stunning reminder of the ways that books transform young lives. The Texas Center for the Book also

sponsors an annual literacy award, funded by our Friends of Libraries and Archives of Texas. The initiative supports nonprofit literacy organizations, such as Women's Storybook Project, which records incarcerated mothers in Texas women's prisons reading books to their children. As another example, the initiative has sponsored Books Are GEMS, an El Paso-based organization that distributes books free of charge to children and teachers to achieve its goal to inspire children and families through literacy.

5. *TSLAC supports family values for educational success by providing students with comprehensive access to information used in K–12 subjects.* In addition to supporting early education through public libraries, TSLAC also works with K–12 libraries to assist students in finding resources they need to support their studies and intellectual growth. Leveraging statewide buying power, TSLAC's TexQuest program provides school districts across the state access to online e-resources, encompassing a vast array of information that would not otherwise be affordable for many districts. TSLAC also works with the Texas Education Agency to set voluntary standards for K–12 library programs to provide guidance in achieving excellence in school library services.

6. *TSLAC promotes digital-based learning for young people and their families.* For young people and their families to be fully engaged in learning and for libraries to fulfill their role as community anchors for technology access and digital inclusion, libraries must be connected to high-speed internet. TSLAC is committed to helping libraries increase their broadband access. In 2018 and 2019, TSLAC assisted 145 library locations in Texas—mostly smaller community libraries—to achieve much higher internet speeds at lower costs by more actively seeking federal E-rate discounts. With these connections, students can more successfully access online networks and resources to further their studies, while communities, families, and individuals can find in the library the connections they need to support work and personal needs. The Smithville Public Library, in partnership with the Smithville Independent School District, the ACE Afterschool Program (Parent University), and the Smithville Area Chamber of Commerce, plans to establish a curriculum in digital literacy and use the course materials to provide workforce and technology training to the unemployed and underemployed residents and small-business owners of Smithville and the surrounding area. Courses will be offered throughout the year and will be recorded and available in an archive as a "webinar" for future reference and online training.

These programs are available to persons in all parts of the state in all sizes of libraries, both urban and rural, regardless of economic status, background, or educational advantage. Libraries ensure that the vital information resources that children, adults, and families need to be successful in school, work, and life are available to everyone.

New Directions

TSLAC will continue to pursue ways to encourage libraries to engage with children and families in their communities. A new position, that of inclusive services librarian, has been created and a new staff member hired to help Texas libraries develop services to historically underserved clienteles. As technology evolves, TSLAC will be a place that will allow young people to interact with new technologies such as virtual reality, augmented reality, and artificial intelligence. TSLAC is also rolling out a completely revised curriculum for its small library management series. This long-standing, signature program will continue to evolve to equip librarians with new skills that will build the capacity of small and rural libraries to assume their rightful place at the center of the educational, economic, and cultural life of the community.

References

Texas State Library and Archives Commission. "Agency Strategic Plan 2019–2023." n.d.-a. https://www.tsl.texas.gov/sites/default/files/public/tslac/landing/documents/TSLAC-strategic-plan-2019-2023.pdf (accessed October 11, 2019).
Texas State Library and Archives Commission. "Grant Recipients for Fiscal Year 2019." n.d.-b. https://www.tsl.texas.gov/ld/funding/lsta/recipients19.html. (Accessed October 11, 2019).

CHAPTER TWENTY-TWO

Public Libraries Adapt to Connect with Families in Times of Crisis

Ashley J. Brown

The world changed in 2020, and it will not return to the one we knew before. Beginning in January of that year, we began experiencing a catastrophic event: a pandemic that by May had affected six million people globally and led to over three hundred thousand deaths (World Health Organization, n.d.). As the coronavirus known as COVID-19 spread, our daily lives rapidly shifted into staying at home, working from home, and schooling from home. For those without homes, it meant moving to different shelters and spaces to live. The simple activity of going to a public library became unsafe for health reasons. Public libraries across the United States closed but also responded in numerous ways to help families and communities weather the crisis.

The COVID-19 global pandemic wasn't the first disaster in which public libraries proactively responded to their communities. During the recession of 2008, many libraries were "doing more with less" as they helped patrons access digital resources for filling out job applications, use workforce development tools, and connect with others in the online world. Some disasters happen regionally or locally, and libraries find ways to meet community needs. After Hurricane Harvey struck the Texas coast in 2017, the Houston Public Library mobilized its resources to serve the community. During the early part of the storm, many Houston branch libraries served as temporary shelters until some of the libraries flooded and had to be evacuated. Branches with minimal damage opened as soon as they were able and offered "one-on-one assistance with storm relief applications, provided access to Wi-Fi and computers, and even offered a safe space so that people could find a quiet refuge" (Houston Library Foundation, 2017).

As of this writing in May 2020, our public libraries are finding creative ways of responding to a global crisis and engaging our society to work toward a better world tomorrow. The Public Library Association (PLA), a division of the American Library Association, surveyed public libraries online between March and April 2020 to find out more about how they were serving their communities during the COVID-19 crisis. While the results do not represent every single public library in the United States, the 2,545 unique responses came from at least one library from every state, and 43 states had 10 percent of their public libraries represented in the survey (American Library Association, n.d.). Results of the survey showed that although many libraries closed their buildings to the public and sent staff home to work, they continued to provide vital informational and community services. Following are examples of how families and communities have benefited.

Easy access to online resources. Libraries removed some of the barriers to access, such as requiring an in-person visit to the library to apply for a library card, and were able to continue serving families. For example, in the PLA survey, the McArthur Library in Biddeford, Maine, reported this: "We have issued 418 library cards in three weeks (since we closed)! Customers can apply on our website, and their barcode number will be emailed to them" (Public Library Association, n.d.).

Expanded digital resources for information, education, and entertainment. Seventy-four percent of libraries responding to the survey had expanded their digital resource offerings (Public Library Association, n.d.). As homes became classrooms, children and families took advantage of library collections. Young children could borrow many titles, and adults could find materials needed for schooling their children at home. For example, the Auburn Public Library, in Auburn, Alabama, offered patrons existing digital services such as cloudLibrary, an e-book lending platform, and Creativebug, which offers over one thousand online crafting classes. Through Homework Alabama, parents new to distance-learning-based homeschooling could get help with harder homework questions via chats with an online tutor. The library also added Kanopy, a digital streaming service, the *New York Times*, the *Washington Post*, and TumbleBooks.

Safe frontline workers to keep communities safe. Some libraries used assets such as 3D printers and hotspots to aid the community. "We have a large 3D print lab, and our lead volunteer is working with the El Dorado Community Foundation to use our printers to print face shields for our local, regional hospitals and county facilities," reported the El Dorado County Library in California. At that point, it had delivered seven hundred face shields and planned to print fifteen thousand more (Public Library Association, n.d.). Since some libraries also allowed workers to bring library equipment home, these library staff and their families were able to work together to create personal protective equipment.

Online literacy support. For many libraries, programs went virtual with the use of conferencing software, such as Zoom. The Dallas Public Library in Dallas, Texas, adapted its Reading Buddies program to make available a virtual reading mentor. Families could make an appointment to read virtually with their favorite librarian. Virtual storytimes created opportunities for families to stay connected to early literacy programming from home.

Fun and safe events for the whole family. Many libraries used their platforms to keep families safe and engaged. For example, Dallas Public Library also offered a variety of scavenger hunts for different neighborhoods across the city. Through the activities, whole families could get in a car or on their bikes to find landmarks as a fun way to keep the family engaged.

New roles for families and communities. Public libraries are serving their communities now with an eye to the future. The San Francisco Public Library is inviting community members to submit photos, blog posts, videos, drawings, and other media that capture how people have been impacted by and responded to this public health crisis. Parents, children, and other community members have a unique opportunity to write history. The San Francisco Public Library is planning to share digital content with families via its online collection platforms and social media accounts (San Francisco Public Library, n.d.).

Conclusion

In times of crisis, public libraries remain the heart of communities responding to what is needed at the moment, whether that is shelter from the storm, access to digital resources, urgent medical supplies, or stories for posterity. To meet the current crisis, libraries are pulling past experiences to innovate and to connect with families creatively. Ramiro Salazar, past president of the Public Library Association, had this to say about the current crisis: "As circumstances change daily for all of us, I am proud of the dedicated and creative work of our public libraries and their staff to serve everyone from toddlers to isolated senior citizens to small business owners" (American Library Association, n.d.).

As for the impact the response of public libraries had for the families in our communities, time will demonstrate both the successes and failures of the responses unfolding now. My neighbors have asked questions and expressed gratitude about what has been offered. They eagerly await the time they can use library spaces and collections in-person again.

References

American Library Association. "Public Libraries Launch, Expand Services during COVID-19 Pandemic." n.d. http://www.ala.org/news/press-releases/2020/04/public-libraries-launch-expand-services-during-covid-19-pandemic-0 (accessed May 21, 2020).

Houston Library Foundation. "Library Recovery." 2017. https://www.houstonlibraryfoundation.org/hpl-recovery.

Public Library Association. "Public Libraries Respond to COVID-19: Survey of Response & Activities." n.d. http://www.ala.org/pla/sites/ala.org.pla/files/content/advocacy/covid-19/PLA-Libraries-Respond-Survey_Aggregate-Results_FINAL2.pdf (accessed May 21, 2020).

San Francisco Public Library. "COVID-19 Community Time Capsule." n.d. https://sfpl.org/locations/main-library/sf-history-center/digital-collections/covid19-time-capsule (accessed May 21, 2020).

World Health Organization. "Coronavirus Disease (COVID-19) Pandemic." n.d. https://www.who.int/emergencies/diseases/novel-coronavirus-2019 (accessed May 21, 2020).

Index

Play, 6, 8, 28, 29, 46, 51, 52, 55, 73,
76, 87, 99, 118, 130–131, 146,
149–160, 169, 170, 171, 196
Policy, 43, 146, 166, 178, 181, 199,
200; federal, 25; fines, xvi, 42, 177,
179, 180, 183, 184; state, 4, 5, 13,
25, 28, 46, 166
Poverty, 89, 110, 120, 136–137, 149,
150, 151, 152, 155, 157, 159, 160,
162, 163, 179, 180, 195
Professional development, 47, 142,
194. *See also* Training
Public Library Association, 153, 160,
208, 209, 210

Qualitative, 22–27, 29, 30, 32, 34,
166, 200
Quantitative, 2, 9, 10, 22, 26, 27, 30,
63, 160
Queens Library (NY), 74

Reading, ix, xv, 3, 5, 6, 7, 8, 13, 31,
36, 39, 41, 51, 53, 59–65, 70, 73,
79–82, 121, 122, 130–131, 147,
150, 151, 152, 153, 154, 155, 160,
164, 173, 174, 196, 204, 205, 209.
See also Literacy; Summer reading/
learning
REFORMA, 37
Research paradigms, xvi, 2, 9, 21–32;
constructivist, 2, 22, 26–28, 36;
critical, 2, 22, 29–31, 36, 156, 169,
174, 187, 200, 201; positivist/
postpositivist, 2, 22, 23–26, 36
Rural, 2, 9, 11, 21, 22, 28, 29, 70,
119–120, 147, 151, 171, 173, 174,
193–201

San Diego Public Library (CA), 146,
177, 178, 179, 180, 181, 183, 184,
188
San Francisco Public Library (CA),
165, 209, 210
San Mateo County Library (CA),
69–72

Science. *See* STEM/STEAM
Scottsdale Public Library (AZ), 45–56
Sevier County Public Library System
(TN), 195
Show Low Public Library (AZ), 10
Smithville Public Library (TX), 205
Social justice, ix, xiii, xv, 4, 12, 20,
29, 30, 145, 146, 147, 148, 193–201
Social media, 41, 88, 89, 95, 97, 111,
190, 209
Space, 1, 4, 5, 6, 7, 8, 13, 20, 21, 28,
30, 36, 38, 43, 48, 52, 53, 63, 99,
101, 110, 117, 125, 131–132, 143,
146, 147, 151, 152, 153, 154, 155,
156, 157, 158, 159, 163, 170, 171,
173, 188, 190, 196, 199, 204, 207,
208, 209
Storytelling, 28, 42, 80, 81, 84, 89,
90, 95, 108, 112–113
Storytime, 5, 26, 28, 40, 43, 46–53,
48, 52, 53, 55, 56, 136, 151, 152,
154, 156, 158, 171, 209
STEM/STEAM, 10, 23, 46, 51, 71,
89–90, 92, 95–97, 99, 111, 137,
147, 152
Summer reading/learning, 5, 6, 14,
39, 40, 71, 95, 120, 122, 132, 141,
147, 204
Survey, 5, 25, 48, 51, 151, 208, 210

Technology, 6, 32, 71, 73, 75, 84, 88,
90, 96, 108, 110, 111, 113, 118,
131, 135–140, 147, 150, 153, 155,
156, 159, 160, 179, 188, 189, 191,
195, 196, 199, 200, 201, 203, 204,
205, 206
Teens. *See* Youth
Theory of change, 36, 47
Training, 54, 55, 66, 84, 142, 146,
150, 155, 164, 165, 170, 189, 196,
200, 201, 203, 205. *See also*
Professional development
Trust, 4, 10, 21, 46, 54, 55, 75, 83, 85,
118–119, 124, 142–143, 172, 173,
189

About the Editors and Contributors

Editors

Margaret Caspe is an educator, researcher, and writer who focuses on how families, early childhood programs, schools, and communities support children's learning. She is coeditor of *Promising Practices for Engaging Families in STEM Learning*, and her work has appeared in *Public Library Quarterly*, *Early Childhood Research Quarterly*, *School Community Journal*, *Young Children*, and *Childhood Education*.

M. Elena Lopez is an independent researcher on the ecology of learning, which includes the home, school, and community. She regularly contributes to research, policy, and practice on family engagement in children's learning. Trained in social anthropology, she is interested in the dynamic interplay of individual agency and system factors in promoting educational equity. As a member of the board of the Mountain View Public Library in California, she seeks to develop policies for greater access and engagement with library programs and services.

Bharat Mehra is a professor and EBSCO Endowed Chair in Social Justice in the School of Library and Information Studies at the University of Alabama. His growing up in India created an awareness and acceptance of human diversity in its multiple forms of expression, thought, and action. His training as an architect in New Delhi made him visually literate and sensitive toward human factors in design. Among his many research interests are diversity and inclusion advocacy, intercultural communication and action, social justice in library and information science, community-engaged scholarship, and critical and cross-cultural studies.

Contributors

Ashley J. Brown is the engagement and outreach librarian at Auburn Public Library in Alabama. She serves (through June 2021) as the cochair of the Public Library Association's Family Engagement Task Force and is a member of the Library Freedom Project.

Donna C. Celano is an assistant professor at La Salle University in Philadelphia. She has conducted research into the differences in how low- and middle-income children gain knowledge through their media usage and is coauthor of the book *Giving Our Children a Fighting Chance*.

Tamela Chambers is the manager of the children's department at the Woodson Regional Library, part of the Chicago Public Library. She has over eighteen years of experience serving children and their families in both public and school library settings. Tamela was a member of the BCALA Reading Is Grand! grant development team and hosted the first program in 2010.

Tamara Lynette Clegg is an associate professor at the College of Information Studies, University of Maryland. Her research focuses on understanding how to help people come to see themselves in new and empowered ways by helping them form new relationships with information.

Olivia Forehand is a master's graduate from the School of Information Sciences at the University of Tennessee. She is interested in a career in public libraries, particularly working with teens, where she hopes to incorporate inclusion and representation of diverse groups of people in her work.

Lisa Guernsey is director of the Teaching, Learning, and Tech program and senior advisor to the Early and Elementary Education Policy program at New America. Her work involves leading teams of analysts and writers to translate research, examine policies, and generate new ideas for developing high-quality learning opportunities for underserved and historically disadvantaged populations.

Nick Higgins is the chief librarian at Brooklyn Public Library in charge of public service across Brooklyn. In 2017 Nick was named "Mover and Shaker" by *Library Journal* for creating a citywide, library-based video visiting service for kids with parents incarcerated on Rikers Island.

Jessica Hilburn is the executive director of Benson Memorial Library in Titusville, Pennsylvania. Before her current role, she worked in local history, adult services, and family programming. Her research interests include the importance of libraries to rural communities. She is the author of *Hidden History of Northwestern Pennsylvania*.

Misty Jones is the director of the San Diego Public Library, overseeing the Central Library and thirty-five branches. She believes libraries are the great equalizer, always inclusive and never exclusive. She is intent on showing that libraries are a vital part of the educational and economic ecosystem and essential to the success of a community and its members.

R. David Lankes is a professor and the director of the University of South Carolina's School of Information Science. His book, *The Atlas of New Librarianship* won the 2012 ABC-CLIO/Greenwood Award for the Best Book in Library Literature. Lankes is a passionate advocate for librarians and their essential role in today's society.

Karen Lemmons is the library media specialist at the Detroit School of the Arts/Detroit Public Schools Community District. She also serves as chair of the Reading Is Grand! Award Committee. Her work with teachers and students focuses on developing information literacy and twenty-first-century skills.

Sarah McNeil is the senior librarian in the early learning department at the Denver Public Library. She leads the department in supporting Denver's children from birth through kindergarten, their adults, their educators, and their advocates with programs, services, and materials in DPL branches and in the community.

Susan B. Neuman is professor of early childhood and literacy education at New York University. Her research interests include early childhood policy, curriculum, and early reading instruction for children who live in poverty. As the U.S. assistant secretary for elementary and secondary education during the George W. Bush administration, she established the Early Reading First program.

Megan E. Pratt is an assistant professor at Oregon State University. She coordinates the Oregon Child Care Research Partnership, which conducts research related to childcare policy at the local and state levels. Her work examines how early learning in both formal and informal community settings can best support families with young children.

Carine Risley is deputy director at San Mateo County Library in California.

Ricarose Roque is an assistant professor in the Department of Information Science at the University of Colorado, Boulder. She explores how to design inclusive learning experiences that enable young people to create and express themselves with new technologies and media, with a special focus on youth from underrepresented groups in computing.

Scott Sikes is the associate director of the Appalachian Center for Civic Life and an instructor in the Civic Innovation Department at Emory & Henry College. As a PhD student at the University of Tennessee, he is studying the use of social media in the 2018 West Virginia teacher's strike.

Mark Smith is director and librarian at the Texas State Library and Archives Commission. His office coordinates strategic planning and budgeting efforts; provides information to the governor, Texas Legislature, and Legislative Budget Board; and ensures that the mission, goals, and objectives of the agency are fulfilled.

Becky Stahl is the youth services librarian at Benson Memorial Library in Titusville, Pennsylvania.

Mega Subramaniam is associate professor and the codirector of the Youth eXperience (YX) Lab at the iSchool, College of Information Studies at the University of Maryland, College Park. She conducts research on enhancing the role of libraries in fostering the mastery of emerging digital literacies among underserved young people.

Michelle Taylor is assistant professor of child development and family studies at California State University, Long Beach. She conducts research on the role of adults in young children's learning and development. She participates in the Partnership for Family-Library Engagement, aimed at understanding and improving the quality of early childhood education programming within public library settings.

Felton Thomas Jr. is executive director of Cleveland Public Library. His vision for the library is that of a strong leader in defining a more prosperous future for Cleveland by battling the digital divide, illiteracy, unemployment, and other community deficits with innovative programming and action at all twenty-seven CPL branches.

Kristen Todd-Wurm is the national coordinator for Family Place Libraries at Middle Country Public Library in New York.

Sandra Toro is a program specialist at the U.S. Department of Education. Previously she was a senior program officer at the Institute of Museum and Library Services.

Laura Walter is a writer and editor at Cleveland Public Library. She teaches writing workshops for Literary Cleveland, Cuyahoga County Public Library, and other literary organizations. Her debut novel, *Body of Stars*, was published in 2021.

Mariko Whelan is the early learning, youth, and teen services coordinator at Scottsdale Public Library in Arizona.

Sari A. Widman is a doctoral candidate at the University of Colorado, Boulder's School of Education. Her research focuses on community-based, intergenerational STEAM (science, technology, engineering, arts, and math) learning, particularly in library settings. She is especially interested in how libraries can support historically marginalized communities and build inclusive and welcoming learning environments.

Kaurri C. Williams-Cockfield has over twenty-five years of work experience in U.S. and international library settings, including public, academic, school, and corporate institutions. She is the director of the Blount County Public Library in Maryville, Tennessee. Her research areas include public libraries; social justice and sustainable communities; and school media center impact on student test outcomes. She is an adjunct instructor for the School of Information Sciences at the University of Tennessee Knoxville.